Kandel *Fuzzy Mathematical Techniques with Applications*
Keene *Object-Oriented Programming in Common LISP*
Klahr & Waterman (Eds.) *Expert Systems: Techniques, Tools and Applications*
Luger & Stubblefield *Artificial Intelligence and the Design of Expert Systems*
Manna & Waldinger *The Logical Basis for Computer Programming.* Vol. 1: *Deductive Reasoning*
Marcus *Prolog Programming: Applications for Database Systems, Expert Systems and Natural Language Systems*
Pearl *Heuristics: Intelligent Search Strategies for Computer Problem Solving*
Richards *Clausal Form Logic: An Introduction to the Logic of Computer Reasoning*
Rogers *A Prolog Primer*
Rogers *A Turbo Prolog Primer*
Sager *Natural Language Information Processing: A Computer Grammar of English and its Applications*
Sager, Friedman & Lyman *Medical Language Processing: Computer Management of Narrative Data*
Silverman (Ed.) *Expert Systems for Business*
Sowa *Conceptual Structures: Information processing in Mind and Machine*
Walker (Ed.), McCord, Sowa & Wilson *Knowledge Systems and Prolog*
Waterman *A Guide to Expert Systems*
Wilensky *Planning and Understanding: A Computational Approach to Human Reasoning*
Winograd *Language as a Cognitive Process.* Vol. 1: *Syntax*
Winograd & Flores *Understanding Computers and Cognition*
Winston *Artificial Intelligence,* 2nd Edition
Winston & Horn *LISP,* 3rd Edition
Wright & Bourne *Manufacturing Intelligence*

Inductive Acquisition of
Expert Knowledge

Turing Institute Press

Managing Editor Jon Ritchie
Academic Editor Dr Peter Mowforth

The Turing Institute, located in Glasgow, Scotland, was established in 1983 as a not-for-profit company, named in honour of the late Alan M. Turing, the distinguished British mathematician and logician whose work has had a lasting influence on the foundations of modern computing.

The Institute offers integrated research and teaching programmes in advanced intelligent technologies – in particular, logic programming, computer vision, robotics and expert systems. It derives its income from research and training contracts, both governmental and industrial, and by subscription from its Industrial Affiliates. It assists Affiliates with the transfer of technology from research to application, and provides them with training for their technical staff, a wide range of software tools and a comprehensive library and information service.

The Turing Institute is an Academic Associate of the University of Strathclyde, and its research staff work closely with different departments of the University on a variety of research programmes.

Other titles published in association with the Turing Institute Press

Applications of Expert Systems (Vol. 1)
J. Ross Quinlan (Ed.)

Applications of Expert Systems (Vol. 2)
J. Ross Quinlan (Ed.)

Structured Induction in Expert Systems
Alen D. Shapiro

Knowledge-Based Programming
Enn Tyugu

Inductive Acquisition of Expert Knowledge

Stephen Muggleton
The Turing Institute, Glasgow

TURING INSTITUTE PRESS
in association with

ADDISON-WESLEY PUBLISHING COMPANY
Wokingham, England · Reading, Massachusetts · Menlo Park, California
New York · Don Mills, Ontario · Amsterdam · Bonn · Sydney
Singapore · Tokyo · Madrid · San Juan

© 1990 Addison-Wesley Publishers Ltd.
© 1990 Addison-Wesley Publishing Company, Inc.
© 1990 Turing Institute Press

All rights reserved. No part of this publication may be reproduced, stored in a retrieval system, or transmitted in any form or by any means, electronic, mechanical, photocopying, recording or otherwise, without prior written permission of the publisher.

Many of the designations used by manufacturers and sellers to distinguish their products are claimed as trademarks. Addison-Wesley has made every attempt to supply trademark information about manufacturers and their products mentioned in this book.

The programs presented in this book have been included for their instructional value. They have been tested with care but are not guaranteed for any particular purpose. The publisher does not offer any warranties or representations, nor does it accept any liabilities with respect to the programs.

Cover designed by Crayon Design of Henley-on-Thames and
printed by The Riverside Printing Co. (Reading) Ltd.
Camera-ready copy produced using LaTeX.
Printed in Great Britain at The Bath Press, Avon

First printed 1990

British Library Cataloguing in Publication Data

Muggleton, S. (Stephen)
 Inductive acquisition of expert knowledge.
 1. Expert systems
 I. Title
 006.3'3

 ISBN 0–201–17561–4

Library of Congress Cataloging in Publication Data

Muggleton, S. (Stephen)
 Inductive acquisition of expert knowledge
 1. Expert systems (Computer science)
 I. Title
 006.3'3   QA76.9

 ISBN 0–201–17561–4

To my wife, Thirza.

Preface

One of the major problems to emerge from the construction of expert systems in the 1970s was the 'bottleneck' of acquiring knowledge from experts. Although experts were found to be good at giving examples of diagnoses, and other forms of decisions making, they found it difficult to express exact rules corresponding to what they knew to be the case. It rapidly became apparent that machines capable of constructing rules from examples would considerably ease this problem. The first demonstration of the feasibility of this idea came in 1980 with Michalski and Chilauski's description (Michalski and Chilauski, 1980) of a successful attempt to inductively acquire expert rules for diagnosing soya beans. In this study the machine-constructed rules were shown to outperform human-constructed rules for the same problem.

The 1980s have seen a great expansion of such techniques. This has led to the development of a new sub-branch of Artificial Intelligence known as Machine Learning. The new subject is now replete with its own journal (the Machine Learning Journal) and yearly conferences.

This book describes some of the successes achieved in the commercial application of inductive inference techniques which have been used to build expert systems. Expert systems are usually embedded within extensive and powerful shells. The commercially available system RuleMaster, described in this book, provides such a shell for inductively constructed expert systems, complete with explanation facilities and abilities to manipulate externally coded routines. RuleMaster has been used by the West German company Brainware to construct what is presently the world's largest expert system, containing around 50,000 rules. This system encodes the many fire regulations for use in the design of buildings. RuleMaster has also been used to develop large industrial expert systems, two of which, WILLARD and EARL, are described in this book. Another simpler system, SHUTTLE, is also described. This was developed by NASA for deciding when to apply the auto-pilot in landing the space shuttle.

The successes of commercial systems such as RuleMaster have led to further theoretical and applied investigations of problems which were not amenable to the first generation of machine learning tools. In the later chapters of this book we describe two such approaches, namely 'sequence induction' and 'constructive induction'. Sequence induction allows the construction of control systems. The examples for sequence induction consist of sequences of situation/action pairs. These are used to construct finite state machines which represent particular control structures.

The Duce system which carries out 'constructive induction' is described in the last chapter of this book. Duce works by automatically decomposing high level problems into lower level ones. This is an essential capability in many expert domains in which it is hard to assess beforehand exactly which relevant features of a problem should be given to a learning system. As is well known from the experience of structured programming, once a problem is hierarchically decomposed each sub-problem is far simpler to encode. Structured systems also have the advantage of being much easier to maintain.

A real world application involving neuro-psychological diagnosis is described in which Duce managed to structure the expert system in a way which was judged by the domain specialist to be both informative and of scientific interest. The structure proposed was in fact strikingly similar to a taxonomy which had been described within the neuro-psychological literature but which had not yet come into wide-scale acceptance.

This result is encouraging in terms of possible applications of inductive techniques to scientifically aided discovery from data, an area which is likely to have a growing importance in future uses of Artificial Intelligence techniques.

Stephen Muggleton
The Turing Institute
Glasgow
1990

Contents

Preface   vii

1 Overview   **1**
  1.1 What are expert systems?   1
  1.2 How expertise is acquired: the debug cycle   3
  1.3 Induction   4
  1.4 Inductive knowledge acquisition environment   8
  1.5 Applications   8
  1.6 Duce applications   10
  1.7 Summary   10

2 Inductive inference   **13**
  2.1 Generalisation   13
  2.2 Examples and rules   14
  2.3 Criteria for inductively generated results   16
  2.4 Languages involved in inductive inference   18
  2.5 Classification learning   19
  2.6 Finite-state automata and strategy learning   24
  2.7 Induction of finite-state automata   30
  2.8 Conclusion   31

3 RuleMaster   **33**
  3.1 Some issues in knowledge engineering   33
  3.2 RuleMaster   34
  3.3 Knowledge acquisition   35
  3.4 Types of expert systems supported   38
  3.5 Radial   39
  3.6 Individual Radial modules   45
  3.7 Operator definitions   50
  3.8 Explanation   51

x   Contents

	3.9	The Rulemaker code generator	53
	3.10	External information sources	60
	3.11	Conclusion	61

4 Robotic applications — **63**
- 4.1 Introduction — 63
- 4.2 The problem: building a five-block arch — 63
- 4.3 The action *arch* — 65
- 4.4 The action *onto* — 66
- 4.5 The action *clear* — 68
- 4.6 A session — 68
- 4.7 GENARCH — 71
- 4.8 Conclusion — 81

5 Expert systems applications — **83**
- 5.1 Introduction — 83
- 5.2 SHUTTLE — 83
- 5.3 WILLARD — 86
- 5.4 EARL — 91

6 Grammatical induction theory — **95**
- 6.1 Introduction — 95
- 6.2 Language identification — 97
- 6.3 Mixed positive/negative presentations — 98
- 6.4 Positive samples — 98
- 6.5 An efficient new algorithm — 109
- 6.6 k-contextual languages — 115
- 6.7 Use of semantic information — 120

7 Sequence induction applications — **127**
- 7.1 Introduction — 127
- 7.2 A simple grammar — 128
- 7.3 1-bit binary adder — 130
- 7.4 Traffic light controller — 131
- 7.5 Reverse motor problem — 134
- 7.6 Algebra problem — 136
- 7.7 Hanging pictures in a room — 140
- 7.8 Conclusion — 143

8 Chess strategies — **145**
- 8.1 Introduction — 145
- 8.2 The problem : KBBKN — 147
- 8.3 Conclusion — 152

9 Duce — **153**
- 9.1 Introduction — 153

	9.2	Background	154
	9.3	Transformation-based induction	154
	9.4	Operators	155
	9.5	The search algorithm	158
	9.6	Animal taxonomy	159
	9.7	Even-parity	162
	9.8	Recreation of the KPa7KR structure	165
	9.9	Neuropsychology application	168
	9.10	Conclusion	169

Appendices

A	**ACLS, ID3 and CLS**		**173**
	A.1	The entropy function	174
B	**Definitions**		**177**
C	**Heuristics used in the literature**		**181**
	C.1	Biermann and Feldman's *k*-tail predicate	181
	C.2	Levine's heuristic	182
	C.3	Miclet's algorithm	182
	C.4	Angluin's algorithm	182
D	**Proofs**		**185**
E	**Example move sequences**		**195**
	E.1	Actions	195
	E.2	Attributes	195
	E.3	Black plays optimally	196
	E.4	Black plays badly	198
F	**Results of sequence induction**		**201**
	F.1	Actions	201
	F.2	Attributes	201
	F.3	State machine	202
G	**Automata after ACLS induction**		**203**
	G.1	Actions	203
	G.2	Attributes	203
	G.3	State description	204
H	**KBBKN Rulemaker induction file**		**205**
I	**KBBKN Radial code**		**207**
Bibliography			**209**
Index			**215**

Chapter 1
Overview

1.1 What are expert systems?

In recent years expert systems have been exciting a great deal of interest, not only in the computational and cognitive sciences but also within the computer industry at large. In 1988, the world market for software products was US$42 000M. Of this, US$595M was in AI products, a large proportion of which was based on expert systems technology[†]. It is the aim of this book to demonstrate that the knowledge for large expert systems is most easily acquired using algorithms which learn from examples. In this context, the Berlin-based company Brainware recently announced that they had constructed the world's largest expert system, containing some 50 000 rules, using the machine learning capabilities of RuleMaster, a commercially available expert system shell sold by Radian Corporation, Austin, Texas. The author of this book was the chief designer of RuleMaster, which is described in Chapter 3.

What is meant by an 'expert system'? An often-repeated but naive definition says that an expert system is a program that solves problems which would otherwise require a highly skilled human for their solution. Powerful, but essentially 'black box' problem solvers, such as autopilots in the aircraft industry or the MACSYMA system (Moses, 1975) for symbolic manipulations, would qualify under such a definition. The definition is generally extended to include the property of self-explanation. Thus Ed Feigenbaum, co-author of the highly influential book on the Japanese fifth generation, *The Fifth Generation: artificial intelligence and Japan's computer challenge to the world*, (Feigenbaum and McCorduck, 1984), required that the system must 'be able to explain its activity; else the question arises of who is in control...' and saw the issue as crucial to user acceptance. However, it would be

[†] *Source*: Coopers and Lybrand/IDC

naive to go to the other extreme and say that an expert system is a computer program which has all the behavioural characteristics of a human expert. Clearly the latter definition is not restrictive enough as we would not expect a computer program to go out for lunch at midday. For the purposes of this book, Michie's definition of an expert system will be adopted:

> *An expert system embodies in a computer the knowledge-based component of an expert skill in such a form that the system can generate intelligent actions and advice and can also on demand justify to the user its line of reasoning.* (Michie, 1985)

With reference to this definition, two important aspects should be stressed. Firstly, an expert system's task performance should be demonstrably at least as good as that of a human expert in the given domain. Secondly, the system must be capable of explaining its line of reasoning on demand. It should be noted that this definition does not exclude problem domains too complex for human specialists to have mastered. If, somehow, a program were constructed which gave an account of its faultless play of the chess endgame of King and two Bishops against King and Knight in terms which endgame specialists could understand and apply, then the program would qualify as an expert system. Expert systems are the knowledge-based sub-category of a larger class of computer programs which display good task performance based upon large amounts of information. (For a definition of the technical meaning of the term *knowledge* used here, see Michie (1982).) This larger category we will call *domain-specific problem solvers*. The information for the latter class may be held implicitly, as in search-driven game-playing programs, or explicitly, as look-up. For the above mentioned expert-inscrutable Bishop-Bishop-Knight ending, a tabulation by K. Thompson (Roycroft, 1983; Thompson, 1986) of the complete space of several hundred million legal positions can be made to yield optimal play. Note that this does not constitute an expert system but does exemplify the larger class.

Both domain-specific problem solvers and expert systems can be partitioned into the following two distinct classes.

1. **Classification systems.** In a classification system like MYCIN (Shortliffe and Buchanan, 1975), it is assumed that the state of the world being classified does not change during the operation of the system. Thus, if some statement could be made about the situation being classified at the beginning of the process of classification, the same statement would hold throughout.

2. **Control systems.** In a control system such as VM (Fagan *et al*, 1979), no such steady-state assumption holds, and, indeed, it is generally part of the function of the system to carry out operations which change the state of the world.

1.2 How expertise is acquired: the debug cycle

Many of the problems of building and using an expert system involve the human interface. The reasons for this, over and above the usual problems of providing user interfaces for normal programs, lie in the fact that an expert system, like an expert's knowledge, is never complete. Once the system has been shown to perform well in some domain, its owner typically seeks either to improve on this proficiency or expand the scope of expertise. Thus expert systems are often continually being debugged. Moreover, this debugging cycle does not only involve a programmer or knowledge engineer but also a human expert. Experts, though knowledgeable in their own field, cannot be expected to be acquainted with programmer-oriented tools. Thus in the study of expert systems, we need to be able to answer at least the following questions.

1. **How does the expert assess a system's present knowledge?** The answer seems to lie in allowing the expert to use example test-cases. The expert checks a natural language representation of the system's reasoning in particular example cases and uses this to infer the reasoning process. This was first shown to be effective in the MYCIN project (Shortliffe and Buchanan, 1975).

2. **How does the expert alter the system's knowledge?** By symmetric analogy to the first answer, we would expect that experts should be allowed to express, by example, their reasoning to the system in a natural format. The system could then infer how its own reasoning process must adapt to fit that of the expert. This methodology was first tested by Michalski and Chilausky who found it gave excellent results (Michalski and Chilausky, 1980).

Algorithms, like that used by Michalski *et al.*, which infer generalised descriptions from example material are collectively termed *inductive inference* algorithms. If the outputs of such algorithms are in user-intelligible and mentally checkable form, then it is customary to speak of *inductive learning* algorithms. The study of inductive learning has in recent years blossomed into the rapidly evolving science of machine learning. It is now widely recognised that machines with the ability to learn knowledge in a similar fashion to human beings are essential for achieving the long-term aims of artificial intelligence. The study of machine learning algorithms and their application in expert system technology forms the main thrust of this work.

1.3 Induction

The following sections give a brief overview of the uses of inductive algorithms. A fuller review of the subject of inductive inference is given in Chapter 2.

1.3.1 Static induction

Logical induction is the process of generating concept descriptions which are more general than some set of examples of that concept. Typically, descriptions generated by inductive algorithms are more compact than the original example set. As these descriptions can generally be executed, induction can also be viewed as an automatic programming technique. Work originated at Illinois by Michalski and Chilauski (Michalski and Chilauski, 1980) and extended at Edinburgh by Shapiro (Shapiro, 1987) has shown the potential for constructing expert knowledge bases in the relaxed framework of concepts generalised from examples. Commercially available packages such as Expert Ease (McLaren, 1984), Extran-7 (A-Razzak *et al*, 1984), and RuleMaster (Michie *et al*, 1984) have proved the power of this approach, with development-time savings in building large expert systems of at least an order of magnitude over the traditional 'deductivist' rule extraction technique. By traditional methods used in systems such as MYCIN, rules are extracted during a series of interviews between the knowledge engineer and the expert. However, it cannot be said that the 'inductivists' have yet completely met their targets. A goal for the constructors of learning/knowledge environments might be a 'laboratory' in which the scientist (expert), unaided by knowledge engineers, uses machines to carry out experimentation and theory formation by mechanisms which learn from mistakes. Some form of inductive engine must surely lie at the core of any such environment.

Under the present inductive regime, examples represent *static descriptions* of world situations to which labels are attached indicating a classification or action to be taken. The world described often has a finite number of distinguishable states or *situations*. Rules may be developed inductively in various different formalisms ranging from decision trees (Quinlan, 1979) to propositional and predicate calculi (see Chapter 9 and also Muggleton (1988); Sammut and Banerji (1986); Zubrick (1988); Van Melle (1980). The most serious problem to emerge from the development of this approach is that, although inductive generators, when presented with sufficient example sets, can generate efficient and correct rules, these rules can be so large and complex that they are incomprehensible to human experts (Quinlan, 1982). Ease of comprehension is a crucial factor in the debug cycle of inductively generated knowledge. Two complementary approaches to this apparent impasse have been suggested:

1. **Structured induction.** Shapiro has shown that large expert domains can be dealt with effectively by employing the techniques of structured programming in an inductive environment (Shapiro, 1987). Thus the expert is expected to structure his knowledge in a top-down fashion *manually*, and then present examples for each part of the hierarchy. These examples are then used to construct the individual rules (or decision trees) automatically. Facilities to aid this structuring process have been built into RuleMaster which is described fully in Chapter 3. Shapiro demonstrated this methodology in the construction of an expert system for classifying two chess endgames as being won or not won for white (Shapiro, 1987).

2. **Human subset languages.** Michie has suggested that by constraining every constituent rule to take one or other of two alternative forms (either linear thresholded sum or linear decision tree) and by also constraining the form of the 'calling diagram' relating linearised procedures to each other, rulebases can be constructed that are easily understood and force builders to structure their problem (Michie, 1984). Arbab (Arbab and Michie, 1985) has implemented a new version of a rule-induction algorithm due to Bratko (Bratko, 1983) which constructs a linear rule where one

exists and otherwise presents the most nearly linear tree which can be constructed from the data.

Manually structured induction is not the ultimate solution. In any expert system building task, the structuring of the problem now becomes the new knowledge acquisition bottleneck. The results of some early attempts at automatically structuring domains from example material (Michalski and Stepp, 1983; Paterson, 1983) were not very promising, with the machine's suggested hierarchies not necessarily having any significance to experts in the domain. However, substantial automatic knowledge structuring has recently been achieved by the author (Muggleton, 1987) using an algorithm called Duce (see Chapter 9). Duce managed to reconstruct an understandable knowledge structure for one of the endgame classification problems studied by Shapiro (Shapiro, 1987). Duce suggested intermediate attributes for the problem which resulted in a structure which was topographically similar, though not identical to Shapiro's original handcrafted structure. In section 9.9 an expert system application of Duce is described in which automatic structuring of the domain was superior to that carried out by a human being.

A new approach to the construction of control systems is also described in this book (see section 1.1). This new approach is called *sequence induction*. The full theoretical basis for sequence induction is developed in Chapter 6, and experimental results are given in Chapters 7 and 8.

1.3.2 Sequence induction

This approach relies on the presentation of example *sequences* to an inductive algorithm. Each element of the sequence is a situation/action pair similar in form to the static descriptions such as those described in section 1.3.1 These sequences can be taken to represent a series of world descriptions which are altered by actions operating on that world. The output of the inductive process is a finite-state control structure in which each state contains a small number of the static description examples concerning the actions and state transitions which should be carried out in various situations. These static description examples can be used by a static induction algorithm to produce rules or a decision tree for each state. Although this does not produce a hierarchical structure, it does achieve some of the aims of structured induction (that is, a set of small, understandable rules) by making use of the additional structural information which lies within each example. Whereas structured static induction seems to be of most use in classification systems, sequence induction lends itself more readily to the construction of control systems (see section 1.1). In terms of automatic programming, sequence induction is used to design the overall branching and looping structure of routines in a program, while static induction is used at a lower level to decide the internal ordering of nested if-then-else statements.

The basis for sequence induction techniques lies in the study of grammatical induction, that is, the inference of grammatical structures from example sentences of a language (see Chapter 6). Under the generative paradigm of computational linguistics, the grammar produced can be viewed as the control structure of a program which generated the example sentences. Some of the earliest work in the area of grammatical induction was done by Biermann and Feldman, who devised an algorithm to induce a finite-state automaton representing a particular language from example strings contained in that language. (Biermann and Feldman, 1972). Although their algorithm was capable of identifying any regular language given a sufficient example set, the algorithm requires an arbitrary complexity parameter and also has rather low *example efficiency* (a large number of examples are needed to infer anything). Angluin has described an algorithm which infers only a limited subset of the regular languages. (Angluin, 1982). She calls this subset the k-reversible languages. By limiting the target result set, Angluin's algorithm requires fewer examples than that of Biermann and Feldman's algorithm.

The author has taken Angluin's algorithm and redesigned it to run in $O(n^2)$ time complexity rather than Angluin's original $O(n^3)$ time (see Chapter 6). Furthermore, an even smaller, but useful subset of the k-reversible languages, called the k-contextual languages has been discovered by the author. The algorithm for inferring members of the k-contextual languages uses fewer examples even than Angluin's, to the extent that inference is possible from samples containing only a single example (all other grammatical inference methods in the literature presuppose more than a single example). A method that circumvents the need for supplying the algorithm with an arbitrary complexity measure, something which is required by all other methods in the literature (Angluin, 1982; Biermann and Feldmann, 1972; Levine, 1982; Miclet, 1980) has also been discovered. This was achieved by making use of the semantic content of static examples in the construction of finite state schemas.

1.4 Inductive knowledge acquisition environment

In order to test the hypothesis that expert *control* knowledge can be acquired conveniently by inductive inference, it is necessary to have an environment which is capable of being used for the routine inductive construction and execution of knowledge-bases. It is desirable that this environment has the following properties:

1. **An induction engine.** Inductive apparatus both for *static* and for *sequence* induction.

2. **A rule language.** This is used to express the output of 1 in a natural and comprehensible fashion. Such a language should provide support for problem structuring and the manipulation of whatever data is needed for the task at hand.

3. **An explanation facility.** According to the definition of section 1.1 this is necessary for the construction of any expert system.

In Chapter 3 RuleMaster is discussed. This has been constructed to meet these requirements and the only requirement listed above not yet fully met is the integration of the sequence induction algorithm and Duce with other tools in RuleMaster.

1.5 Applications

1.5.1 Applications of static induction

RuleMaster has been tested in the construction of two major expert classification systems. The techniques used for the construction of both of these were based on the structured static induction methodology first advocated and tested by Shapiro and Niblett (1982). The systems were:

1. **WILLARD.** WILLARD (Zubrick, 1984) is an expert system for predicting the likelihood of severe thunderstorms occurring in the central USA. The system was written by Steve Zubrick, a meteorologist at Radian Corporation. Extensive testing of the system (Zubrick, 1988) has shown that it is capable of producing predictions which usefully complement those of the US National Weather Service. A fuller description of WILLARD can be found in Chapter 5.

2. **EARL.** EARL (Riese, 1984) is a system for diagnosing imminent break-down in large oil-cooled electrical transformers. The system was constructed by Charles Riese who is a software engineer working for the Hartford Steam Boiler Company. When EARL was tested against 859 test-cases, it managed a diagnostic success rate in excess of 99%. EARL is now in routine industrial use. A fuller description of EARL can be found in Chapter 5.

The author gave help and advice in the structuring and example acquisition of both the above systems. Details of a smaller control system called ARCH are given in Chapter 4.

1.5.2 Applications of sequence induction

Sequence induction can be applied successfully to a diverse set of problems, including automatic VLSI circuit synthesis, user modelling in a mathematical educational environment and generalisation of robot plans.

Using sequence induction, the author successfully built an expert system for playing a fragment of the chess endgame domain of King and two Bishops against King and Knight (see Chapter 8). This endgame is so complex that even the chess endgame specialist, John Roycroft, failed, after months of continuous study aided by unlimited access to machine-generated facts and variations, to acquire more than a partial and patchy understanding of it. However, when presented with the expert system built from his example move sequences, he easily recognised and agreed with the various states of the generalised structure which had been built. The most complex states (in terms of the number of static examples placed), were precisely those which Roycroft had spent most time describing in the sequence acquisition stage. The induced automaton is given in Appendix G in a form which can be directly translated into a Rulemaker induction file. Appendix H shows the result of applying Radial's static induction algorithm to produce decision trees for each state of the automaton of Appendix G. Appendix I represents a runnable Radial expert system which, although compact, is easily comprehended.

1.6 Duce applications

In Chapter 9 we describe an ongoing research project investigating a novel form of machine learning in which the learner's vocabulary is enriched by the machine suggesting useful new descriptive terms for the user to accept or reject. An algorithm called Duce has been shown to be effective along these lines in developing and extending propositional theories within a chess endgame domain and a diagnostic domain of neuro-psychology.

1.7 Summary

In this chapter the topic of expert system research was introduced, following Michie's definition of an expert system. Expert system development involves continuous debugging of knowledge structures. It was argued that the two most important tools in this debugging process are first an *explanation facility* and second an *inductive knowledge acquisition mechanism*. The major topic of interest within this book is that of inductive inference.

Two different forms of induction were described. *Static induction* algorithms take examples of descriptions of world situations to which labels are attached. These labels indicate a classification or an action to be taken. On the other hand, *sequence induction* relies on the presentation of example sequences to an inductive algorithm. Each element of the sequence is a situation/action pair similar in form to the static descriptions.

The author was involved in the construction of the expert system environment RuleMaster. This comprises an *induction engine*, a *rule language* and an *explanation facility*. Although RuleMaster in its present form only has facilities for static induction, it would be a simple matter to introduce a sequence induction package based on the techniques developed in this book.

Generally, whereas static induction techniques have been found to be effective knowledge-acquisition methodologies in classification domains such as chess classification (Quinlan, 1982; Shapiro and Niblett, 1982; Shapiro, 1987), weather forecasting and transformer diagnosis (see Chapter 5), the author believes sequence induction to be similarly promising as a strategy-acquisition methodology in control domains such as robot planning (see Chapter 7) and chess endgame play (see Chapter 8).

Lastly, a novel new technique for automatically structuring knowledge with two large applications involving chess and neuropsychological diagnosis is described in Chapter 9. In the case of the chess endgame domain, Duce managed to reconstruct Shapiro's KPa7KR structure from example data alone. In the second case, Duce automatically extracted a new expert-understandable knowledge structure directly fom raw data.

Chapter 2
Inductive Inference

2.1 Generalisation

Deduction is the process of deriving specific statements from more general ones. For instance, let a list be an ordered set. Thus

["John", "Mary", "Harry"]

is a list of people's names. A legitimate corresponding general statement concerning the members of a list might be the following

X is a member of the list L if X is the first element of L or if X is a member of the list formed by removing the first element of L. (2.1)

Many statements are deductively derivable from the statement of list membership. For instance

"John" is a member of the list L, where L = ["John", "Mary", "Harry"] since "John" is the first element of L. (2.2)

Statement 2.1 can be expressed in first-order logic as follows.

$$\forall x, y, l'(Member(x, x.l') \wedge (Member(x, l') \rightarrow Member(x, y.l'))) \quad (2.3)$$

Statement 2.3 is called a *well-formed formula* of first-order predicate calculus since it obeys the syntax of the calculus. We can define the generality relation between two well-formed-formulae, A and B, as follows

A is more general than B iff $A \vdash B$

13

where $A \vdash B$ should be read as 'A entails B' or alternatively 'B is provable from A'. In this book we will not be studying the process of generalisation for arbitrary first-order formulae (though the author has done so elsewhere (Muggleton and Buntine, 1988)). Instead, we will be looking at inductive inference methods for particular restricted formalisms, such as those for grammars, decision trees and propositional clauses. In these cases, it is straightforward to map sentences from these restricted formalisms into first-order logic, thus defining the generality relation in a uniform fashion. In this way, if we imagine defining a suitable mapping m from English sentences to first-order calculus, we could show that statement 2.1 $\vdash^m$ statement 2.2, where $\vdash^m$ indicates that entailment holds relative to the appropriate mapping.

The inductive algorithms described in this book take a set of descriptive statements E, the example set, and propose a new set of descriptive statements R, the rule set, such that $R \vdash^m E$. Clearly, there may or may not exist a descriptive statement $e' \notin E$, such that $R \vdash^m e'$. Such a descriptive statement e' which is derivable from R but not originally given in E must be treated as a 'guess'. These guesses are usually introduced in order to compact R as much as computational trade-offs permit (see the later discussion of Popper's philosophical comment on inductive generalisation). However, a strategy which applies algorithm information compression to guide generalisation can achieve strong statistical support for such guesses even with small amounts of information compression (Muggleton, 1988).

The advantage of employing an inductive algorithm in developing expert systems seems to lie not necessarily in the inductive algorithm's ability to 'guess' the classifications of previously unseen examples, but rather in a particular psychological fact: whereas experts can easily suggest particular situations to which they can apply their knowledge, it is much more difficult for them to formulate general rules.

2.2 Examples and rules

Expert systems carry out tasks relating to a particular (though not necessarily explicit) *world*. For instance, in medical expert systems, the world is the set of possible states of a patient's body together with relevant anatomical and physiological laws, while in game-playing domains (such as chess) the world might be the set of legal arrangements of pieces on a board together with the laws of chess. Often the program will contain a model of the world, which is some simplified and abstracted representation of the world in question containing enough detail for the program to work on.

For any particular model of the world, there exists a set of *situations* or arrangements of the model. For example, in the chess domain, a 'ground model' might have as its set of situations the complete set of different arrangements of pieces on the board. These situations can be abstracted by defining a set of *attributes* (relationships between parts of the world) in terms of which a particular situation can be described. In the chess world, one possible attribute might be *the black king is in check*.

In a classification problem, such as deciding whether a chess endgame is a win-for-white (see Chapter 9 and also Shapiro, 1987), an *example* consists of a particular situation described in terms of the values of all relevant attributes together with the classification given. For instance, we might have

Example: win-for-white if A and B and C and D and E

where A, B, C, D, and E are a set of attributes, observable from the world model, which are used to decide whether white can force a win. A general rule derived from this example might be

Example: win-for-white if B

Note that the rule does not necessarily use all the attributes necessary to describe a particular world situation: an ideal rule uses as few attributes as possible. In the case of Shapiro's work, one such simple rule for the KPa7KR domain was that *white wins if it can safely capture the black rook*.

In general, we call the input to an inductive algorithm the *example set* and the output the *rule set*. Examples and rules may take a very different form from those shown above, for instance in sequence induction (Chapters 6, 7, 8).

2.2.1 Ordering

Ideally we would not want the order in which examples are presented to an inductive algorithm to affect the results given. In fact, this is true for all inductive techniques dealt with in this book. Not only is the order of examples essentially irrelevant to these techniques but also the order of attributes given has no effect on the result. In contrast, in sequence induction the internal ordering within particular examples does, justifiably, affect results of induction (see Chapters 6, 7, 8), remembering that, in this context, an 'example' includes the specification of a particular ordering.

2.2.2 Types of example material

Examples presented to an inductive algorithm are said to be either *positive* or *negative* in the sense that they respectively exemplify or counter-exemplify the concept being conveyed. The nature of example material also differs according to the method in which it is employed. In this book, a source of examples is referred to as an *oracle* when it can be interrogated interactively by an inductive algorithm. Alternatively, when examples are given according to some fixed presentation scheme, the source of examples is said to be *text*. All inductive algorithms in this book, except Duce (Chapter 9), use textual example material. Duce uses both text and an oracle.

2.3 Criteria for inductively generated results

It is important to be able to make sound statements about

1. **algorithmic effectiveness.** What results do we expect the algorithm to be able or unable to produce, or not produce?

2. **validity of induced results.** Since any inductive process potentially involves the assertion of hypotheses which are not originally given, the question arises as to how confident one can be when applying the resulting information.

These problems are investigated in the following sections.

2.3.1 Effectiveness

Suppose an inductive algorithm A conjectures a series of rule sets

$$R_1 R_2 R_3 \ldots$$

in response to an enumeration of instances of a given rule set R. Each R_{i+1} is proposed as soon as the rule set R_i is found to be inconsistent with the instance source (oracle or text). The algorithm A is said to *identify in the limit* the rule set R if and only if there exists a finite natural number i such that A proposes the rule set R_i, which is equivalent to R, and does not subsequently change this proposal. The notion of 'identification in the limit' is discussed further in Chapter 6 in the context of sequence induction.

Clearly, the ability to prove that an algorithm will identify in the limit some rule set from a class of rule sets *effectively* imbues the user with confidence in that algorithm. However, from the outsider's viewpoint, if the specification of the target total set is not available, it will never be clear that any particular guess made by such an algorithm will not be subsequently changed. This means that one cannot necessarily ever have complete confidence in any particular result generated by such an algorithm if it is known only that a correct rule-set will eventually be generated – it is necessary to have some independent means of verifying inductive results.

Recently Haussler (1988) and others have extensively investigated an alternative framework for discussing the convergence properties of learning algorithms. In terms of this model, one describes the expected number of examples required for a given learning algorithm to converge with high probability on a concept which is approximately the same as the target concept.

2.3.2 Verification of inductive results

Induction is believed by some to be logically and philosophically unsound since it is not possible in general to prove a generalisation based on some set of observations. It is only possible to disprove such a generalisation (Popper, 1970). Thus we might, on the basis of experience of a number of example cases, have hypothesised the descriptive law that the sun will rise every morning. This hypothesis could not be positively proved, only disproved. Although these objections are perfectly valid, it is widely agreed that much of human and animal knowledge is acquired on the basis of experience. Thus it is not the usefulness of inductive inference which is in question, but rather the way in which confidence can be gained in its results.

Let us separate the class of computable functions into the subclasses F (finite) and I (infinite). Functions within F have a finite domain while functions within I have an infinite domain. Clearly, hypothesised functions within F have a finite number of instances. These could, therefore, in principle be completely verified by enumerating all expressible problems and checking the solution's results against an oracle. However, functions hypothesised within I cannot be exhaustively proved like this since a potentially infinite number of instances exist for any function within I. Instead, we might turn to the method of *mathematical induction*[†] for a proof here. Using this technique we attempt to find an incremental operator which, if applied repetitively, can deductively derive all possible instances from a set of base statements. If the base statements are found to be valid according to the oracle, and an arbitrary application of the operator to non-base statements also produces statements consistent with the oracle, then we can infer the entire set of statements to be correct. As this method of proof is often used to prove human-generated programs it seems reasonable to use the same technique for machine-generated programs. This latter technique has not been applied to inductively generated programs in this book, but is believed to be a pressing topic for further research.

2.4 Languages involved in inductive inference

If inductive inference is to be used as an automatic programming tool, as is the case with RuleMaster, it should be recognised that there are three languages involved.

1. **Implementation language.** In terms of logic, this is a metalanguage which is used to transform examples into rules inductively. In RuleMaster the implementation language for the inductive rule generator is the programming language C.

2. **Example language.** This language comprises a simplified symbolic representation of decision-making in the world being modelled. In this book, as explained in Chapter 1, we deal with two distinct forms of example material:

    (a) *Static* examples, represented by ⟨situation/classification⟩ pairs.

    (b) *Dynamic* or *sequence* examples, consisting of sequences of ⟨situation/action⟩ pairs which represent a changing situation controlled by actions carried out on the world.

[†]Note that this is not related in any simple way to 'induction' as used generally in this book.

3. **Rule language.** The rule language expresses descriptive or prescriptive statements about the world. In an inductive programming environment, such rules are fragments of some executable program or knowledge-base. In the Radial language, classification rules are expressed as multi-branching decision trees. Control information is expressed in the format of recursive transition networks – a set of finite state automata (see section 2.6) – which call each other. A desirable feature of a rule language in expert systems work is that its expressions should correspond well with the expert's own conceptual representations.

2.5 Classification learning

Simple concepts can be stated in logic as propositions in the propositional calculus. For instance, we might define the concept of *bird* as follows

fred-is-bird if fred-has-wings and not(fred-is-aeroplane)

Note that this could either be viewed as an *example* of a bird or as a general *rule* for recognising birds. The example language of Quinlan's ID3 inductive algorithm (Quinlan, 1979) (see Appendix A) recognises only tabulated disjunctions of conjunctions where each conjunction (or example) could be directly translated into a statement such as that shown above.

ID3's rules are generated as binary decision trees in a language having the equivalent of the context-free grammar

    rule → TRUE
    rule → FALSE
    rule → IF attribute THEN rule ELSE rule

where *attribute* is simply the name of a test. Although simple, a generalised form of ID3 called ACLS (see Appendix A) is shown to be useful in the construction of large expert systems (see Chapters 3, 4 and 5). However, a small artificial example developed in the following sections shows the limitations imposed by the expressibility of the output of such inductive inference.

Attribute-1	Attribute-2	Attribute-3	Attribute-4	CLASS
false	false	false	false	TRUE
false	false	false	true	FALSE
false	false	true	false	FALSE
false	false	true	true	TRUE
false	true	false	false	FALSE
false	true	false	true	TRUE
false	true	true	false	TRUE
false	true	true	true	FALSE
true	false	false	false	FALSE
true	false	false	true	TRUE
true	false	true	false	TRUE
true	false	true	true	FALSE
true	true	false	false	TRUE
true	true	false	true	FALSE
true	true	true	false	FALSE
true	true	true	true	TRUE

Figure 2.1 Examples of even-parity

2.5.1 Parity problem (unstructured)

Imagine that we want to develop inductively a rule for deciding whether a set of four truth values contains an even number of *trues*. This is normally called the problem of *even-parity*. We give ID3 a full tabulation of all examples as shown in figure 2.1. *CLASS* is the value of even-parity for the particular situation. ID3's result is shown in figure 2.2.

Far from compacting the data in this case (as ID3 generally does), the decision tree has as many leaves as examples and is very difficult to understand due to its bulk. This is admittedly a worst-case problem for ID3, but it should be questioned how problems of this type can be solved, as similarly difficult problems may turn up in real world situations. Shapiro and Niblett (1982) have suggested the use of structuring to simplify the solution of such problems. Can structuring help in solving the parity problem?

```
IF Attribute-1 THEN
    IF Attribute-2 THEN
        IF Attribute-3 THEN
            IF Attribute-4 THEN        TRUE
            ELSE                       FALSE
        ELSE IF Attribute-4 THEN       FALSE
        ELSE                           TRUE
    ELSE IF Attribute-3 THEN
        IF Attribute-4 THEN            FALSE
        ELSE                           TRUE
    ELSE IF Attribute-4 THEN           TRUE
    ELSE                               FALSE
ELSE
    IF Attribute-2 THEN
        IF Attribute-3 THEN
            IF Attribute-4 THEN        FALSE
            ELSE                       TRUE
        ELSE IF Attribute-4 THEN       TRUE
        ELSE                           FALSE
    ELSE IF Attribute-3 THEN
        IF Attribute-4 THEN            TRUE
        ELSE                           FALSE
    ELSE IF Attribute-4 THEN           FALSE
    ELSE                               TRUE
```

Figure 2.2 ID3 decision tree for even-parity

2.5.2 Parity problem (structured)

One structuring method is the following. Let the top-level decision, 'even-parity' be based on two sub-attributes

1. **First-half-even**. This checks whether the attributes *Attribute-1* and *Attribute-2* have an even number of trues between them.

2. **Second-half-even**. This checks whether the attributes *Attribute-3* and *Attribute-4* have an even number of trues between them.

Figures 2.3, 2.4 and 2.5 show the examples for the new 'even-parity', 'first-half-even' and 'second-half-even' sub-problems respectively.

Note that, although the examples are still fully tabulated, only 12 examples are needed rather than the original 16 for figure 2.1.

First-half-even	Second-half-even	CLASS
false	false	TRUE
false	true	FALSE
true	false	FALSE
true	true	TRUE

Figure 2.3 Even-parity

Note also, coincidentally, that, since all three example sets are identical in terms of the examples present, we only show the new decision tree for 'even-parity' in figure 2.6, the other two decision trees having the same outline. ID3 can do no compaction in generating these trees, though this time, since the tree is small, it is easier to understand.

In Chapter 9 an algorithm which is capable of automatically structuring the 'even-parity' problem is described.

2.5.3 Example and description complexities

It is interesting to note the number of examples, size of description and description execution time for unstructured and structured solutions of the parity problem. Let N be the number of primitive attributes used (the original number of truth-values being dealt with). By primitive attributes we mean those that are not described hierarchically in terms of any sub-attributes. No decision can be made about even-parity without considering all primitive attribute values.

We will consider the unstructured solution first. In this solution it is necessary to present ID3 with all possible examples in order to

Attribute-1	Attribute-2	CLASS
false	false	TRUE
false	true	FALSE
true	false	FALSE
true	true	TRUE

Figure 2.4 Examples of first-half-even

Attribute-3	Attribute-4	CLASS
false	false	TRUE
false	true	FALSE
true	false	FALSE
true	true	TRUE

Figure 2.5 Examples of second-half-even

obtain a correct decision tree. That is to say 2^N examples are required, so in figure 2.1 there are $2^4 = 16$. Again, since all primitive attribute values must be considered in making any decision on even-parity, all leaves of the unstructured decision tree will need to be at maximum possible depth in the tree, depth N. There must be 2^N leaves in such a decision tree (one for each example), and by simple summation of nodes at different levels there must be $2^{N+1} - 1$ nodes (in figure 2.2 that is $2^{4+1} - 1 = 31$). When executing the tree, the number of decisions made in gaining any particular result is always N, the maximum depth of the tree. Thus we say that the unstructured solution requires $O(2^N)$ examples, $O(2^N)$ description space and $O(N)$ time to execute the description.

Let us now consider the structured solution. We can extend the solution shown in figures 2.3–2.5 to deal with any number of primitive attributes N, by using sub-attributes which repeatedly break the attribute set in half. For instance, given 8 attributes, 'first-half-even' would have the sub-problems of 'first-first-half-even' and 'second-first-half-even' instead of Attribute-1 and Attribute-2 (see figure 2.4). It works out that the number of examples needed for N primitive at-

```
IF First-half-even THEN
    IF Second-half-even THEN      TRUE
    ELSE                          FALSE
ELSE IF Second-half-even THEN     FALSE
    ELSE                          TRUE
```

Figure 2.6 New ID3 decision tree for even-parity

tributes is $4(N-1)$ (in the solution of figure 2.3–2.5 there are $4\times 3 = 12$ examples). The descriptive size of the solution, the total number of nodes in all trees in the solution, is $7(N-1)$ (21 in the solution of the example set of figures 2.3–2.5). In order to decide on even-parity using the structured set of trees, it is necessary to execute all internal nodes of all trees in the solution, which in general amounts to $3(N-1)$ nodes (9 nodes in the solution of figures 2.3–2.6). Therefore the unstructured solution requires $O(N)$ examples, $O(N)$ description space and $O(N)$ time to execute the description. The complexity results for various representational methods of describing the parity problem are summarised later in figure 2.8.

The author is not aware of any such quantitative analysis of worst case for structured and unstructured induction presented elsewhere. However, these results are in line with Shapiro's observation in his chess endgame solution for the domain of KPa7KR, that, while the execution time for structured solutions is not noticeably different from that of unstructured solutions, considerably fewer examples are needed and the total size of description produced is smaller (Shapiro, 1987).

Structuring can, therefore, be an effective technique both for compaction and for understandability. However, let us change the parity problem slightly and try to build a decision tree for checking even-parity of an arbitrarily long stream of truth-values. Suppose that an inductive algorithm has a training phase in which examples of even-parity are presented and a rule set is produced. With either the unstructured or structured ID3 solution, an example set can only define a window into a finite portion of the stream of truth-values. Remembering that no decision can be made about even-parity without checking all primitive attribute values, the generated decision tree will work only for segments of the truth-value stream which are less than or equal to the length (number of attributes) described by the example set. In order to deal with sequences of arbitrary, unbounded, or even infinite length, using a finite amount of training, we must turn to finite-state machine theory.

2.6 Finite-state automata and strategy learning

A *finite-state automaton* is a mathematical model of a controller which has a discrete set of inputs and outputs. This controller has a predefined fixed set of internal states through which it passes when carrying

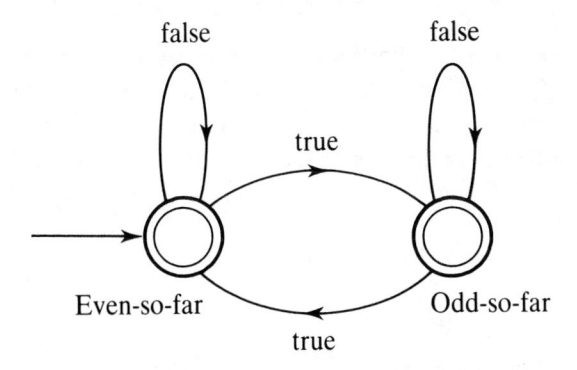

Figure 2.7 The even-parity finite-state acceptor

out its function. The output response of the controller to any set of inputs presented to it is determined not only by the input values, but also by the value of its internal state.

2.6.1 Finite-state acceptors

A finite-state *acceptor* is a limited form of finite-state automaton which has an output repertoire of accept, reject when applied to any particular series of symbols.

2.6.2 Parity example revisited

Let us reconsider the parity problem discussed in section 2.5, and pose this as a problem for a finite-state acceptor. The allowable symbols for any element of a sequence presented to a parity checking automaton are chosen from the set true, false. The acceptor has two states, 'even-so-far' and 'odd-so-far'. When in state 'even-so-far' the acceptor will report with the action 'accept', and will give the answer 'reject' when in the state 'odd-so-far'. If the string of symbols terminates leaving the acceptor in the state 'even-so-far', we will know that there were an even number of trues, otherwise there were an odd number. Figure 2.7 illustrates such an automaton. In figure 2.7, circles represent states. A state is denoted by a double circle when it is associated with an *accept* output and by a single circle for the output being *reject*. Labelled arrowed arcs joining circles represent transitions that are taken between states on recognition of particular symbols in the input sequence. The unlabelled arc leading into the state 'even-so-far' from the left indicates that this is the state in which the automaton starts when presented with the first symbol in the sequence.

Finite-state acceptors have special importance in the theory of formal languages. It can be shown (Hopcroft and Ullman, 1979) that the class of languages accepted by finite-state automata is exactly that of the regular languages. In these terms, strings of true/false values accepted by our even-parity acceptor would be sentences in the language of even-parity.

2.6.3 Formal definition of finite-state acceptors

We formally denote a finite-state acceptor by a 5-tuple $(Q, \Sigma, \delta, I, F)$ where Q is a finite set of states (even-so-far, odd-so-far as in the example), Σ is a finite input alphabet (true, false in the example), $I \subseteq Q$ is the set of initial states (even-so-far in the example), $F \subseteq Q$ is the set of final or accepting states (even-so-far in the example) and δ is the transition function mapping $Q \times \Sigma$ to Q (the labelled arcs of figure 2.7). That is, $\delta(q, a)$ is a state in Q for each state q and input symbol a.

2.6.4 Complexity measure for the finite-state parity solution

In terms of the complexity measures of section 2.5.3, it can be seen that two decision nodes are needed in the finite-state solution of figure 2.7 irrespective of the number of truth-values inspected. Thus the descriptive complexity is constant, which we denote $O(0)$. In terms of execution steps, as always we need to look at all N of the values in any particular string of values to decide on even-parity. Thus the time complexity is still $O(N)$. In Chapter 6 (example 6.13, section 6.5.5) it is shown that parity acceptors can be built by the KR induction algorithm using a fixed number of examples. The example complexity using this algorithm is thus constant, or $O(0)$.

Figure 2.8 sums up the various complexity results for different representations of the even-parity problem solution.

2.6.5 Mealy and Moore machines

Although finite-state acceptors are a powerful model for representing predicates which decide whether or not a string of symbols belongs to a particular set of such strings, a general purpose controller needs to be able to produce more than the two outputs accept, reject. There are two different formalisms used to generalise the notion of finite-state

	Unstructured tree	Structured trees	Finite-state machine
Example complexity	$O(2^N)$	$O(N)$	$O(0)$
Description complexity	$O(2^N)$	$O(N)$	$O(0)$
Execution time	$O(N)$	$O(N)$	$O(N)$

Figure 2.8 Complexity results, $N =$ number of binary variables dealt with

acceptors to automata capable of producing a selection of more than two outputs.

1. **Moore machines.** The output values are paired with particular states. Figure 2.9 shows the Moore machine version of an 'even-parity' finite-state automaton. Note that if the machine in figure 2.9 had more than two outputs it would need more than two states.
2. **Mealy machines.** The output value is paired with particular inputs. Figure 2.10 shows the Mealy machine version of an 'even-parity' finite-state automaton.

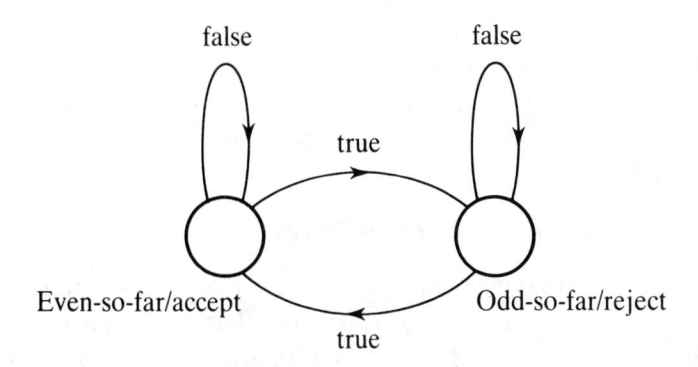

Figure 2.9 The even-parity Moore machine

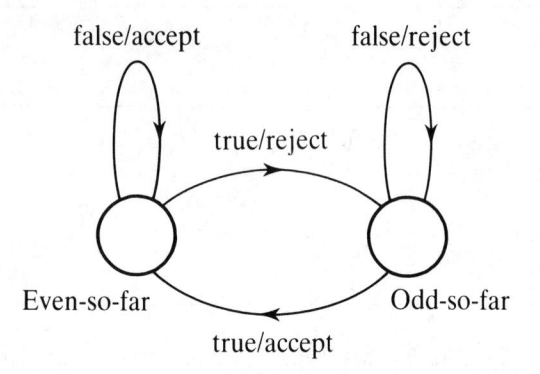

Figure 2.10 The even-parity Mealy machine

A specific form of Mealy machine, the deterministic uniquely terminated Mealy machine (DUTMM) is described in Chapter 6. DUTMMs are the basis of the control within modules of Radial programs (see Chapter 3). These machines have a unique goal state, entry into which causes termination of the module's execution. The input and output symbol pairs which label the arcs of a Mealy machine equate to particular situations which cause actions to be fired, with a simultaneous state transition. In turn, the situation vectors represent sets of callable Radial modules, each of which returns a value. The action is a callable Radial module which does not return a value. In the next section we investigate the expressive power of Radial modules.

2.6.6 Expressive power of DUTMMs

In order to show that DUTMMs have more expressive power than decision trees, it is necessary to show first that they can describe all decision-tree solutions to problems and that at least one other problem solution can be described using a finite-state automaton, but not using any structured or unstructured set of decision trees. The first condition, that DUTMMs can describe all decision-tree solutions to problems, is shown to be true by figure 2.11. In this figure each situation/classification pair s_i/c_i $(1 \leq i \leq n)$ derivable from some decision tree is used to label the arcs leading from the start state of the DUTMM to the goal state, the particular decision c_i being returned on recognition of situation s_i. Clearly, an automaton such as that in figure 2.11 can be constructed to be behaviourly equivalent to any given decision tree.

The second condition is apparent from the fact that a one-way infinite lengthed string parity problem is insoluble by use of decision trees (see end of section 2.5.3), as any decision tree must be finite, though it is simply soluble as a Mealy machine (figure 2.10) which reports parity-so-far for any prefix of the one-way infinite string.

2.6.7 Limits on expressive power of finite-state machines

Finite-state automata, in turn, have limits, and form only one rung in the ladder of arithmetic expressiveness. Figure 2.12 describes a simple version of this hierarchy, Universal Turing machines being the most expressive computational formalism.

In fact the only difference between a finite-state machine and a Universal Turing machine is the latter's ability not only to read from a tape of symbols which can be moved backwards and forwards, but also to *write* symbols onto that tape. In our example, the tape of symbols was the string of truth values which the finite-state machine was allowed to read from. The extra ability to write to the tape equates to the use of variables and program stack in computer programs. As shown in the next section, the Radial language has these abilities, and therefore has the expressivity of a Universal Turing machine.

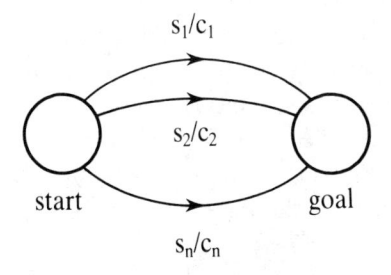

Figure 2.11 DUTMM equivalent of decision trees

```
                    Universal Turing machines
                                |
↑ Expressive        Finite-state automata
  power                         |
                       Decision trees
```

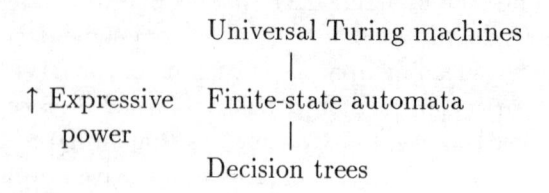

Figure 2.12 Hierarchy of arithmetic expressiveness

2.6.8 Recursion and variables

The Radial language caters for recursively defined functions and procedures by allowing situational conditions and actions to be evaluated by the mechanism of procedure call. To complete the requisites of full computational expressiveness, any high-level language must allow for the creation and manipulation of variables. Radial permits the use of variables by the standard methods of variable declaration, value assignment and module parameterisation. The use of variables and recursion are illustrated in Chapters 3 and 4.

2.7 Induction of finite-state automata

Although in the last section we emphasised the expressivity of finite-state representations over simpler classification formalisms, this aspect is secondary to human comprehensibility of these description formats. The transition mechanism of finite-state automata has a direct parallel with the *goto* statement of many programming languages. As unconstrained use of *goto* in programs is known to lead to highly opaque code which is difficult to create and maintain, it might be felt that we are trying to re-open a 'Pandora's box' which had almost been closed. In practice, though, knowledge engineers using RuleMaster without any way of inducing finite-state control from sequence information have largely preferred to avoid the use of multiple state modules, and limited themselves to building classification systems by structuring a hierarchy of single-state modules in the manner proposed and tested by Shapiro (1987).

However, human beings seem to find it easy and natural to generate 'control plans' consisting of sequences of ⟨*situation/action*⟩ pairs. If such 'plans' could be used by an inductive algorithm to produce finite-state automata, the problem of origination and maintenance would be made considerably easier. Algorithms which do so are presented, together with examples of their use in Chapters 6–8.

This still leaves the problem of opacity of automatically generated finite-state automata. This might be approached in a similar fashion to that suggested by Michie (1984) for decision trees. Thus inductive algorithms would be limited, by some constraint, so that only humanly comprehensible finite-state automata were produced. For instance, the two-state automaton shown in figure 2.10 seems quite comprehensible, though a twenty-state automaton with arbitrary transitions would be very difficult to understand. One approach that becomes immediately obvious is to place an upper limit on the product of the number of states and transitions which is acceptable in an automatically generated finite-state automaton. However, in this book we have not dealt with these aspects of comprehensibility.

2.8 Conclusion

In this chapter the nature of inductive algorithms has been characterised. Inductive algorithms use various types of example material to generate hypotheses in various rule formats. By definition, inductive algorithms make 'guesses' concerning unknown facts. These guesses must be shown to be sound according to some demonstrable criteria.

In sections 2.5 and 2.6 the 'parity' problem was used to illustrate properties of various rule representations. In figure 2.8 a table of complexity results for the three chosen representations was given. This table showed that, for this problem at least, it is preferable to use a finite-state machine representation rather than a decision-tree based one. Finite-state machine representations were shown to have more expressive power than those of propositional calculus and decision trees. However, there exist formalisms, such as Universal Turing machines, which have even more expressive power than finite-state machines. One might ask whether formal power is the ultimate criterion for deciding between representations. It was stated that, for expert system applications, *expert comprehensibility* is more relevant to the choice of an appropriate representation than *formal power*.

Chapter 3
RuleMaster

3.1 Some issues in knowledge engineering

Expert systems differ from other computer programs in the following aspects.

1. **Explanation.** Expert systems can be debugged by using execution traces to 'explain' the link between certain factors being investigated and the conclusions which they support. This has been found to be a useful and sometimes necessary debugging tool for the development of expert systems (see section 3.8).

2. **Problem type.** Expert systems are more suitable than an algorithmic approach for problems which involve a large amount of branching.

3. **Partial certainty.** Expert systems are usually able to deal with a set of values between true and false which represent the partial certainty of a proposition. RuleMaster, described in this chapter, does not provide facilities to deal with partial certainty.

It has been stated by Feigenbaum (1979) that the most difficult part of expert system building lies in the acquisition of knowledge from experts. A key issue here is the difference between dialogue acquisition of rules and the use of inductive learning. The latter approach relieves experts of much of the burden of generating rules directly, allowing them merely to present instances of correct decision making, while the machine produces generalisations from these decisions.

One of the goals of AI programming language design (as pursued, though not yet fully attained, by the logic programming school) is that users should be able to tell the machine relevant facts, theories, advice and so on in the order that it occurs to them rather than in a fixed sequence as demanded by traditional programming languages. A degree of order-independence which has so far eluded every Prolog interpreter can be supplied by a new style of programming based on inductive rather than deductive mechanisms. Strictly speaking, inductive programming involves the user in creating operational specifications which can be transformed by the inductive mechanism into well sequenced, efficient programs.

Large knowledge bases can become unwieldy and difficult to understand and experts tend to organise their knowledge as a set of *interrelated* factors. By making a hierarchy of attributes explicit Shapiro (1986) has shown it is possible to make the interrelationship of problem attributes easier to understand and maintain. Furthermore, he has also shown that structuring even pays off in terms of strict store cost and processor cost (see also section 2.5.3). Even though this approach involves the human overhead of structure formation, its advantages outweigh this disadvantage.

As explained in section 1.1, expert systems can be broadly divided into two main categories: classification, such as MYCIN (Shortliffe and Buchanan, 1975) and control, such as VM (Fagan *et al*, 1979). Often expert systems require a combination of these abilities but in many systems the form of knowledge representation supports one of these approaches while impeding the other.

Practical expert systems require information sources other than the rules which the expert uses when making decisions. For instance, a medical diagnostic system might read biomedical sensors, access patient records and do mathematical modelling of bodily processes. Facilities for linking to external routines may therefore be considered as an essential component of modern expert system software.

3.2 RuleMaster

3.2.1 Overview

RuleMaster is a general purpose expert system building tool. It consists of two major components: Radial and Rulemaker. Rulemaker is an inductive generator of executable expressions in a rule language called Radial. Rulemaker allows users to describe their knowledge in a declarative form, while Radial executes the more procedurally oriented form generated by Rulemaker. Rulemaker is discussed further in section 3.3 on knowledge acquisition, while some of the special features of

Radial are described in later sections.

It is a well-recognised fact that over 50% of the time taken creating an expert system is spent on building support facilities for carrying out calculations, reading instrumentation or accessing databases. As a high-level language Radial combines the ability to represent conditional rules and to carry out calculations and communicate with procedures written in other languages (see section 3.10). While other high-level languages might have provided similar facilities in this respect, Radial is unique in its ability to provide explanations of its reasoning as an integral part of the program specification.

The development of RuleMaster was motivated by a desire to solve the knowledge engineering issues involved in building large expert systems (described in Section 3.1). ACLS (Paterson and Niblett, 1982), described in Appendix A, a refinement of ID3 (Quinlan, 1979), is the inductive algorithm used by Rulemaker. A methodology for structuring inductively generated rule sets was developed and tested by Shapiro and Niblett (1982) and the explanation facility used by the Radial interpreter is derived from a proposal by Shapiro and Michie (1986). The Radial environment is the academic counterpart of the commercial product RuleMaster (Michie et al, 1984).

The original version of RuleMaster was largely designed and coded by the author. It is written as a set of interrelated C programs running under the UNIX[†] operating system. The entire RuleMaster environment is composed of around 15,000 lines of C code. There are current working versions running on the following machines: DEC VAX, SUN Microsystems, IBM PC/XT and PC/AT, and AT&T UNIX machine.

3.3 Knowledge acquisition

The approach to knowledge acquisition taken in RuleMaster differs considerably from that employed when hand crafting rules. It is well known that experts explain complex concepts to human apprentices implicitly, by way of examples, rather than explicitly, by stating principles. The apprentice intuitively generalises these sample decisions to form more widely applicable rules. A computer can learn in the same way as the human apprentice if it is able to produce general rules from specific instances.

RuleMaster allows the expert system builder to use rules written

---

[†]UNIX is a trademark of Bell Laboratories.

either explicitly by an expert or by the machine from examples. The machine builds rules by a process called *rule induction*. In induction of classification rules, rules are induced by generalisation from *examples* of expert decision-making. An example is expressed as a vector of values concerning attributes of the decision, together with the expert's classification. For instance, in a very simple case, if we are trying to build a rule to classify animals, the attributes of the decision might be *colour* and *size*. A possible classification is *Elephant*. Given the example:

Colour	*Size*		*Class*
grey	big	⇒	Elephant

the induction algorithm would generalise this example to the rule:

Irrespective of the animal's colour or size, it is an ELEPHANT

In order to get a more accurate generalisation, more examples would need to be added, and a more complex rule would be induced. For instance, with the following example set:

Colour	*Size*		*Class*
grey	big	⇒	Elephant
yellow	big	⇒	Giraffe
grey	small	⇒	Tortoise

the following decision tree is generated:

If the animal's colour is

 (a) yellow, then it is a Giraffe
 (b) grey, then if the animal's size is
   (i) big, then it is an Elephant
   (ii) small, then it is a Tortoise

In RuleMaster, a class is composed of an action and a next-state. The action specifies what to do in the example situation, and the next-state says which context must be entered after the action has been carried out. The induction subsystem which supports this is known as Rulemaker. The syntax and semantics of Rulemaker are described in section 3.7.

An illustration of the power of inductive inference to weed out irrelevance is shown in the following example taken from the WILLARD expert system (see section 5.3). Contained within a widely used meteorological manual (NTIS: *Use of SkewT, Log P Diagram in Analysis*

Vertical Divergence	Vertical Motion	Vertical Thickness		Change in Lapse Rate
divergent	descending	shrinking	⇒	more stable
divergent	ascending	shrinking	⇒	more stable
divergent	ascending	stretching	⇒	less stable
convergent	descending	shrinking	⇒	more stable
convergent	descending	stretching	⇒	less stable
convergent	ascending	stretching	⇒	less stable
divergent	none	shrinking	⇒	more stable
convergent	none	stretching	⇒	less stable
divergent	ascending	no change	⇒	no change
convergent	descending	no change	⇒	no change
none	ascending	stretching	⇒	less stable
none	descending	shrinking	⇒	more stable

Figure 3.1 Table found in NTIS Air Weather Service Manual used in lapse rate determination

and Forecasting) is a table (given here as figure 3.1) of three attributes used to determine the expected change of lapse rate.

The rule generated from these examples used only one of the three given attributes. This rule was as follows:

> *If the thickness (distance between the two constant pressure surfaces)*
>
> *(a) shrinks, the lapse rate becomes more stable*
> *(b) stretches, the lapse rate becomes less stable*
> *(c) does not change, the lapse rate does not change*

This simple relation was never spotted by meteorologists although the table had appeared for years in standard texts. The rule was found to be correct and consistent with a physical model of the atmosphere (based on the hypsometric equations).

Entering rules by examples has several distinct advantages over writing production rules. When the example set has insufficient information to cover the entire problem space, Rulemaker will generalise these examples in order to produce a decision tree which covers all the possible situations. If the knowledge is entered directly as rules, no generalisation is carried out. When too many attributes are present (as in the case shown in figure 3.1), redundant information is ignored by Rulemaker. Again, production systems do not have this ability to compact knowledge.

The knowledge is given as examples in a more implicit declarative form than in production systems, and this is automatically transformed into a more explicit procedural form than that of production systems. Thus experts can enter and revise knowledge without regard to order, while reviewing and executing an economical procedural form constructed for them by the system. In logic programming, the equivalent of Rulemaker's example set would be an arbitrarily ordered set of Horn clauses in a propositional subset of first order logic.

3.4 Types of expert systems supported

A wide range of approaches may be taken in the construction of expert systems. These approaches employ varying knowledge representations, including: production systems (as by Shortliffe and Buchanan, 1975), first-order predicate logic (as by Niblett, 1985), frames (as by Minsky, 1975), inference networks (as by Duda *et al*, 1979), causal models (as by Mozetic *et al.*, 1984), object-oriented models (as by Bobrow and Stefik, 1983) or hybrid approaches (as by Intellicorp, 1989). The best understood of these are classificatory in nature. However, expert system packages made by removing the knowledge component from an expert classification system, as was done with EMYCIN (Van Melle, 1980), often have difficulty in handling procedural actions. RuleMaster was designed from the start to allow a wide range of control strategies, so that the system could be applied to a broad set of problem types.

An expert system application built with RuleMaster consists of a set of Radial modules. These modules consist of a transition network of states, each of which contains a single decision tree. When invoked, each decision tree carries out a sequence of tests until a decision is reached to perform an action. After execution of this action, control is passed to a new state within the calling module. Control only moves from one module to another via the mechanism of procedure call. The ability to do conditional branching together with that of calling modules recursively allows the building of arbitrarily complex control structures (see sections 2.6.6 and 2.6.7 for a discussion of the expressivity of the Radial language). More details concerning the Radial language are given in the next section.

The large RuleMaster expert systems described in Chapter 5 are primarily classificatory and only use a subset of the Radial language. However, small but effective control expert systems have been built. For example, an expert system which builds an arch out of a set of blocks from an arbitrary starting position to a given goal position was constructed inductively from sample arch-building action-decisions. This is discussed further in Chapter 4. Although this was only a demonstration of RuleMaster's capabilities, the domain contains several features of non-classificatory applications such as simple design and scheduling.

3.5 Radial

Radial is a language for the run-time orchestration of an incremental library of C-coded procedures. It accordingly leaves all actual computations to these, including I/O. It could be said that all that a Radial program ever does is to execute rules and control statements and assign strings to variables.

3.5.1 Finite automata

The language has its formal basis in finite-automata theory (see section 2.6). The subclass of finite-state automata which are of interest here, DUTMMs (see sections 2.6 and 6.6), consists of machines whose output signal is entirely dependent on the combination of their input signals and their internal machine state.

More formally, the behaviour of the machine is described by the 6-tuple $\{Q, \Sigma, \Delta, \delta, q_0, q_g\}$ in which

1. $Q = \{q_0, q_1, \ldots\}$ is a set of machine *states*.

2. Σ is a set of legal *inputs*.

3. Δ is a set of legal *outputs*.

4. δ is the *next state function* which gives the next state based on the current state and the current situation (in the case of a machine measuring the situation on the basis of two binary values we have $\delta : Q \times \{0, 1\} \times \{0, 1\} \rightarrow Q$)

5. q_0 is the *start state* of the automaton.

6. q_g is the unique *goal state* of the automaton.

7. δ can be described by a tabulation of inputs and outputs related to particular states. This is usually called the *state transition*

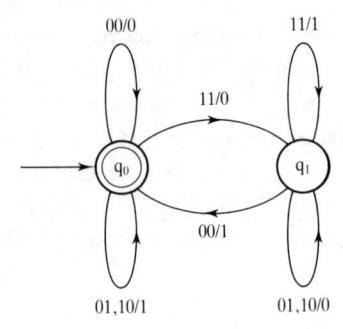

Figure 3.2 A binary adder as a finite-state machine transition diagram.

table. However, a finite-state function is often more clearly represented in terms of a *state transition diagram*. Figure 3.2 depicts a finite state diagram of an automaton capable of taking two streams of binary input digits and producing one stream representing their sum using the states q_0 and q_1 to represent the 'carry'. The initial state is indicated by a start arrow, and the state transition arcs are labelled with the two input digits read-in, together with the one output digit produced. At any moment in time, the machine's situation is the pair of values being read in, for example, $\langle 0, 1 \rangle$. The action chosen will either be to output '0' or to output '1'.

By analogy with the above, we could imagine a sequential procedure being represented in the style of figure 3.3, with conditional tests replacing the input symbols, and procedure calls replacing the output symbols. The figure is a diagrammatic representation of a possible Radial program module. The module, while in state 'in bed', decides to do the action 'sleep' and stay in state 'in bed' if the conditions 'tired' and 'not-hungry' are true. Alternatively, if 'tired' is untrue or 'hungry'

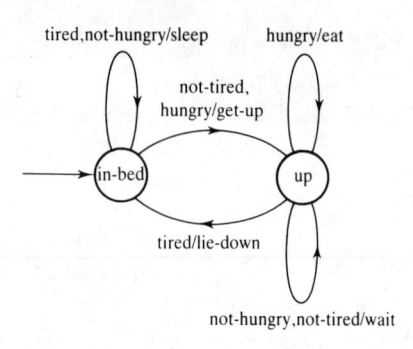

Figure 3.3 A simple daily routine. ',' means 'or'

Finite state automata	Production rule systems
state	context
situation	antecedent
action	consequent
transition arc	goto ⟨context⟩

Figure 3.4 Relationship between finite-state automata and production rules

is true, then action 'get up' is carried out, and the module enters state 'up'. It is left to the reader to follow the remaining transitions.

An approximate correspondence between this formalism and the production-rule formalisms more familiar to knowledge engineers is shown in the table of figure 3.4. We shall follow EMYCIN in the use of the term 'context' to denote a self-contained bundle of rules which can be entered from another context as a result of firing an action which contains a 'goto'.

In terms of algorithmic programming (an inductively generated application can be viewed as an efficient block-structured program), we have the correspondence of figure 3.5.

3.5.2 Radial syntax

Figure 3.6 shows the syntax of Radial as a syntax diagram. The following sections use illustrative examples to describe the structure of Radial programs.

Radial	Algorithmic
module	routine (may or may not return value)
state	labelled if-then-else block
situation	set of callable value-returning routines
action	non-value-returning routine
transition arc	goto ⟨label⟩

Figure 3.5 Relationship between Radial and Algorithmic languages

42   Inductive Acquisition of Expert Knowledge

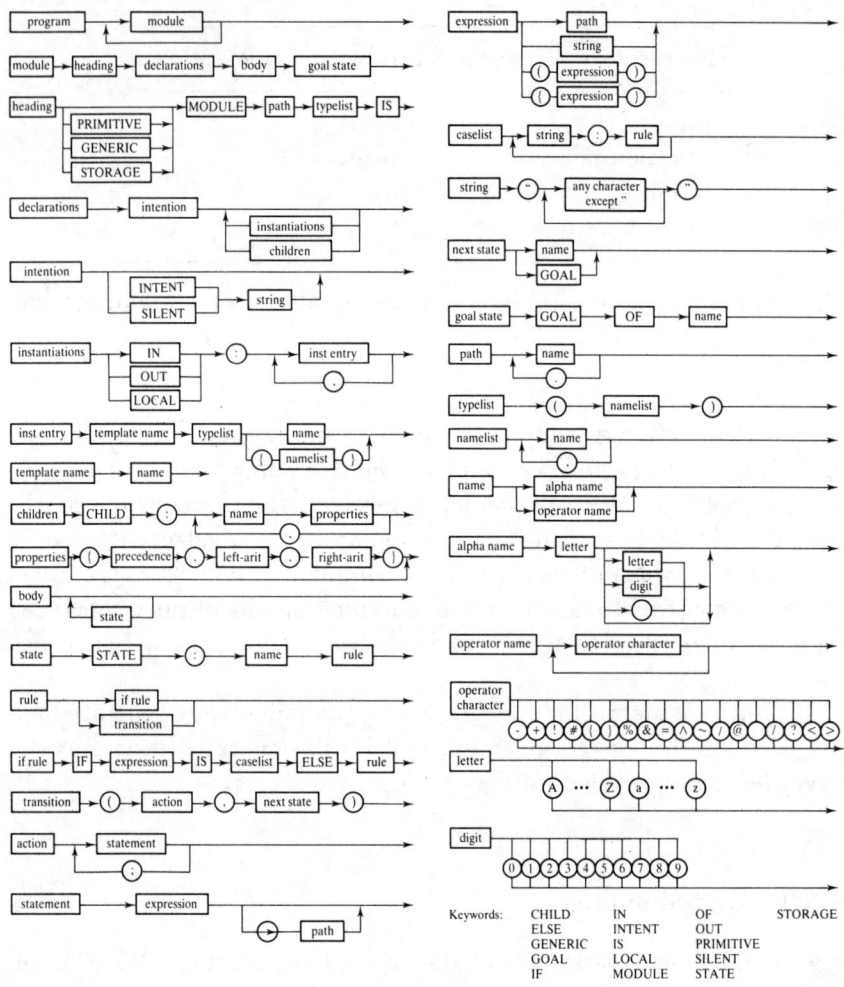

Figure 3.6   The syntax of Radial

3.5.3   Radial program structure

A Radial program consists of a collection of interrelated modules. An individual module can represent either an executable procedure or a piece of data. In order to aid the imposition of a structure on these modules, they are arranged in a tree. The scope of referencing a module from any other is limited by a recursive scope rule called *visibility*. Visibility is defined (figure 3.7) as follows:

> module m2 is visible to module m1 iff
>   m2 is a child of m1 or
>   m2 is visible to the parent of m1

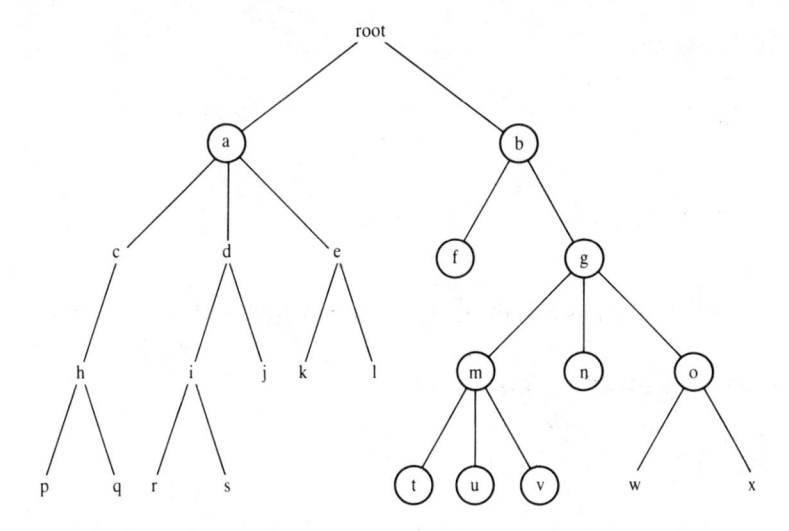

Figure 3.7 The visibility of module m

Figure 3.7 represents a hypothetical program tree with modules named by the letters of the alphabet. Note that the highest module in the tree, root, by the definition of visibility cannot be referenced by any module in the tree. The circular modules are those visible to module 'm'. Rather than using block bracketing to indicate the tree structure of a Radial program, each module is identified using its unique path from the root in the program tree, so module m's complete name is 'b.g.m.'

3.5.4 Form of individual states

Each Radial module consists of a declaration section together with a number of named states. Each state in a module has a single decision tree associated with it which decides, on the basis of a number of tests, what action should be taken, and which state within the present module to enter subsequently. The decision trees have tests at internal nodes and action/next state pairs at the leaves.

The state shown in figure 3.8 is from a module to decide whether or not to use an umbrella.

The decision tree is expressed as nested 'case statements' each of form

IF ⟨test⟩ IS
  ⟨val1⟩ : ⟨tree1⟩
  ⟨val2⟩ : ⟨tree2⟩
  ...

  ELSE ⟨treeN⟩

where each ⟨treex⟩ is either of the same form or of the form

$$(\langle action \rangle, \langle next-state \rangle)$$

In figure 3.8:

1. 'weather', 'inside' and 'soaked' are tests producing the quoted string values shown (e.g., weather can be "wet,sunny" or some other value).

2. "USE" → result and "DONTUSE" → result are actions indicating the assignment of the string literals "USE" and "DONTUSE" to the variable 'result'.

3. 'goal' is the name of a special state which is found in every Radial module. When entered, it merely returns control to the calling module.

```
STATE: decide
IF (weather) IS
   "wet" : IF (inside) IS
      "yes" : ("DONTUSE" → result, goal)
      ELSE IF (soaked) IS
         "yes: ("DONTUSE" → result, goal)
         ELSE ("USE" → result, goal)
   "sunny" : ("DONTUSE" → result, goal)
   ELSE ("DONTUSE" → result, goal)
```

Figure 3.8 Decision tree within state which decides whether to use an umbrella

Type	Module labelling	Meaning
0	MODULE	A normal callable procedure
1	PRIMITIVE MODULE	Callable C-coded procedure
2	GENERIC MODULE	A module which can be instantiated for operation on different types
3	PRIMITIVE GENERIC MODULE	Unused combination
4	STORAGE MODULE	Unused combination
5	PRIMITIVE STORAGE MODULE	Unused combination
6	GENERIC STORAGE MODULE	User-defined abstract data type
7	PRIMITIVE GENERIC STORAGE MODULE	System-defined abstract data type

Figure 3.9 The interpretation of the eight different types of Radial module

3.6 Individual Radial modules

A Radial module can be labelled with certain combinations of:

1. PRIMITIVE.

2. GENERIC.

3. STORAGE.

Figure 3.9 tabulates the meaning of the eight different combinations of these three labels.

These various module types are explained in the following sections.

3.6.1 Type 0 modules: Normal Radial modules

There are two basic classes of type 0 module: modules which return a value to the calling module and modules which do not. When applied to expert systems, this distinction is between modules which carry out some diagnostic value-returning test that does not affect the state of the

```
            MODULE main.rain IS
            INTENT: "decide whether to use an umbrella"
            CHILD: weather, inside, soaked
            OUT: string result
            STATE: decide
            IF (weather) IS
              "wet" : IF (inside) IS
                "yes" : ("DONTUSE" result, GOAL)
                ELSE IF (soaked) IS
                  "yes: ("DONTUSE" result, GOAL)
                  ELSE ("USE" result, GOAL)
              "sunny" : ("DONTUSE" result, GOAL)
                ELSE ("DONTUSE" result, GOAL)
            GOAL OF rain
```

Figure 3.10 A value-returning Radial module

world and modules which carry out non-value-returning control actions which are intended to affect the world (see section 1.1 for an explanation of the distinction between classification and control). Figure 3.10 shows an example of the former type of module while figure 3.11 shows an example of the latter. Figure 3.10 is the complete Radial module from which the state shown in figure 3.8 was taken.

The module *rain* exists in the program tree as a child of *main* (hence the path name is *main.rain*). The system will use the string following the keyword *INTENT* when referring in explanation to the execution of this module. *rain* is a single-state module, the state being called 'decide'. Examples of modules containing multiple states are given in section 3.9.3. The module *rain* has five sub-modules, *weather*, *inside*, *soaked*, *incar* and *result*. *result* is an instantiation of the primitive generic storage module string and is used as the output variable of *rain*.

The module *oax* in figure 3.11 plays nought's side of the game noughts and crosses by asking a number of questions about the board state, such as "is board full". On the basis of these questions it advises an action, such as "take any free space". Paired with this action is the next state which can either be the present state, *decide*, which causes looping, or the special module exit state, *GOAL*, which causes termi-

```
MODULE oax IS
  INTENT: "play noughts and crosses"
  STATE: decide
    IF (ask "is board full" "yes,no") IS
      "yes" : (advise "Board full - end of game", GOAL)
      ELSE IF (ask "can O win immediately" "yes,no") IS
        "yes" : (advise "complete line to win", GOAL)
        ELSE IF (ask "can X win immediately" "yes,no") IS
          "yes" : (advise "block X", decide)
          ELSE IF (ask "is middle free" "yes,no") IS
            "yes" : (advise "take centre", decide)
            ELSE IF (ask "Is there a corner free" "yes,no" ) IS
              "yes" : (advise "take the corner with most WEIGHT",
                decide)
              ELSE (advise "take any free space",
GOAL OF oax
```

Figure 3.11 A non-value-returning Radial module which plays noughts and crosses

nation of play. Note that the major difference between the modules shown in figures 3.10 and 3.11 is the respective presence and absence of the OUT declarations.

3.6.2 Type 1 modules: C-coded procedures

Radial programs can call programs written in other languages (presently C and FORTRAN) by the mechanism of PRIMITIVE MODULE. Figure 3.12 shows the interface to the primitive module *ask* which is called by the noughts and crosses-playing module of figure 3.11. Note that the explanation string for *ask* is labelled with the keyword *SILENT* here, rather than *INTENT*, since we do not want the workings of *ask*

```
PRIMITIVE MODULE ask IS
  SILENT: "the answer to '$1'"
  IN: string prompt
  OUT: string answer
GOAL OF ask
```

Figure 3.12 The primitive module 'ask'

to be shown in any explanation of execution (see section 3.8). The input prompt string (*IN: string prompt*) is substituted for the $1 in the explanation string. Any occurrence of a '$' followed by some number, N, causes the runtime substitution of the Nth input argument into the explanation string when an explanation of execution is given.

The Radial interpreter executes PRIMITIVE modules either by mapping each call via a look-up table to a unique C-function compiled into the interpreter, or, failing this, by requesting 'remote' execution of the procedure in a 'slave' process which runs as a concurrent process connected by a UNIX pipe to the Radial interpreter.

3.6.3 Type 2 modules: generic modules

Generic modules are code segments which can be multiply instantiated to act on different data types. For instance, the module *square* of figure 3.13 can be multiply instantiated as in modules *sqri* and *sqrf* to operate on either integers or floating point numbers. The interpreter automatically infers the appropriate meaning for '*' in the instantiated modules from the types of its operands.

3.6.4 Type 6: user-defined abstract data types

When experts describe their problem, they prefer to state it using the terminology of their subject. Thus a thrust force of 5000 N is to a turbo engineer more than the integer value '5000'. Abstract data types

```
GENERIC MODULE square (type) IS
  IN: type val_in
  OUT: type val_out
  STATE: calculate
 (val_in * val_in → val_out, GOAL)
GOAL OF square

MODULE m IS
  LOCAL: square (integer) sqri, square (float) sqrf
  STATE: show
    (print sqri 5 ; print sqrf 5.0, GOAL)
  GOAL OF m
```

Figure 3.13 Generic modules and instantiations

GENERIC STORAGE MODULE coordinate IS
  LOCAL: float x,y,z
  CHILD: read, print
GOAL OF coordinate

MODULE m IS
  LOCAL: coordinate top,bottom
  STATE: getshow
    (read "Bottom? " → bottom; read Top? → top; print bottom, GOAL)
GOAL OF m

Figure 3.14 The abstract data type 'coordinate'

allow experts to invent their own data types and the operators for manipulating them. Users can define their own abstract data types within a Radial program by the declaration of GENERIC STORAGE MODULES. The direct children of a generic storage module are taken as being operators which act only on data of the corresponding type. Thus figure 3.14 describes a new type of object called a 'coordinate' which consists of three values, x, y and z. The operations which can be carried out on a coordinate are 'read' (which reads a coordinate value from the user), 'print' (which prints a coordinate value onto the screen) and 'offset' (which adds a 2D offset to a coordinate position). Note that since this is a storage module, it has no executable body.

3.6.5 Type 7: system-defined abstract data types

The Radial language has no inherent data types built into its syntax. All variables are stored internally as strings for the convenience of inter-process communication. However, certain data types are supplied to the interpreter along with any application. Such base types are declared as PRIMITIVE GENERIC STORAGE MODULEs. In all other ways primitive generic storage modules are identical to the GENERIC STORAGE MODULEs of section 3.6.4. The Radial interpreter at present supports the following data types

    string
    integer
    float
    list

PRIMITIVE GENERIC STORAGE MODULE integer IS
   child: + {20,1,1},
               - {20,1,1},
               * {30,1,1},
               ** {50,1,1},
               / {30,1,1},
               < {15,1,1},
               leq {15,1,1},
               > {15,1,1},
               >= {15,1,1},
               == {10,1,1},
               != {10,1,1},
               i_to_s,
               s_to_i,
               real,
               read,
               print {8,0,1}
GOAL OF integer

Figure 3.15   Integer data-type operators

3.7   Operator definitions

In several languages, including Prolog, programmers are provided with the ability to declare procedures (or predicates in Prolog's case) in such a way that they can be called using infix, prefix or postfix notation within expressions. Such a facility is also provided in the Radial language by allowing the declaration of 'operator properties' together with the definition of modules. Figure 3.15 illustrates the use of such operator properties in the definition of the integer data type operators.

In the definition + *{20,1,1}* of figure 3.15, the three numbers stand respectively for *precedence*, *left arity* and *right arity*. The first of these, precedence, indicates +'s binding strength within an expression. Imagine an expression depicted in the standard form as a tree, hanging downwards from the root. The lower the precedence, the lower the operator will be in the tree. Left and right arity indicate the number of arguments expected on the left and right side of the operator. Clearly the sum of the left and right arities should be equal to the number of input arguments expected by the corresponding procedure. Note that in figure 3.15 the operators *i_to_s*, *s_to_i*, *real* and *read* have no declared operator properties. In such a case, the interpreter assigns a default precedence of *100*, a left arity of *0* and a right arity equal to the number of input arguments. Operators have a maximum precedence of *511*.

3.8 Explanation

The Radial interpreter has the ability to explain its line of reasoning at any time during a session. When an expert system is consulted, the reasoning behind a piece of advice may influence whether or not it is accepted. For example, if the explanation indicates that a critical factor has been ignored, the user may decide to reject the advice. Requests for explanation during hypothetical test cases can also be used to instruct novices. Explanation has additional value at development time. In explanation-driven development, the expert checks that correct decisions are reached, and that they are reached for the right reasons. This increases the likelihood that situations outside the training set will be dealt with correctly. A case in point occurred during the validation of the EARL expert system (see Chapter 5), when it was discovered that, in 4 cases out of the 859 tested, EARL reached the correct conclusion for the wrong reasons. Without the ability to validate the result *and* the explanation against the expert, this would never have come to light.

This implementation of explanation follows that described in Shapiro and Michie (1986), though the irrelevance-suppression option which Shapiro and Michie regarded as important has not been incorporated; instead the explanation is presented in rule-sized chunks so as not to overburden the user.

Each Radial module requires a text segment containing optional slots for run-time substitution of the input arguments of that module (such as the *INTENT* statement of figure 3.10 and the *SILENT* statement of figure 3.12). These pieces of text are combined in a standard set of masks to produce English phrases. An algorithm orders the individual phrases to form a proof which justifies the reasoning by building from axiomatic facts towards the final conclusion. The explanation is given piecemeal, the most relevant portion being presented first, with further elaboration on demand. Actions and tests are dealt with differently by the presentation algorithm. Users can request explanation at any time that they are asked a question or given advice and they can also interrupt the system at any time to find out what is happening. Furthermore, a full report of the line of reasoning leading to some final conclusion can be produced at the end of a session. Although the

FULL EXPLANATION OF THE FORECAST:
Since upper level cold air advection causing increased
        upwards vertical velocities is present
    it follows that the upper-level destabilisation
        potential is sufficient   (1)
Since the K Index is strong
    when the Lifted Index is strong
    it follows that the stability indices condition
        is favourable   (2)
Since daytime heating acting as a possible trigger mechanism
        for potential instability release is strong
    when (2) the stability indices condition is favourable
    it follows that low-level destabilisation potential
        is favourable   (3)
Since an approaching 500 millibar short wave trough is present
    it follows that the vertical velocity field
        is favourable   (4)
Since a high 850 mb dew point is present
    when surface dew point classification is moderate
    it follows that the low-level moisture field
        is marginal   (5)
Since (1) the upper-level destabilisation potential is sufficient
    when (3) low-level destabilisation potential is favourable
    and (4) the vertical velocity field is favourable
    and (5) the low-level moisture field is marginal
    it was necessary to advise:
        "There's a MODERATE CHANCE that thunder-
        storms occurring 12 hours from now will be
        severe at this location."
    in order to actually forecast the chance of severe
    thunderstorms

Figure 3.16   Sample WILLARD forecast explanation

ordering is revised, this form of explanation is similar to that given by MYCIN.

An example of automatically generated explanation is given in figure 3.16.

It should be noted that the bracketed numbers in figure 3.16 are not produced by the present version of RuleMaster, but are included in the diagram for ease of reading. This would be a simple and desirable

```
            A
          /   \
         /     \
        B       C
       /|\     /|\
      D E F   G H I
```

gives:

　　　Since D
　　　　when E
　　　　and F
　　　　　it follows that B
　　　Since G
　　　　when H
　　　　and I
　　　　　it follows that C
　　　Since B
　　　　when C
　　　　　it follows that A

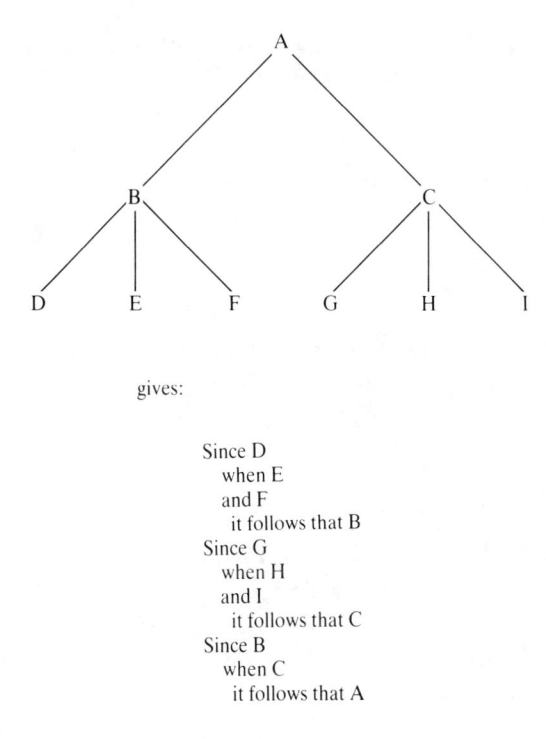

Figure 3.17 Method of ordering explanation

addition to the system's capabilities.

The following example illustrates the mechanism by which explanation is ordered. The Radial interpreter saves a full trace of a program's execution as a proof tree. When an explanation is demanded, the proof tree is presented in postfix order with keywords (such as *Since*), inserted. Thus, if in figure 3.17 the tree represents the execution proof tree, with A being proved by the conjunction of B and C being true and so on, the explanation would be presented bottom-up, as shown in the same diagram. This explanation shows how axioms are presented before lemmas, which are in turn presented before the final theorem is proved. This is the normal convention used in the presentation of mathematical proofs.

3.9 The Rulemaker code generator

Experts using RuleMaster have the freedom to build their expert system without ever having to write actual Radial code, generating it instead from example decisions. For this purpose Rulemaker uses the ACLS algorithm (see Appendix A and Paterson and Niblet, 1982) to generate a single rule for each state of the module. Rulemaker distinguishes between 'test' and 'action' modules, in that whereas the former returns a value, the latter does not.

3.9.1 Rulemaker syntax

For every Radial module there exists a Rulemaker file which was used to generate that module. Figure 3.18 shows the syntax of Rulemaker files. In the following sections we use illustrative examples to describe the structure of these files.

3.9.2 Single-state module

The Radial module shown in figure 3.10 was generated automatically from the induction file given in figure 3.19. The module has only one state where the action is to return a string giving the decision. An informal description of the keywords and major sections of this Rulemaker file is given below.

1. **TEST:** is followed by the path of the Radial module to be induced, "main.rain". Following this are return value options. In this case the return value is a string with two possible values: "USE" and "DONTUSE".

2. **DECLARATIONS:** introduces a piece of text (between square brackets) to be placed at the top of the module produced. The declarations indicate the modules associated with "rain".

3. **STATE:** is followed by the name of a state in the object module. The actions, conditions, and examples define the rule for that state.

4. **ACTIONS:** indicates a set of action-names found in the implication of example clauses. Each action name is followed by a piece of Radial code in brackets, which is substituted for the action name in the object program. In the umbrella example, the actions are simple assignments of strings to the output argument 'result'.

5. **CONDITIONS:** are a set of value-producing expressions. Like actions, each condition name is followed by a piece of Radial substitution code in square brackets. Following this in curly brackets

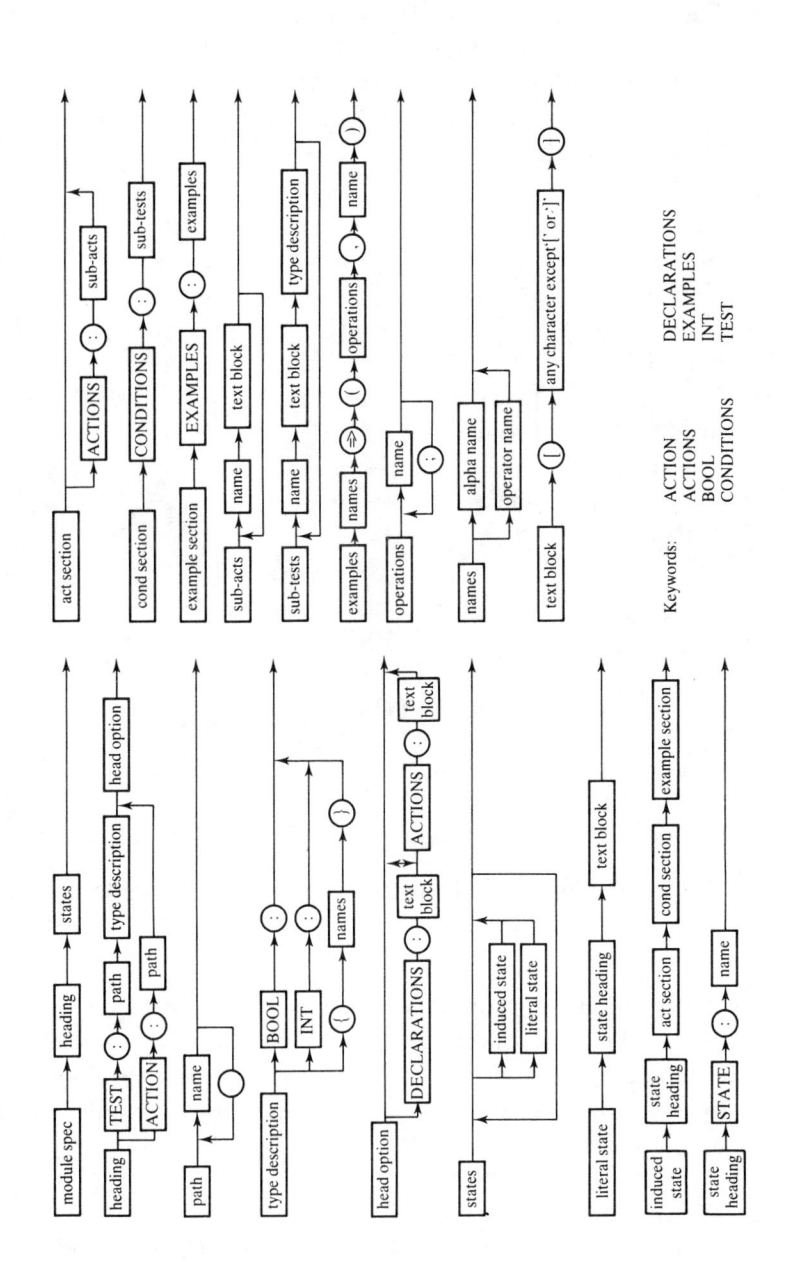

Figure 3.18 The syntax of Rulemaker

TEST: main.rain { USE DONTUSE }

DECLARATIONS:
[CHILD: weather, inside, soaked, incar
  OUT: string result]

STATE: decide
ACTIONS:
    DONTUSE   ["DONTUSE" → result]
    USE   ["USE" → result]
CONDITIONS:
weather   [weather]   {wet sunny blustery }
    inside   [inside]   {yes no }
        soaked   [soaked]   {yes no }
            incar   [incar]   {yes no }
EXAMPLES:

sunny   -   -   -   ⇒ (DONTUSE, goal)
blustery - -   -   ⇒ (DONTUSE, goal)
wet yes -   -   ⇒ (DONTUSE, goal)
wet no yes no   ⇒ (DONTUSE, goal)
wet no no yes   ⇒ (DONTUSE, goal)
wet no no no   ⇒ (USE, goal)

Figure 3.19 Rulemaker induction file for Radial module of figure 3.10

is the set of values that can be produced by this conditional expression. The conditions have a one-to-one correspondence with the example value vectors. For this reason, the condition descriptions are stepped in order to line up with the columns of the example set.

6. **EXAMPLES:** are vectors of values, one value from each condition expression, each followed by an ⇒ and an (action, next state) pair. These are used to induce the decision tree for this state. A '-' in an attribute column is called a *don't care* value. *Don't care* values are interpreted as representing all possible values which the corresponding attribute could take. Thus an example containing one *don't care* value for an attribute with N possible values, ac-

tually represents N distinct examples. An example with more than one *don't care* value represents a number of examples equal to the product of all the numbers of attribute values for which the *don't care* values are present.

3.9.3 Multiple-state module

The next example file (figure 3.20) defines a routine with two states. The rules instruct an individual on the 'Heimlich method' – the actions to be taken in case of an adult victim who is choking standing up. The conditions to be checked are the victim's airway, consciousness, pulse, and whether or not the patient is breathing.

One new feature seen here is compound Radial statements, joined by ';', as the action implicated by examples. The statements may be expressions or assignments. Radial modules named in expressions will often be primitives written in C. For example, 'prints' and 'reads' are C utility routines for printing and reading strings. Each application will typically add its own set of domain-dependent utility routines.

Each of the two induced states sometimes passes control to the other induced state, and sometimes to the goal state. Thus looping control algorithms can be induced from a set of example files. In figure 3.20:

1. Under **DECLARATIONS**, 'ar' (artificial respiration) is a child of choke, and is called as one of the ACTIONs of choke in the STATE called 'unconscious'.

2. There are three **ACTIONS** sections. The first describes actions which are global to both the STATEs 'conscious' and 'unconscious'. Each STATE also has local ACTIONS to be used only for the rule in that STATE. All ACTIONS apart from 'ar' call the C-coded primitive 'prints' to print a message to the user.

3. No *global* **CONDITIONS** are represented in the induction file, but, both states have *local* CONDITIONS. These all involve calling 'reads' to prompt the user for an answer. However, a more complex example might call a TEST module to test the condition.

The induction file presented in figure 3.20 is transformed by Rulemaker into the Radial module of figure 3.21.

3.9.4 Induction of a hierarchy of rules

Much of RuleMaster's power to solve industrial-scale problems derives from its ability to induce a hierarchy of rules from a set of example

58   Inductive Acquisition of Expert Knowledge

```
MODULE: main.choke

    DECLARATIONS:
        [ CHILD: ar ]
    ACTIONS:    /* global actions */
        hit     [prints "hit victim's back 4 times\n"]
        sweep   [prints "sweep victim's mouth with finger\n"]
        ok      [prints "comfort the victim\n"]
    STATE: primary
        ACTIONS:
            squeeze   [prints "squeeze victim's chest 4 times\n"]
            brace     [prints "brace victim to prevent falling\n"]
            amb       [prints "call an ambulance\n"]
        CONDITIONS:
        freed         [reads "Is the obstruction clear?"]
                            {yes no }
            falling   [read "Is the victim falling? "]
                            {yes no }
                conscious [reads "Is the victim conscious? "]
                            {yes no }
        EXAMPLES:

        yes yes yes  ⇒ (brace; ok, GOAL)
        no  no  yes  ⇒ (hit; squeeze; sweep, primary)
        no  yes yes  ⇒ (brace; hit; squeeze; sweep, primary)
        -   -   no   ⇒ (amb, unconscious)
        yes no  yes  ⇒ (ok, GOAL)
    STATE: unconscious
        ACTIONS:
            thrust    [prints "apply 4 chest thrusts\n"]
            ar        [ar] /* Artificial respiration */
            cpr       [prints "apply cpr: 15 compressions, 2 breaths\n"]
            emt       [prints "let EMT staff take over\n"]
            ok        [prints "You just helped save a life\n"]
        CONDITIONS:
freed              [reads "Is the obstruction clear?"]
                            {yes no }
    breathing      [read "Is the victim breathing? "]
                            {yes no }
        pulse      [reads "Is there a pulse? "]
                            {yes no }
            conscious [reads "Is the victim conscious? "]
                            {yes no }
                amb [reads "Has the ambulance arrived? "]
                            {yes no }
        EXAMPLES:

no yes yes no  no  ⇒ (hit; thrust; sweep, unconscious)
no no  yes no  no  ⇒ (ar, unconscious)
yesno  yes no  no  ⇒ (ar, unconscious)
yesno  no  no  no  ⇒ (cpr, unconscious)
no no  no  no  no  ⇒ (hit; thrust; sweep; cpr, unconscious)
yesyes yes yes no  ⇒ (ok, primary)
-   -   -   -  yes ⇒ (emt, GOAL)
```

Figure 3.20   Induction file for the choke problem

```
MODULE main.choke IS
 CHILD: ar
  STATE: primary
   IF (reads "Is the victim conscious? ") IS
    "yes" : IF (reads "Is the obstruction clear? ") IS
     "yes" : IF (reads "Is the victim falling? ") IS
      "yes" : (prints "brace victim to prevent falling\n";
               prints "comfort the victim\n", GOAL)
      ELSE (prints "comfort the victim\n", GOAL)
     ELSE IF (reads "Is the victim falling? ") IS
      "yes" : (prints "brace victim to prevent falling\n";
               prints "hit victim's back 4 times\n";
               prints "squeeze victim's chest 4 times\n";
               prints "sweep victim's mouth with finger\n", primary)
      ELSE (prints "hit victim's back 4 times\n";
            prints "squeeze victim's chest 4 times\n";
            prints "sweep victim's mouth with finger\n", primary)
    ELSE (prints "call an ambulance\n", unconscious)

  STATE: unconscious
   IF (reads "Has ambulance arrived? ") IS
    "yes" : (prints "let EMT staff take over\n", GOAL)
    ELSE IF (reads "Is the obstruction clear? ") IS
     "yes" : IF (reads "Is there a pulse? ") IS
      "yes" : IF (reads "Is the victim breathing? ") IS
       "yes" : (prints "You just helped save a life!\n", primary)
       ELSE (ar, unconscious)
      ELSE (prints "apply cpr : 15 compressions, 2 breaths\n", unconscious)
     ELSE IF (reads "Is the victim breathing? ") IS
      "yes" : (prints "hit victim's back 4 times\n";
               prints "apply 4 chest thrusts\n";
               prints "sweep victim's mouth with finger\n", unconscious)
      ELSE IF (reads "Is there a pulse? ") IS
       "yes" : (ar, unconscious)
       ELSE (prints "hit victim's back 4 times\n";
             prints "apply 4 chest thrusts\n";
             prints "sweep victim's mouth with finger\n", unconscious)
GOAL OF choke
```

Figure 3.21 Radial module produced from the Rulemaker file of figure 3.19

files. A list of actions, conditions and examples is supplied for each rule in the system, and the automatic induction process generates both the individual rules for each state, as well as the connections between states in a module, and between modules.

The choke example above uses a sub-module called 'ar' (artificial respiration) as an ACTION module. The example file of figure 3.22 defines the ar routine. The induction file was transformed by Rulemaker into the Radial program shown in figure 3.23.

ACTION: main.choke.ar/* artificial respiration */
  STATE: arproc
    ACTIONS:
        airway   [prints "tilt head - open airway\n"]
        breath   [prints "give 1 breath/5 sec\n"]
        ok   [prints "reassure victim\n"]
        stop   [prints "stop applying ar\n"]
        monitor   [prints "monitor victim\n"]
        cpr   [prints "apply cpr -15/2\n"]
    CONDITIONS:
  pulse   [reads "Is there a pulse?"]
                      yes no
      breath   [read "Is victim breathing?"]
                      yes no
          breath   [read "Is victim conscious?"]
                      yes no
    EXAMPLES:
  yes no no ⇒ (airway;breath, arproc)
  yes yes no ⇒ (stop;monitor, arproc)
  yes yes yes ⇒ (ok, GOAL)
  no no no ⇒ (cpr, arproc)

Figure 3.22 Induction file for artificial respiration

3.10 External information sources

Virtually all large expert system applications will require access to external information sources, such as sensors, files, databases, and specially written or existing programs and external resources can be used to incorporate alternate reasoning approaches into a system. External output to control devices to update data bases may be desired.

To deal with these demands, RuleMaster allows the developer to set up separate processes under the operating system. Communication with these other processes is defined by a simple interface which allows external programs to be called in the same manner as Radial modules (see section 3.6.2). At execution time, instructions and data are passed across a UNIX pipe between RuleMaster and the external programs. These programs can be written in any language supported by UNIX (FORTRAN, C, LISP, Prolog).

```
MODULE main.choke.ar IS
  STATE: arproc
    IF (reads "Is victim breathing?") IS
      "yes" : IF (reads "Is victim conscious?") IS
        "yes" : (prints "reassure victim\n", GOAL)
        ELSE (prints "stop applying ar\n";
              prints "monitor victim\n", arproc")
      ELSE IF (reads "Is there a pulse?") IS
        "yes" : (prints "tilt head - open airway\n";
                prints "give 1 breath /5 sec\n", arproc)
        ELSE (prints "apply cpr - 15/2\n", arproc)
GOAL OF ar
```

Figure 3.23 Radial module produced from the Rulemaker file of figure 3.22

3.11 Conclusion

RuleMaster is an expert system building package intended to solve many of the problems involved in the construction of large knowledge based programs. An inductive learning system (Rulemaker) allows rapid and effective acquisition of expert knowledge. The Radial language allows structured organisation of large quantities of knowledge acquired in such a manner. Radial also provides a facility for presenting ordered explanation of reasoning to the level of elaboration required. However, RuleMaster does not explicitly support any form of reasoning based on partial certainty.

In comparison to other expert system approaches, although knowledge representation, in the form of decision trees, is no better than that of production systems, the fact that knowledge can be presented in the form of examples from which rules can be refined means that the process of knowledge acquisition is greatly eased. It has often been noted during the construction of Radial-based applications that, whereas designers using dialogue acquisition methodologies talk of constructing prototype systems in terms of years, Radial-based applications have consistently been prototyped in around six man-months.

Typical expert system applications contain aspects of both classification and control tasks. RuleMaster provides a consistent knowledge representation for these disparate problem elements. Furthermore, an interface to external sources and sinks of information is provided.

A method of inducing the state transition structure of Radial modules from trace information would be desirable. The theoretical basis for such a mechanism is given in Chapter 6.

Chapter 4
Robotic Applications

4.1 Introduction

In this chapter it is described how a planner for 'blocks world' problems can be inductively generated using RuleMaster. The problem chosen is identical to that attempted by Dechter and Michie (1984). Whereas Dechter and Michie used Expert-Ease (McLaren, 1984), the choice of Radial for the re-implementation overcame several of the problems which they encountered.

Planning is the sub-field of artificial intelligence concerned with programs which carry out a sequence of actions, or plan to achieve some specified goal (Nilsson, 1980). Typically, a planning program is given a description of the start situation, a set of actions which can alter that situation, and a goal situation. The program must discover a sequence of actions which transforms the start situation into the goal situation.

For every goal, there is a set of plans, each corresponding to an initial situation, for achieving this goal. Given such a goal, a situation is classified to the first action in the plan for achieving this goal from this situation. Accordingly, for every goal, a set of examples which partially describe the relationships between situations and actions can be created. For this set of examples, a conditional rule is induced. Thus, given an initial situation, the induced rules can be used to select the appropriate action.

4.2 The problem: building a five-block arch

The problem involves generating a plan for the simple activity of building an arch out of five blocks named A, B, C, D and *beam*. Five plat-

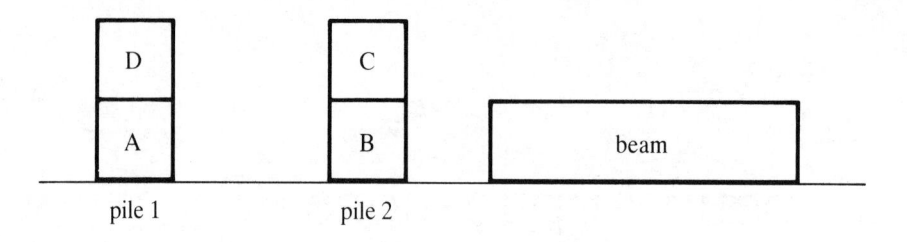

Figure 4.1 An initial situation

forms are used to hold the blocks. These platforms are called *pile1*, *pile2*, *beam store*, *right arch* and *left arch*. In the initial world situation, the blocks A, B, C, D are stacked on pile1 and pile2. The beam is placed on the beam store. Figure 4.1 illustrates a typical initial situation.

The goal is to build an arch on the *right arch* and *left arch* platforms in the configuration shown in figure 4.2.

The problem was divided into a hierarchy of sub-problems for Rule-Master. This hierarchy is shown in figure 4.3. Dechter and Michie (1984) showed that, without such problem decomposition, inductively generated decision-tree solutions require an unmanageable number of examples. However, whereas the package used by Dechter and Michie did not allow the creation and iterative execution of a hierarchy of decision trees, RuleMaster does (see section 3.9.4).

The action *main* merely calls the top-level action *arch*.

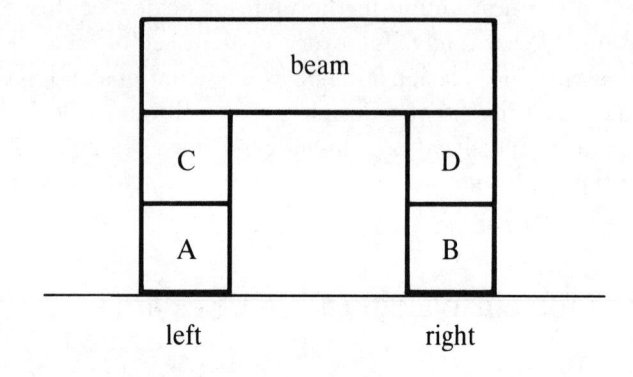

Figure 4.2 The goal situation

Robotic applications 65

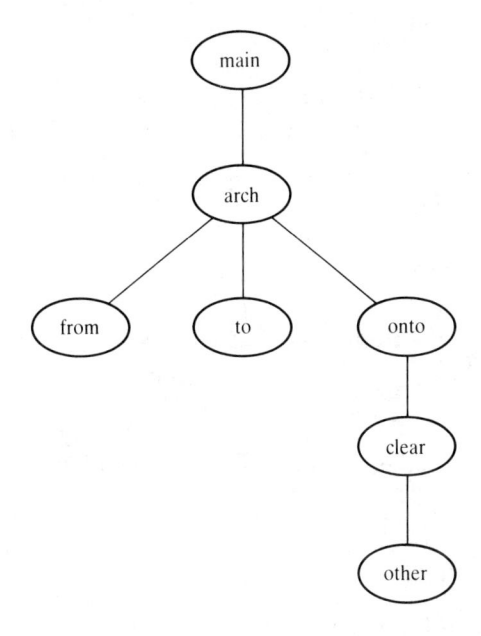

Figure 4.3 Hierarchical breakdown of the problem

4.3 The action *arch*

The top-level action, *arch*, defines the order in which five different goals must be reached, that is, the way A, B, C and D must be moved to their respective positions and the beam placed across the top. In figure 4.4 the Rulemaker file which describes this top-level goal is given. Note that, at this level, no examples are needed as the task can be described by a simple sequence of goals.

main.arch is the path leading from the root of the problem hierarchy to this action node. *arch* has three children in the problem hierarchy. These are *onto*, *from* and *to*. *onto* produces a plan which will move a particular block onto its goal position. *from* and *to* are actions which, given that a block is clear of other blocks, respectively pick up a block from a given position and place it at some other given position. The action names are used as infix operators (see section 3.7) in expressions like

"A" onto "the left arch"

and

"BEAM" from "beam store" to "C and D"

ACTION: main.arch

    DECLARATIONS:
      [CHILD: onto 100,1,1, from 110,1,1, to 100,1,1]
  STATE: only
   [("A" onto "the left arch";
    "B" onto "the right arch";
    "C" onto "A (left arch)";
    "D" onto "B (right arch)";
    "BEAM" from "beam store" to "C and D",
    GOAL)]

Figure 4.4 Rulemaker file describing the top level goal

Thus the declaration

    CHILD: onto 100,1,1, ...

says that *onto* has a precedence of 100 and takes one argument on the left, and one on the right. This allows a more English-like statement of the required activity than that produced by Dechter and Michie.

4.4 The action *onto*

The action *onto* is described by the Rulemaker file of figure 4.5.

    onto has two INput parameters called *block* and *place*, as described in the previous section. It also has one child in the problem hierarchy. *onto*, like all the modules within ARCH is a single state module. The examples use a number of ACTIONS which are described between square brackets as small pieces of Radial code such as

    block from "pile1" to place

says that the block given to *onto* as a first parameter must be picked up from pile1 and put onto the place given as *onto*'s second parameter. The possible situations are described using the CONDITIONS xon, clearx and pilex. These merely invoke questions which are directed at the user. In terms of these three CONDITIONS, a set of EXAMPLES is given which specifies what to do under different circumstances. The action done for each circumstance is paired with the next state to enter,

```
ACTION: main.arch.onto
    DECLARATIONS:
        [ IN: string block, place
          CHILD: clear]
    STATE: decide
        ACTIONS:
            x1toplace      [block from "pile1" to place]
            x2toplace      [block from "pile2" to place]
            clearx1        [clear block "pile1"]
            clearx2        [clear block "pile2"]
            null           [null]
        CONDITIONS:
        xon
                [reads "is " # block # " on " #
                    place # "? (yes/no) "]
                yes no
            clearx
                [reads "is " # block #
                    " clear of blocks? (yes/no) "]
                yes no
              pilex
                [reads "which pile is " #
                    block #
                    " on? (pile1/pile2) "]
                pile1 pile2
        EXAMPLES:
        yes   -    -        ⇒   (null, GOAL)
        no   yes  pile1     ⇒   (x1toplace, GOAL)
        no   yes  pile2     ⇒   (x2toplace, GOAL)
        no   no   pile1     ⇒   (clearx1; x1toplace, GOAL)
        no   no   pile2     ⇒   (clearx2; x2toplace, GOAL)
```

Figure 4.5 The Rulemaker file describing the action 'onto'

which for each of these is GOAL. Entering the GOAL state returns control from the action being carried out.

Note the use of parameterisation (block and place) in this module. This was found by Dechter and Michie to be particularly awkward to simulate using Expert Ease.

4.5 The action *clear*

The action *clear* is described by the Rulemaker file given in figure 4.6.

In the examples for *clear*, if there is nothing on the block being cleared, then the goal has been reached. If one of the blocks A–D is on the block being cleared, then *clear* is recursively called for the upper block. Once the upper block has been cleared, it is moved to the other pile.

The use of recursion in an inductively generated solution for clearing blocks was suggested by Dechter and Michie. However, again because of the limitations of Expert Ease, a separate decision tree needed to be developed for clearing A, clearing B, clearing C and clearing D. As shown, this can be avoided when using RuleMaster by careful use of parameterisation.

However, figure 4.6 illustrates a weakness of RuleMaster which was noted by Dechter and Michie with reference to Expert Ease – actions and condition values cannot be parameterised. With the solution shown in figure 4.6 it would have been useful to be able to write examples of the form

```
CONDITIONS:
   onX        ...
EXAMPLES:
   nothing     ⇒ (null, GOAL)
   Y           ⇒ (clear(Y); to_other(Y), GOAL)
```

4.6 A session

Given the initial situation presented in figure 4.1, the Radial program produced from the Rulemaker files for this problem produces the interaction shown in figure 4.7. User answers are shown in italics and primitive operations in the plan are shown in bold print.

ACTION: main.arch.onto.clear

    DECLARATIONS:
    [IN: string block, place
    CHILD: other 120,0,1]
STATE: decide
    ACTIONS:

Aother	["A" from place to other place]
Bother	["B" from place to other place]
Cother	["C" from place to other place]
Dother	["D" from place to other place]
clearA	[clear "A" place]
clearB	[clear "B" place]
clearC	[clear "C" place]
clearD	[clear "D" place]
null	[null]

CONDITIONS:
    onx
        [reads "which block is on " # block
        # "? (A/B/C/D/nothing) "]
    nothing A B C D
EXAMPLES:

nothing	$\Rightarrow$ (null, GOAL)
A	$\Rightarrow$ (clearA; Aother, GOAL)
B	$\Rightarrow$ (clearB; Bother, GOAL)
C	$\Rightarrow$ (clearC; Cother, GOAL)
D	$\Rightarrow$ (clearD; Dother, GOAL)

Figure 4.6 Rulemaker file describing the action 'clear'

is A on the left arch? (yes/no) *no*
is A clear of blocks? (yes/no) *no*
which pile is A on? (pile1/pile2) *pile1*
which block is on A? (A/B/C/D/nothing) *C*
which block is on C? (A/B/C/D/nothing) *nothing*
 !! pick up C from pile1
 !! put C onto pile2
 !! pick up A from pile1
 !! put A onto the left arch
is B on the right arch? (yes/no) *no*
is B clear of blocks? (yes/no) *no*
which pile is B on? (pile1/pile2) *pile2*
which block is on B? (A/B/C/D/nothing) *D*
which block is on D? (A/B/C/D/nothing) *C*
which block is on C? (A/B/C/D/nothing) *nothing*
 !! pick up C from pile2
 !! put C onto pile1
 !! pick up D from pile2
 !! put D onto pile1
 !! pick up B from pile2
 !! put B onto the right arch
is C on A (left arch)? (yes/no) *no*
is C clear of blocks? (yes/no) *no*
which pile is C on? (pile1/pile2) *pile1*
which block is on C? (A/B/C/D/nothing) *D*
which block is on D? (A/B/C/D/nothing) *nothing*
 !! pick up D from pile1
 !! put D onto pile2
 !! pick up C from pile1
 !! put C onto A (left arch)
is D on B (right arch)? (yes/no) *no*
is D clear of blocks? (yes/no) *yes*
which pile is D on? (pile1/pile2) *pile2*
 !! pick up D from pile2
 !! put D onto B (right arch)
 !! pick up BEAM from beam store
 !! put BEAM onto C and D

Figure 4.7 User interaction for blocks problem

Clearly, although rather a lot of questions are asked, a plan is produced which satisfies the goal.

4.7 GENARCH

4.7.1 Introduction

In the rest of this chapter we will describe a generalised version of the RuleMaster arch-building solution. The new system was constructed by Barry Shepherd of the Turing Institute Glasgow, and will be referred to as GENARCH. The simple arch-building system described in previous sections will be referred to as ARCH.

ARCH cannot be considered a practical solution since it solves the problem only in simulation and then only in a symbolic manner. Although the planning aspects of the problem are solved the (mainly numerical) complexities of actually directing a robot to pick up and move the various blocks are not tackled. GENARCH is a practical solution to a more general arch-building problem and has also been generated using RuleMaster. GENARCH can be run either in simulation or in a real environment using a Puma 200 robot.

The problem solved by GENARCH is an extension of the simple arch problem considered by ARCH. Again, the arch consists of two piles and a beam, but now the piles can contain any number of blocks which can be of any size, although the final heights of the piles must be equal. In addition, each block within a pile can itself be an arch, and the beam can also be an arch. This nesting can be to any level. Initially the blocks and beams are stacked in any order in any number of work piles.

An example of a structure which can be categorised as a general arch is shown in figure 4.8.

4.7.2 Structure of the solution

The problem is divided into a hierarchy of sub-problems for RuleMaster, this hierarchy is shown in figure 4.9.

The RuleMaster modules 'buildarch', 'onto', 'pickup' and 'placeat' perform high-level actions. The lowest level actions which are specified in RuleMaster are the set of robot primitives:

moveto(x y z o a t)
grasp

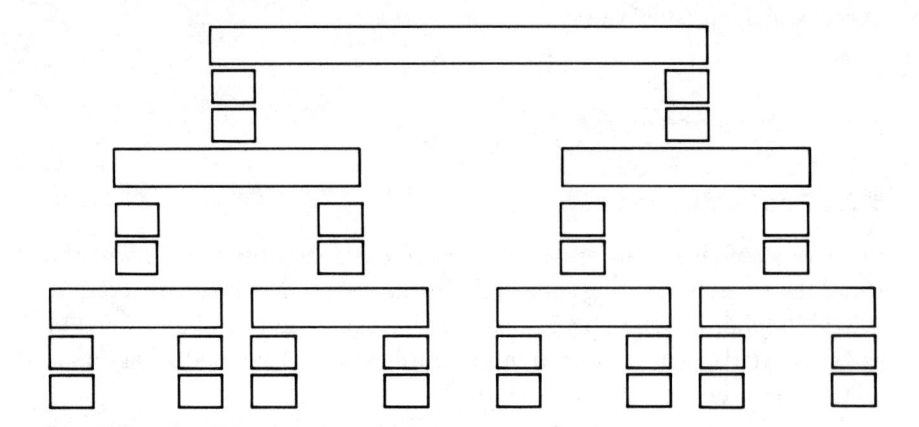

Figure 4.8 Example of a general arch

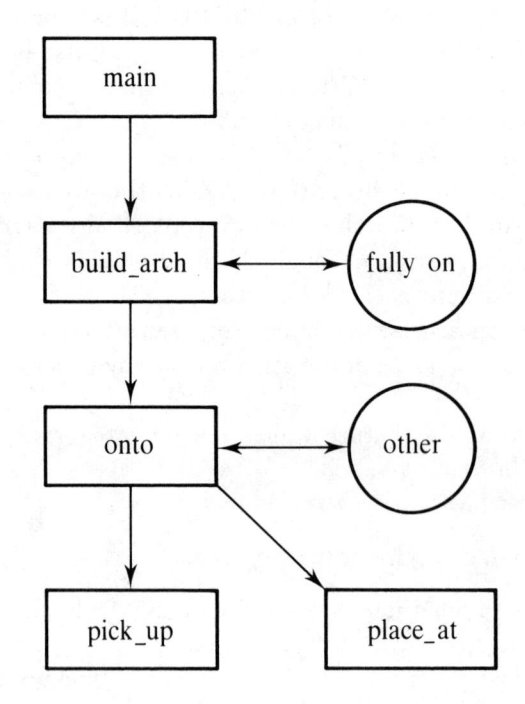

Figure 4.9 Solution structure

release
   home
   setspeed

These robot primitives are coded in C and provide a basic device-independent interface between RuleMaster and the robot chosen to perform the task. At present, they have been created for a Puma 200, and a Rhino XR-1.

The RuleMaster modules 'fullyon' and 'other' return high-level, problem-specific information about the current state of the assembly task. However, GENARCH is a 'blind' solution and thus requires detailed knowledge of the state of the world at all times. This knowledge must be both relational ('what's on redblock1?') and numerical (the position, orientation and size of redblock1). A C-coded world model has been created in order to store this information. This is described in more detail in a later section. The following primitives are an example of the interface between RuleMaster and this world-model:

   above(objectname)
   topof(pilename)
   property(objectname,propertyname)

Note: All objects (whether blocks, beams, piles, arches or places) are stored in the same manner in the world model and are referenced by RuleMaster using only their names.

4.7.3 The Rulemaker induction modules

Listings of all of the RuleMaster modules are given later (see sections 4.7.9–4.7.11).

4.7.4 The action module *buildarch*

A major part of the solution is the module 'buildarch'. This takes as its input the name of a place where an arch is to be built and the names of all of the components of the arch:

   buildarch(location, leftlist, rightlist, beam)

where 'leftlist' and 'rightlist' are lists of the names of those objects (in the correct order) which are to be used to make the arch leftpile and rightpile (call these 'component lists'), and beam is the name of the object to be used as the arch beam. For example, buildarch("tabletop" "[redblk,greenblk]" "[blueblk,blueblk]" "yellowbeam")

In summary, buildarch examines each constituent object in turn and checks to see if it is in position (using the module 'fullyon'). If it is not, it moves the object to the correct position (using the module 'onto'); this may entail clearing the top of the object if it is not already clear.

4.7.5 The query module *fullyon*

In the module 'buildarch' an object in the left or right pile is assumed to be in its final position if it is on top of the object which occurred before it in the object list for that pile. The beam is in position if it is on top of both the left pile and the right pile. The module

object fullyon place

checks to see if the named object (whether a primitive object or a structure) is fully located on the stated place. If the object is a primitive object then the world model primitive 'above' can be used on its own to answer this question. If the object is itself an arch, its status (fully assembled or partially assembled) must also be checked.

4.7.6 The action module *onto*

The module

objectname onto place/objectname

moves an object (a primitive or a structure) onto another object (a primitive object, structure or place). If the object to be moved is a primitive object and it is clear, it can be picked up by the robot (module 'pickup') and placed on the correct location (module 'placeat'). If the object is a structure (an arch) in this case it cannot be moved as a single entity by the robot but must instead be re-assembled (using 'buildarch') at the specified location.

4.7.7 RuleMaster modules

The modules *pickup, placeat* and *other* were not derived inductively but were written directly in RuleMaster. *pickup* takes as an argument an object name, extracts its position and orientation from the world model and generates a series of 'moveto' instructions in order to move the robot gripper horizontally from its home position to a point directly above the object and then down onto the object, close the gripper and return back the way it came. *placeat* takes as its argument the name of a place and operates similarly to *pickup* in order to put the held object on the place so that the centroid of the object is directly above that of the place and their orientations (the orientation of a block is the direction of its principal axis) align. *other* takes the name of an object as an argument and returns the name of the smallest workpile other than the one in which it is currently located.

4.7.8 The world model

The world model consists of a hierarchy of lists. Each object in the problem, whether it is a primitive object (a block), a structure (an arch) or a place (a workpile) is represented in the model by a list. This list contains the properties of that object and also sublists representing the objects contained within that object (none if it is a primitive object). An object can have any number of properties but most objects will possess the following:

> name
> type (eg: cuboid, sphere, disc, pile, arch, surface etc)
> position (x, y, z) usually the position of its centroid.
> orientation (o, a, t) the orientation of its principal axis.
> dimensions (length, width, height).

Examples of other properties that could be included in the sub-list are colour, material, weight and so on.

Any property of an object can be extracted from the world model using the primitive:

> property(objectname, propertyname)

Frequently used properties can also be extracted using individual primitives: X(objectname), Len(objectname).

All objects are referenced using their name. Object names do not have to be unique – many identical blocks can all be called 'redblock'; however, distinct objects do require individual entries. When an object is referenced, the first object found when doing a search of the world-model will be the one which is used. If a particular object is required its 'path' in the world-model (which is unique) can be used instead of the object name.

Relational information can be obtained from the position of the object in the world model. For example, a structure consisting of a pile of blocks will be represented in the world model by a list which will contain (in addition to its own properties) a sub-list for all of those objects contained in the pile. The order in which these occur is the physical order in which they are stacked on top of each other. This ordering has different meanings for different types of structure/place and so on.

The following primitives are used by GENARCH to extract relational information from the model:

>above(objectname)
>bottomof(pilename)   bottom of a pile or stack.
>topof(pilename)   top of a pile or stack.

In order to initialise the model, the following primitive is used:

>newobject(placename, objectname, propertylist)

This will create a new object with the name and properties specified and insert it into the world model at the specified place.

The movement of objects within the model resulting from real actions performed by the robot is achieved using:

>modeltohand(objectname)

This extracts the stated object, and it can now be referenced using the name 'heldobject'.

>handtomodel(placename)

inserts the held object into the stated place.

4.7.9 Specifying a particular task

The modules described so far contain a strategy for building a general arch given the names of the components of that arch. Hence a specific arch could be built with the following 'main' module:

>MODULE GENARCH
>STATE: start
>(initialisemodel;
>   buildarch("tabletop" "[redblk,redblk]" "[blueblk,blkblk]"

```
            "grnbeam"),
        goal
)
        GOAL OF GENARCH
```

where 'initialisemodel' creates entries in the world model for all of the primitive objects (the blocks and beams), the work-piles and the place the arch is to be built on (the tabletop). If one component of this arch was another arch then the above 'main' module would be inadequate. This is solved by creating what can be called a 'task description module' which gives the names and composition of all of the structures in the complete arch.

The task description module for the arch shown in the introduction (tower1) is given below.

```
MODULE build
    INTENT:    "build 1at2"
    IN:        string    object,place
    STATE:     start
    if (object) is
    "tower": (buildarch(object place
                    "[towL]" "[towR]" "towbm"),goal)
    "towL": (buildarch(object place
                    "[towLL]" "[towLR]" "towLbm"),goal)
    "towR": (buildarch(object place
                    "[towRL]" "[towRR]" "towRbm"),goal)
    "towLL": (buildarch(object place
                    "[Y1,Y2]" "[Y3,Y4]" "Ybm1"),goal)
    "towLR": (buildarch(object place
                    "[B1,B2]" "[B3,B4]" "Bbm1"),goal)
    "towRL": (buildarch(object place
                    "[Y5,Y6]" "[Y7,Y8]" "Ybm2"),goal)
    "towRR": (buildarch(object place
                    "[B5,B6]" "[B7,B8]" "Bbm2"),goal)
    "towbm": (buildarch(object place
                    "[G1,G2]" "[G3,G4]" "Gbm1"),goal)
    "towLbm": (buildarch(object place
                    "[R1,R2]" "[R3,R4]" "Rbm1"),goal)
    ELSE (buildarch(object place "[R5,R6]" "[R6,R7]" "Rbm2"),goal)
GOAL OF build
```

The 'main' module for GENARCH can now be

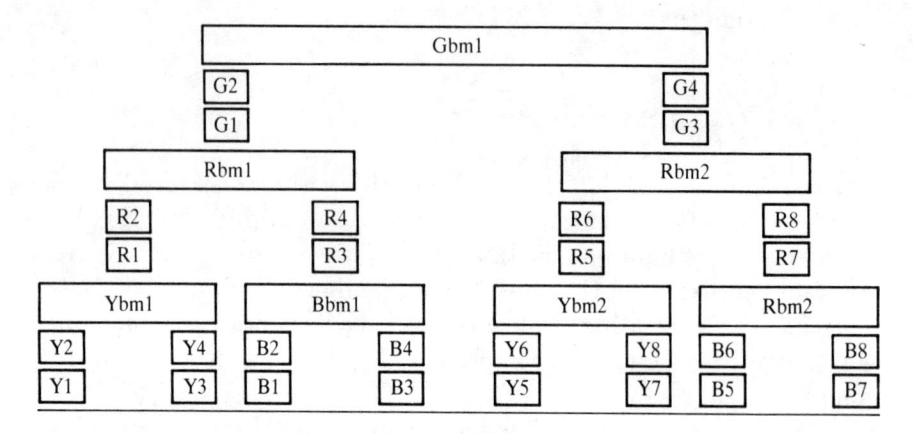

```
                    ┌─────────────────────────────────────┐
                    │               Gbm1                  │
                    ├──────┐                       ┌──────┤
                    │  G2  │                       │  G4  │
                    ├──────┤                       ├──────┤
                    │  G1  │                       │  G3  │
          ┌─────────┴──────┴───────┐     ┌─────────┴──────┴──────┐
          │        Rbm1            │     │        Rbm2           │
          ├──────┐          ┌──────┤     ├──────┐         ┌──────┤
          │  R2  │          │  R4  │     │  R6  │         │  R8  │
          ├──────┤          ├──────┤     ├──────┤         ├──────┤
          │  R1  │          │  R3  │     │  R5  │         │  R7  │
   ┌──────┴──────┴──┐  ┌────┴──────┴──┐ ┌┴──────┴──────┐ ┌┴──────┴──────┐
   │     Ybm1       │  │    Bbm1      │ │    Ybm2      │ │    Rbm2      │
   ├────┐     ┌─────┤  ├────┐   ┌─────┤ ├────┐   ┌─────┤ ├────┐   ┌─────┤
   │ Y2 │     │ Y4  │  │ B2 │   │ B4  │ │ Y6 │   │ Y8  │ │ B6 │   │ B8  │
   ├────┤     ├─────┤  ├────┤   ├─────┤ ├────┤   ├─────┤ ├────┤   ├─────┤
   │ Y1 │     │ Y3  │  │ B1 │   │ B3  │ │ Y5 │   │ Y7  │ │ B5 │   │ B7  │
```

Figure 4.10 A goal state for tower1

    MODULE GENARCH
    STATE: start
    (initialisemodel;
            build("tower" "tabletop"),
            goal
)
    GOAL OF GENARCH

(*Note*: The module 'onto' is changed to call the 'build' module instead of the 'buildarch' module when a structure is to be moved).

This mechanism for defining arches can easily be extended to other structures such as walls, steps, pyramids and so on. For example in the arch defined above the component, towL can be defined as a wall by replacing its definition line with:

    "towL":   (buildwall(place name "redblock" 6 5));

where 'buildwall' is a strategy for building a wall using redblocks which is six blocks long and five blocks high.

4.7.10 Example structures

The structure shown in the introduction to this section (tower1) contains 28 blocks and 7 beams. One particular goal state is shown in figure 4.10 and this has been built using the Puma from the initial state shown in figure 4.11.

Another structure which has been build using GENARCH (simulation only) is shown in figure 4.12 (tower2). One set of initial positions

[Figure 4.11 diagram]

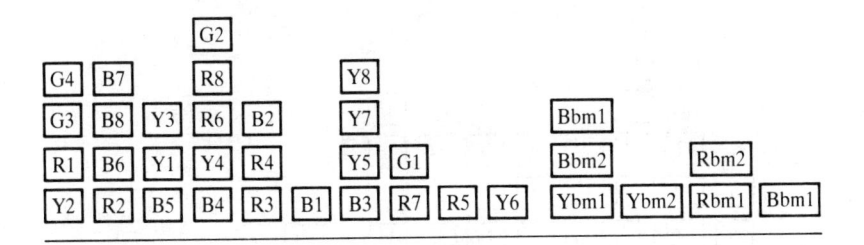

Figure 4.11 An initial state for tower1

is also shown (figure 4.13), this initial state required 83 moves in order to reach the goal.

The task specification module for 'tower2' is shown below. Note that this structure can be built simply by replacing the task specification module for 'tower1' with that for 'tower2'.

4.7.11 Task specification module for tower2

```
MODULE build IS
    INTENT:    "construct 1at2"
    IN:        string    name,place
    STATE: doit
```

[Figure 4.12 diagram]

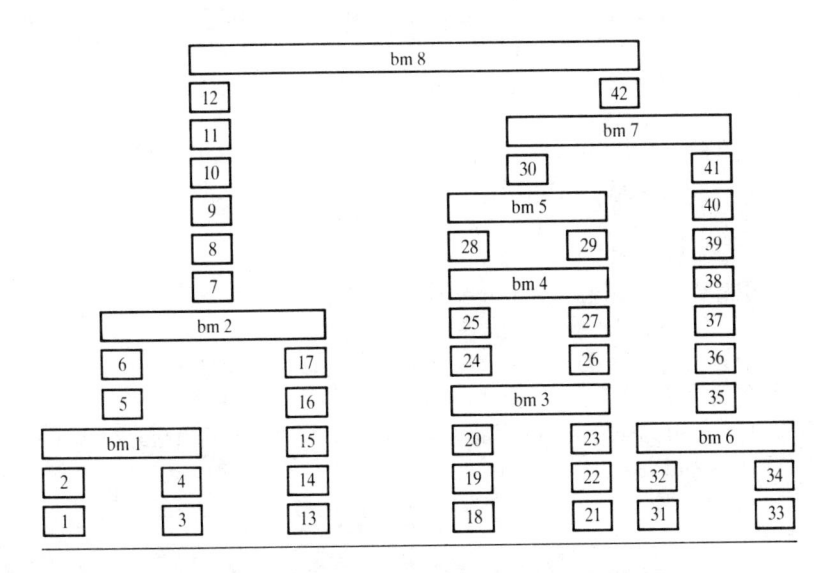

Figure 4.12 Goal state for tower 2

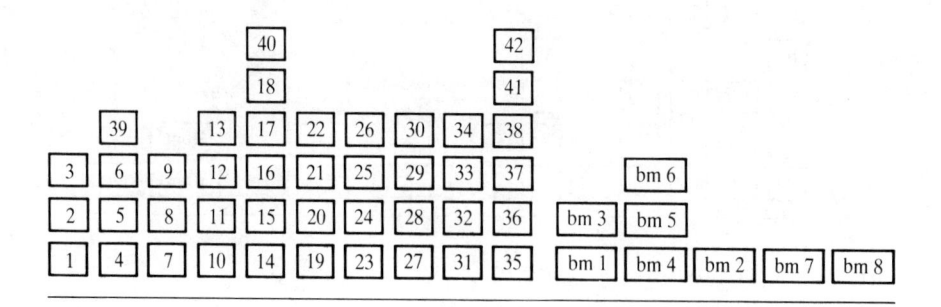

Figure 4.13 Initial state for tower2

```
IF (name) IS
"tower"   : ( buildarch(name place "[towL]" "[towR]"
            "bmTm" ) , goal )
"towL"    : ( buildarch(name place "[towLL]" "[13,14,15]"
            "bmTL") , goal )
"towR"    : ( buildarch(name place "[towRL1,towRL2,towRL3]"
            "[towRR,35,36,37,38,39,40]" "bmTR" ), goal )
"bmTm"    : ( buildarch(name place "[07,08,09,10,11,12]" "[42]"
            "bm08" ),goal)
"towLL"   : ( buildarch(name place "[01,02]" "[03,04]"
            "bm01" ) , goal )
"bmTL"    : ( buildarch(name place "[05,06]" "[16,17]"
            "bm02" ) , goal )
"towRL1": ( buildarch(name place "[18,19,20]" "[21,22,23]"
            "bm03" ) , goal )
"towRL2": ( buildarch(name place "[24,25]" "[26,27]"
            "bm04" ) , goal )
"towRL3": ( buildarch(name place "[28]" "[29]"
            "bm05" ) , goal )
"towRR"  : ( buildarch(name place "[31,32]" "[33,34]"
            "bm06" ) , goal )
ELSE ( buildarch(name place "[30]" "[41]" "bm07" ) , goal )
GOAL OF build
```

4.8 Conclusion

Arch building is a classic artificial intelligence problem in which search-based planners are often employed. RuleMaster facilitates the development of an elegant inductive solution to the ARCH problem by supporting hierarchical problem decomposition, the use of variables, parameterisation and user definable expression syntax. Whereas a classical search-based planning solution to this problem might be able to deal with four or five brick problems before computational overheads became too high, Barry Shepherd of the Turing Institute has shown that the solution presented here can be extended to thirty or forty brick problems without overwhelming overheads (see section 4.7). The advantage of search-based planning over merely programming a solution lies in the fact that the specification is simple, declarative and compact. However, inductive specifications also have these advantages.

Further work needs to be done to allow the use of variable condition values in examples.

Chapter 5
Expert Systems Applications

5.1 Introduction

Many different engineering expert systems applications have been made using RuleMaster. These include TITAN, an expert system to assist in troubleshooting for the Texas Instruments 990 Minicomputer and TURBOMAC, an expert system to aid in the diagnosis of cause of vibration-producing problems in large turbomachinery. In this chapter we describe three expert system applications: SHUTTLE, WILLARD and EARL. In section 5.2 NASA's autolander for the space shuttle is described. In section 5.3 we describe Steve Zubrick's implementation of WILLARD and discuss the validation methods that have been used to assess WILLARD's performance. The author aided in suggesting the structuring methodology used in WILLARD.

In section 5.4 Charles Riese's implementation of EARL is described and the validation that has been used to assess EARL's performance is discussed. EARL is presently in routine industrial use. The author also aided in suggesting the structuring methodology used in EARL.

5.2 SHUTTLE

Michie (1984) has described a RuleMaster application carried out by NASA for guiding the landing of the Space Shuttle. A group of space engineers, led by Roger Burke, were attending a course at Radian Corporation, Texas. During this course they were asked to suggest a class exercise for learning how to use RuleMaster. They decided to try out a problem which had been vexing them for some days. This was the problem of producing a complete and correct decision procedure for deciding whether to use the autolander in landing the Space Shuttle.

MODULE: shuttle
STATE: one
ACTIONS:
    noauto   [advise "Don't use autoland"]
    auto   [advise "Use autoland"]
CONDITIONS:
    stab   [ask "stable?" "stab,xstab"]stab xstab
    error   [ask "errors?" "XL,LX,MM,SS"]XL LX MM SS
    sign   [ask "sign?" "pp,nn"]pp nn
    wind   [ask "winds?" "head,tail"]head tail
    mag   [ask "magnitude?" "L,M,S,O"]L M S O
    vis   [ask "visibility?" "y,n"]y n
EXAMPLES:

-	-	-	-	-	n	$\Rightarrow$	(auto,goal)
xstab	-	-	-	-	y	$\Rightarrow$	(noauto,goal)
stab	LX	-	-	-	y	$\Rightarrow$	(noauto,goal)
stab	XL	-	-	-	y	$\Rightarrow$	(noauto,goal)
stab	MM	nn	tail	-	y	$\Rightarrow$	(noauto,goal)
-	-	-	-	O	y	$\Rightarrow$	(noauto,goal)
stab	SS	-	-	L	y	$\Rightarrow$	(auto,goal)
stab	SS	-	-	M	y	$\Rightarrow$	(auto,goal)
stab	SS	-	-	S	y	$\Rightarrow$	(auto,goal)
stab	MM	pp	head	L	y	$\Rightarrow$	(auto,goal)
stab	MM	pp	head	M	y	$\Rightarrow$	(auto,goal)
stab	MM	pp	tail	L	y	$\Rightarrow$	(auto,goal)
stab	MM	pp	tail	M	y	$\Rightarrow$	(auto,goal)
stab	MM	pp	head	S	y	$\Rightarrow$	(noauto,goal)
stab	MM	pp	tail	S	y	$\Rightarrow$	(auto,goal)

Figure 5.1 Rulemaker file for space shuttle application

The decision whether or not to use the autolander was up till then left to each shuttle pilot. Eventually it was realised that the autolander had not been used, not because it had never been necessary, but because of hubris – none of the pilots wanted to be remembered as the first to rely on the non-manual method of touch-down.

    The engineers were easily able to jot down the six attributes shown in the Rulemaker file of figure 5.1.

    It was also straightforward for them to enumerate the various ex-

```
MODULE shuttle IS
   STATE: one    IF (ask "visibility?" "y,n") IS
                    "y": IF (ask "errors?" "XL,LX,MM,SS") IS
                       "XL" (advise "Don't use auto land", goal)
                       "LX" (advise "Don't use auto land", goal)
                       "MM": IF (ask "stable?" "stab,xstab") IS
                          "stab": IF (ask "sign?" "pp,nn") IS
                             "pp": IF (ask "magnitude?" "L,M,S,O") IS
                                "L": (advise "Use auto land", goal)
                                "M": (advise "Use auto land", goal)
                                "S": IF (asks "winds?" "head,tail") IS
                                   "head": (advise "Don't use auto land", goal)
                                   ELSE (advise "Use auto land", goal)
                                ELSE (advise "Don't use auto land", goal)
                             ELSE (advise "Don't use auto land", goal)
                          ELSE (advise "Don't use auto land", goal)
                          ELSE IF (ask "stable?" "stab,xstab") IS
                             "stab": IF (ask "magnitude?" "L,M,S,O") IS
                                "L": (advise "Use auto land", goal)
                                "M": (advise "Use auto land", goal)
                                "S": (advise "Use auto land", goal)
                                ELSE (advise "Don't use auto land", goal)
                             ELSE (advise "Don't use auto land", goal)
                       ELSE (advise "Use auto land", goal)
                    GOAL OF shuttle
```

Figure 5.2 Radial code for autolander decision for Space Shuttle

amples giving circumstances in which they would apply the autolander. What they found difficult was to be able to turn this knowledge into an efficient decision procedure. Figure 5.2 shows the decision tree that RuleMaster produced automatically.

In this case, it was not the inductive algorithm's ability to generalise over unseen examples that was useful: the specification given in figure 5.1 is virtually complete. Rather it was the ability to enumerate cases and know that the resultant decision tree would agree with the input/output relation defined by those cases.

5.3 WILLARD

WILLARD (Zubrick, 1984) is an expert system for predicting the likelihood of severe thunderstorms occurring in the central USA. The system was written by Steve Zubrick, a meteorologist at Radian Corporation. Extensive testing of the system has shown that it is capable of producing predictions which can usefully complement those of the US National Weather Service (USNWS) (Zubrick, 1988). The author gave help and advice in the structuring and example acquisition of WILLARD.

On average, over 1000 severe thunderstorms are reported each year in the central United States, causing the loss of many lives and billions of dollars of property damage. The National Weather Service defines severe thunderstorms as the occurrence of one or more of the following conditions:

Wind gusts greater than 50 knots,
Tornados, and/or
Hailstones greater than 3/4 inch in diameter.

Severe thunderstorm forecasting for the entire US is currently done by highly skilled meteorologists at the National Severe Storms Forecast Center (NSSFC).

This time-consuming task entails the continuous analysis of vast amounts of raw data and numeric modelling of the results, much of which turns out to be irrelevant. An expert system might automatically screen the data, providing the meteorologists with suggested forecasts together with justifications for these forecasts.

A large number of specific case studies of occurrences of severe thunderstorms have been documented and analysed in the meteorological literature. However, no coherent system of rules covering all possible cases has yet been synthesised. For this reason, an inductive rule generator would appear to be a powerful tool for generalising this accumulated knowledge.

5.3.1 The system

For the purposes of rapid development, an initial set of examples provided by the expert were used to build the prototype expert system. Additional cases of real weather data have subsequently been applied in the ongoing refinement of WILLARD. An illustration of the use of inductive inference in the development of WILLARD is given in figure 3.1 (section 3.3).

Expert systems applications 87

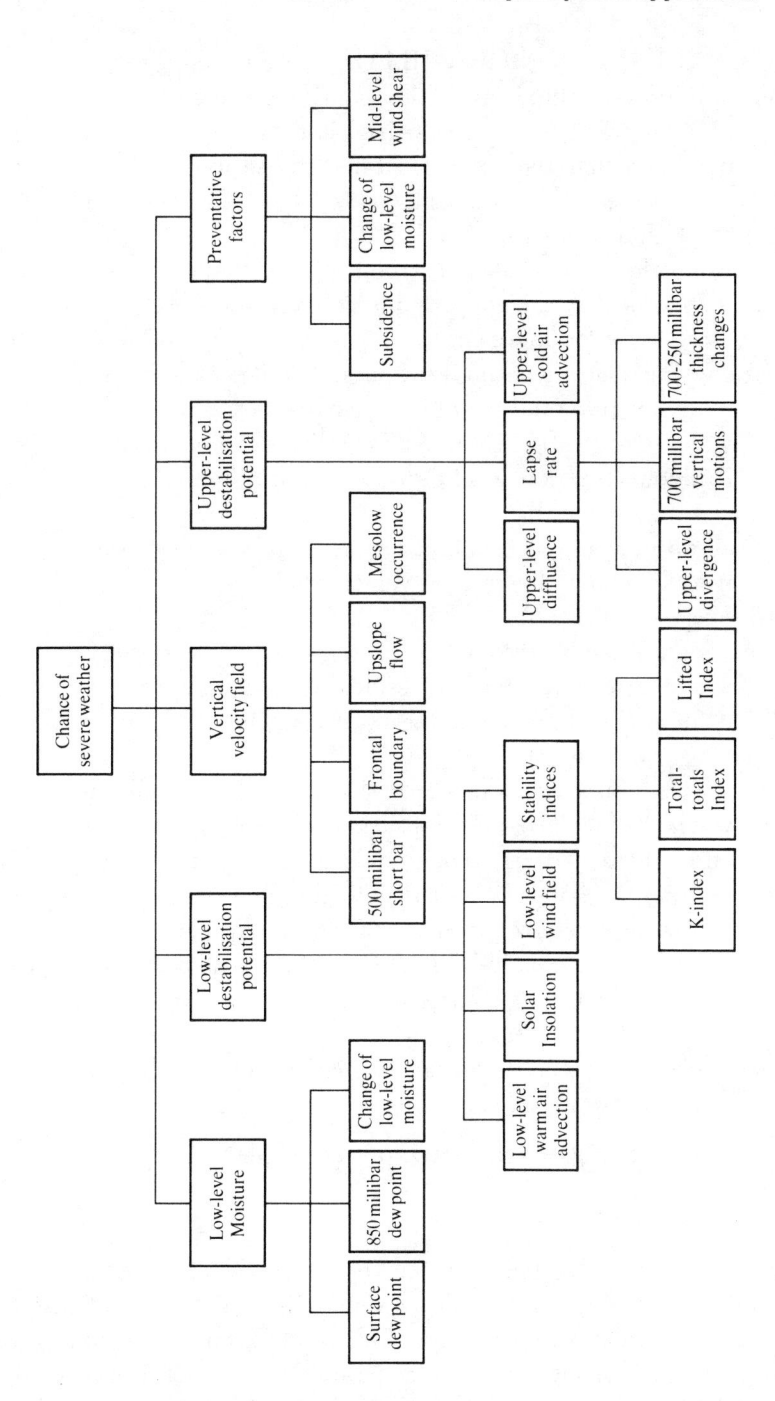

Figure 5.3 WILLARD structure

88 Inductive Acquisition of Expert Knowledge

FULL EXPLANATION OF THE FORECAST:
Since upper level cold air advection causing increased
        upwards vertical velocities is present
    it follows that the upper-level destabilisation
        potential is sufficient   (1)
Since the K Index is strong
    when the Lifted Index is strong
    it follows that the stability indices condition
        is favourable   (2)
Since daytime heating acting as a possible trigger mechanism
        for potential instability release is strong
    when (2) the stability indices condition is favourable
    it follows that low-level destabilisation potential
        is favourable   (3)
Since an approaching 500 millibar short wave trough is present
    it follows that the vertical velocity field
        is favourable   (4)
Since a high 850 mb dew point is present
    when surface dew point classification is moderate
    it follows that the low-level moisture field
        is marginal   (5)
Since (1) the upper-level destabilisation potential is sufficient
    when (3) low-level destabilisation potential is favourable
    and (4) the vertical velocity field is favourable
    and (5) the low-level moisture field is marginal
    it was necessary to advise:
        "There's a MODERATE CHANCE that thunderstorms
        occurring 12 hours from now will be severe
        at this location."
    in order to actually forecast the chance of severe
    thunderstorms

Figure 5.4   Sample WILLARD forecast explanation

    The WILLARD expert system is composed of a hierarchy of 30 modules, each of which contains a single decision rule (see figure 5.3).
    This hierarchy is, on average, four levels deep. All modules' rules were developed using inductive generalisation. A total of around 140 examples were used in building WILLARD. WILLARD has a domain size of approximately nine million measurably different situations.
    For the top-level module, the inductive algorithm was able to order

the critical meteorological factors in a manner consistent with the way forecasters perform their analysis. For example, if the key factors are unfavourable, then a decision can be made rapidly, otherwise, more parameters are investigated until a decision can be reached.

Although WILLARD is essentially an expert classification system, RuleMaster facilitates the use of control loops required for top level control and the monitoring of incoming data.

WILLARD can operate in interactive or automatic forecast mode. In interactive mode, the system asks questions of the meteorologist about pertinent weather conditions for the forecast area and produces a complete, reasoned forecast.

In automatic mode, WILLARD obtains all necessary information from National Meteorological Center data files. External FORTRAN functions were interfaced to WILLARD to access and operate on these data files. The user may specify an area in which WILLARD will generate a grid of nodal values for the chance of severe thunderstorms for that area. A sample explanation of a forecast is shown in figure 5.4.

5.3.2 Validation

Steve Zubrick, with help from the USNWS, has carried out comparisons of WILLARD's forecasting ability versus that of the standard collective outlook issued by forecasters of the Severe Local Storms Unit (SELS) (Zubrick, 1988).

The validation data used spanned a 24-day period in the spring of 1984. Severe thunderstorm outlooks were given by both WILLARD and SELS in terms of the following three aerial density/risk categories.

1. Slight risk: 2 to 5 per cent aerial coverage.

2. Moderate risk: 6 to 10 per cent aerial coverage.

3. High risk: greater than 10 per cent aerial coverage.

Three statistics were quantified over all of the WILLARD and SELS predictions. These were

x severe storm reports correctly predicted (those reports found within a severe risk outlook area);

y severe storm reports not predicted (those lying outside the severe risk outlook area);

z non-severe weather predicted to be severe.

90 Inductive Acquisition of Expert Knowledge

In terms of these values WILLARD and the SELS predictions were compared according to three criteria which are believed by meteorologists to give a good indication of predictive skill. These criteria were

1. Probability of detection (PoD). This is defined as

$$PoD = \frac{x}{(x+y)}$$

2. False alarm ratio (FAR). This is defined as

$$FAR = \frac{z}{(z+x)}$$

3. Critical skill index (CSI). This is defined as

$$CSI = \frac{x}{(x+y+z)}$$

Figure 5.5 shows a comparison of WILLARD and SELS in terms of these three criteria over a representative selection of days during the

Date	PoD (%) SELS/WILLARD	FAR SELS/WILLARD	CSI SELS/WILLARD
25 04 84	82/57	.46/.22	.49/.49
26 04 84	88/20	.44/.41	.52/.81
29 04 84	85/54	.51/.34	.45/.42
25 05 84	100/68	.58/.48	.43/.42
26 05 84	33/91	.74/.90	.17/.10
27 05 84	89/26	.50/.21	.47/.24
04 06 84	70/50	.54/.89	.39/.10
06 07 84	92/71	.44/.31	.54/.54

Figure 5.5 Comparison of WILLARD and SELS forecasts

test period. From this we can see that, although WILLARD's probability of detection is generally lower than that of the SELS predictions, it has a generally better false alarm rate. The critical skill index gives us the clearest overall view of skill, and shows WILLARD to have skill which although generally lower than SELS, is still comparable.

5.4 EARL

EARL (Riese, 1984) is a system for diagnosing imminent break-down in large oil-cooled electrical transformers. The system was constructed by Charles Riese who is a software engineer working for the Hartford Steam Boiler Inspection and Insurance Company (HSB). When EARL was tested against 859 test cases, its diagnosis was correct in 99.5% of the cases studied.

Large oil-filled transformers are used by utilities for power distribution. These transformers sometimes fail due to insulation deterioration, overheating due to overload, failure of bolted or compression joints, corona, arcing, and overheating from inadvertent grounded core. All of these failure modes involve some form of heating of the oil and/or insulation. These materials decompose when heated and some of the decomposition products are hydrogen and hydrocarbon gases which dissolve in the oil. The concentrations of these gases can be measured with conventional gas chromatographs. Over the past 20 years, techniques have been developed to diagnose transformers' conditions from analysis of dissolved gas in the oil.

When large transformers (in excess of 10 MW) fail, the service interruption and repair or replacement costs may run into millions of dollars. This provides financial incentive to detect the onset of transformer failures before catastrophic damage occurs. HSB insures industrial equipment and has sponsored the development of a RuleMaster-based expert system which utilises oil sample analyses to prepare transformer condition reports and to make recommendations on repair action.

The classificatory portion of the expert system contains 27 modules, each having one or more induced rules. Since this is a developing field, the theory relating gas concentrations to faults is not well worked out or documented. It was necessary to rebuild the expert system structure several times, as better organisations of the knowledge became apparent. The induction of rules from examples proved valuable in this rule construction and testing process.

The rules can be divided into several categories. First there are rules to check the validity of data, to determine if there was a leak during sample transport or a chemical analysis error. Other rules determine the presence of failure symptoms: Is there low or high temperature heating? Is heating near insulation? and so on. A third set of rules diagnoses particular faults from the symptoms and gas concentrations, and the final set of rules decides which corrective actions to recommend.

The primary system is used for screening the gas analysis results at the chemistry laboratory. Experts seem to make better use of their time, and to be able to check more transformers.

5.4.1 Validation

Owing to the high cost involved in incorrect diagnoses (in the order of millions of dollars), the accepted rate of human diagnostic failure in this domain is below 0.1

EARL was tested using 859 test cases for which gas concentration data was available. In 208 of these cases, EARL and the expert concurred that a problem existed and that the transformer needed to be overhauled, while in the other 651 cases they both agreed that no problem existed. Out of the 208 cases in which they decided that a problem existed, in 204 cases the expert's explanation was the same as EARL while in the remaining 4 cases the expert's explanation differed from EARL. This highlights the importance of explanation in the 'debugging' stage of expert system development. Without explanation, these 4 cases would have been taken as EARL delivering a correct decision, without it being realised that it was based on the wrong reasoning. The danger of this is that erroneous reasoning could later be used to reach the wrong conclusion, with potentially serious consequences.

In 10 of the 204 cases in which both EARL and the expert agreed on the diagnosis, engineers overhauling the transformers checked to find what the real problem was (this is done rarely as it is very expensive), and in all 10 cases found that EARL and the expert's joint opinion had in fact been correct.

According to these statistics, EARL gave the the same advice as the expert for the same reason in 99.5% of cases tested. In the remaining 0.5%, EARL actually gave the the same advice as the expert, but for different reasons.

It is not known to the author exactly what the estimated cost advantage of using EARL is, nor what the typical rate of inter-expert disagreement is.

5.4.2 Conclusion

EARL is now in full-time field use and automatically drafts textual reports for HSB clients. Both the expert and the knowledge engineer involved in building EARL were satisfied with the RuleMaster expert system environment. Inductive knowledge acquisition allowed the expert system to be constructed to field test standard in an order of magnitude less time than that expected using dialogue acquisition techniques.

Chapter 6
Grammatical Induction Theory

6.1 Introduction

(Since this chapter is somewhat technical the casual reader might either wish to skip to later chapters or else merely browse through the theorems which give the major theoretical results.)

All necessary definitions of theoretical terms and concepts from set theory and formal language theory used in this chapter have been collected in Appendix B. Formal descriptions of methods from the literature can be found in Appendix C. All proofs of lemmas and theorems are given in Appendix D.

RuleMaster in its present form demands that the control structure of RuleMaster finite-state machines be hand-coded. In this chapter we investigate techniques for automatically constructing finite-state structures from trace information. The techniques are based on 'grammatical induction' – the discovery of grammar from example sentences. First we present a survey of algorithms which infer a regular language from a given subset of that language. We introduce a general algorithm for this task which has a low order polynomial time complexity. Several previously devised algorithms are demonstrated by way of adaptations to this general algorithm. For the reader's convenience some of the details concerning finite state machines found in Chapter 2 are repeated here.

We have limited the scope of investigation to the inference of *regular languages* (for a general survey of inductive inference methods see Angluin and Smith, 1983). As an example of the kind of problem which we intend to solve, let us suppose that the inductive inference program with the following sample of strings is presented

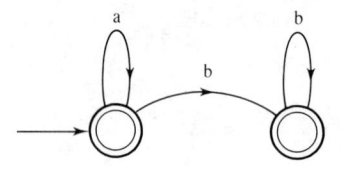

Figure 6.1 The finite-state acceptor representing the language a^+b^+

> $aaabbb$
> ab
> abb

We might expect it to return with the rule

> a^+b^+

This represents the regular language

> *one or more a followed by one or more b*

Alternatively, we can describe a machine which accepts strings of this kind diagrammatically as a finite-state acceptor. Indeed, it has been shown by Hopcroft and Ullman (1988) that any regular language can be recognised by some finite-state acceptor – as has been done in figure 6.1. As the converse is also true – any finite-state acceptor can be expressed as a regular expression – these representations are equivalent.

The aim of this investigation is to develop an algorithm for inducing Radial modules (see Chapters 2 and 3) from traces of their intended execution (sequences of calls to predefined tests and actions). Finite-state acceptors differ from the type of finite-state automata which represent Radial modules, in that the arcs of finite-state automata are labelled with pairs of tokens rather than singlets. Although the methods of induction presented here are for finite-state acceptors, adaptations of these algorithms to produce finite-state automata are presented in section 6.7. These adapted algorithms build automata in Mealy machine form from trace information. We call this adapted form of grammatical induction *sequence induction*.

Most papers on this subject suggest particular solutions to the problem. The algorithms presented are tailored to be as efficient as possible for the heuristic being used. For the sense in which *heuristic* is used here, see section 6.4 and Appendix C. We show that by devising a general algorithm ('IM1', section 6.4.2 below) which can be specialised to any one of a number of existing grammatical inference schemes eases comparison of the properties of the latter. In sections 6.2 and 6.3 we present a brief résumé of the background of this research. In section 6.4 we give the theoretical results of grammatical induction from positive samples. In section 6.4.4 the issues of section 6.4 are discussed in an informal fashion by use of examples which illustrate the behaviour of various algorithms. Section 6.5 describes an efficient version of Angluin's algorithm for inferring k-reversible languages (Angluin, 1982). Section 6.6 introduces k-contextual languages, a subclass of k-reversible languages, and provides an efficient algorithm for inferring such languages. Lastly, in section 6.7, the ways in which the additional information contained in situation/action sequences can be used to choose an appropriate value of k for k-reversible and k-contextual inference algorithms automatically is discussed.

6.2 Language identification

Gold's theoretical study of *language learnability* introduced an abstract setting for the problem of grammatical induction(Gold, 1967). The grammatical induction problem is that of deciding which language L from a class of languages C is characterised by a set of examples E. An example from the set E can be positive or negative in the sense that it is stated whether it is inside or outside L. Thus, supposing C is the set of regular languages over the symbol set $\Sigma = \{0,1\}$, then

$\mathrm{E} = \{\ \langle 00, in\rangle\ \langle 1,\ out\rangle\ \langle 11,\ in\rangle\ \langle 00011,\ in\rangle\ \langle 01000,\ out\rangle\ \ldots\ \}$

might exemplify the regular language $L = (0, 10^*1)^*$ containing only binary strings of even parity. (This is the same problem as that of section 2.6.2 with *0* and *1* replacing false and true respectively.) In Gold's work, inference is carried out on an infinite list of examples containing one or more occurrences of every possible string along with an indication of whether it is in the target language. Gold defined an inference algorithm I as *identifying a language in the limit* if and only if, after a certain number of examples are provided, I chooses the correct explanation and does not subsequently change this explanation as more examples are presented.

Next, Gold introduced the general inference technique of *identification by enumeration* in which a generator exhaustively postulates in some fixed order $L_1, L_2, L_3, \ldots$ all languages L_i from the set C and returns the first which is consistent with the examples so far.

Gold went on to show that for any class of languages C containing all finite languages (those with a finite number of legal sentences) and at least one infinite language, it is impossible for an inference algorithm to identify an arbitrary element of C using only positive examples. This can easily be seen by taking C to be the set of regular languages over the symbol set Σ and showing that for any positive example set E there are at least two languages which can be postulated; namely the universal language Σ^* and the finite language containing only the members of E.

Gold distinguishes between two types of presentation of mixed positive/negative examples. A presentation can be *text*, in which case the inference algorithm I is presented with a passive list of facts. Alternatively, I can be supplied with an *informant* or *oracle*, an agent which answers membership questions about the unknown language.

6.3 Mixed positive/negative presentations

Although regular sets can be identified from positive and negative *text*, Angluin (1978) has shown that the problem of finding a minimal regular expression from such samples is NP-hard. Furthermore, Gold (1978) showed that the corresponding problem of finding a minimal finite acceptor from positive and negative samples is also NP-hard.

Given an *oracle*, Moore (1956) has shown that it is possible to identify a language only if we are also given additional information about L. Moore's algorithm has an NP complexity bound, and requires an upper bound on the number of states in the canonical (state-minimal) acceptor of L as additional information. Pao and Carr (1978) and later Angluin (1982) suggest the use of a representative sample of L, that is, a finite subset of L that exercises every transition in the canonical acceptor of L. Whereas Pao and Carr's enumerative algorithm is NP in the number of queries made of the oracle, Angluin's algorithm requires only a polynomial number of queries for the same problem.

6.4 Positive samples

In section 6.2 we stated Gold's theorem which says that particular classes of languages cannot be identified in the limit from positive examples only. This does not imply necessarily that negative examples are an imperative, only that some form of additional constraint must be used in order to guarantee identification in the limit. In this section algorithms which use parameterised constraint predicates which allow identification of languages in the limit from positive example sets are investigated. As might be expected, all these algorithms have the property that the proposed language L does at least contain the sample set S.

As far as the author is aware, there are only four algorithms in the literature for inducing finite state automata from positive examples. A general algorithm is given in section 6.4.2 which, with suitable alteration of the driving heuristic, produces the same results as all of the existing algorithms except Angluin's.

6.4.1 Properties of induced acceptors

All the inference algorithms considered in section 6.4.4 start with a prefix tree acceptor, and generalise this by merging states. Angluin (1982) proves the following property of the results of such algorithms.

Lemma 6.1 *Let S^+ be a positive sample of the regular language L, and let A_0 be the prefix tree acceptor for S^+. Let $\pi_{Pr(S+)}$ be the partition π_L restricted to $Pr(S^+)$. Then $A_0/\pi_{Pr(S+)}$ is isomorphic to a subacceptor of $A(L)$. Thus $L(A_0/\pi_{Pr(S+)}) \subseteq L$.*

Corollary 6.2 *$L(A_0/\pi_{Pr(S+)})$ is contained in L.*

The following Lemma is due to Fu and Booth (1975).

Lemma 6.3 *Every acceptor $A/\pi_{Pr(S+)}$ derived from the prefix set S^+ is a valid solution.*

This theorem gives an indication of why Gold's results hold. The set of logical constraints provided by a positive example set is insufficient for the determination of a unique language which fits the examples. The heuristics described in later sections of this chapter provide a set of possible additional constraints which have been used to make such a unique determination.

6.4.2 Algorithm IM1

We now present a simple, though general, algorithm for carrying out inference by merging the states of $PT(S^+)$. Many of the algorithms in the literature are special cases of this algorithm. Describing these algorithms in terms of the algorithm IM1 facilitates their presentation and comparison. To the author's knowledge, no algorithm similar to IM1 has appeared in any publication previously.

IM1 applies the characteristic predicate $\chi_{\pi_{Pr(S^+)}}(u,v)$ (hereafter called $\chi(u,v)$) to every pair $u,v \in Pr(S^+)$. If χ returns *true*, IM1 merges the blocks containing u and v. The resultant acceptor A_0/π_f is non-deterministic. Hopcroft and Ullman (1979) give an algorithm which can be used to convert this to the equivalent minimal deterministic acceptor.

Algorithm IM1
Input: a nonempty positive sample S^+
Output: the acceptor $A_0/\pi_{Pr(S^+)}$
Initialisation
Let $A_0 = (Q_0, \Sigma, \delta_0, I_0, F_0)$ be $PT(S^+)$.
Let π_0 be the trivial partition of Q_0.
Let i = 0.
Merging
For all pairs (u,v) in Q_0 do
begin
  If $\chi(u,v)$ then
    begin
      Let $B_1 = B(u, \pi_i)$, $B_2 = B(v, \pi_i)$.
      Let π_{i+1} be π_i with B_1 and B_2 merged.
      Increase i by 1.
    end
end
Termination
Let $f = i$ and output the acceptor A_0/π_f.

6.4.3 Time complexity of IM1

As every pairwise test of elements of Q_0 is made, χ is applied $n(n-1)/2$ times where $n = |Q_0|$. Thus the time complexity of the algorithm is $O(n^2)$.

6.4.4 Informal description of heuristics

In this section the heuristics used in grammatical learning algorithms from the literature are described. Formal definitions of these heuristics are provided in Appendix C.

Having been presented with a sample of a particular regular language, the first step in our general method of finding an appropriate candidate acceptor is to form the unique *prefix-tree acceptor* corresponding to the sample. This prefix-tree acceptor is itself a finite ac-

Sample, S^+: ab,bb,aab,abb
Prefix tree acceptor, $PT(S^+)$:

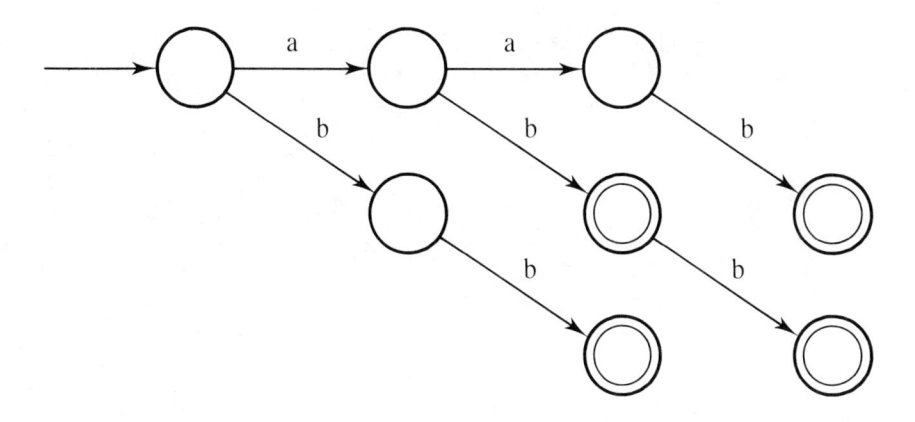

Figure 6.2 A positive sample and its corresponding prefix tree acceptor

ceptor. It is formed by taking each string in the sample and using it to extend a path from the tree root to one of the leaves. The individual segments of the string are used as the labels of the arcs along this path. Moreover, any state at which a string terminates is marked in a special manner with a double circle, and called an *accepting state*. Note that whereas all leaves are accepting states, accepting states can also be found at some internal nodes of the tree. Figure 6.2 illustrates the relationship between the sample and the prefix tree.

Clearly, this finite acceptor will accept no more and no less than the strings presented in the sample. As with any tree, we can name each node uniquely by describing the path from the root to that node. In the case of the prefix tree acceptor shown above, we can represent the states as the set of all prefixes of strings in the sample,

$$Pr(S^+) = \{\lambda, a, b, aa, ab, bb, aab, abb\}$$

where λ is the empty string representing the root node, or start state.

By *merging* some of the nodes of the acceptor of figure 6.2 it is possible to form a smaller acceptor which will still accept only the strings represented in the sample. This new acceptor is shown in figure 6.3. The acceptor of figure 6.3 is in fact the smallest, or *canonical* acceptor which will accept only the sample (this has been confirmed algorithmically).

Language accepted, S^+: ab,aab,abb,bb
Canonical acceptor, $A(S^+)$:

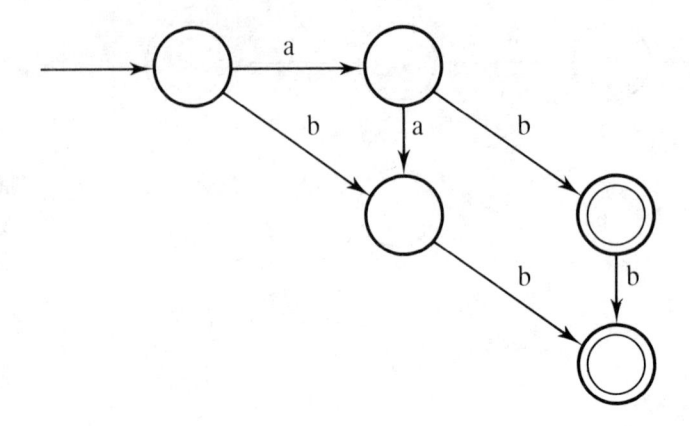

Figure 6.3 The canonical acceptor of the sample

By further merger of the states of the acceptor of figure 6.3 we produce acceptors which accept successively more and more strings. In this way it is possible to infer languages which are generalisations of the original sample, and of which the sample is a proper subset. To illustrate this figure 6.4 shows an acceptor formed by the merger of three of the states of the acceptor of figure 6.3.

This process of merger, if carried on in an arbitrary manner will, in the limit, produce an acceptor containing a single state and single

Acceptor of L:

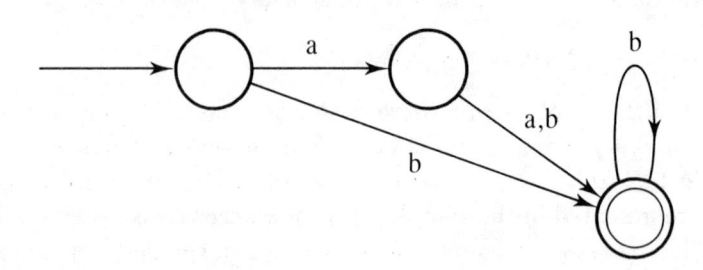

Figure 6.4 A new acceptor derived from that of figure 6.3

Acceptor of L:

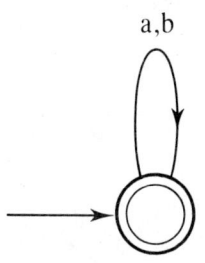

Figure 6.5 The universal acceptor for the symbol set a,b

arc. Such an acceptor, called a *universal* acceptor, accepts *any* string consisting of symbols present in the original sample. This is shown in figure 6.5.

This result is almost certainly an *over-generalisation* of the target grammar. Therefore it is necessary to introduce a restraining factor into the inference process. This is done by using a predicate to qualify the merger of candidate states. This predicate is called the *characteristic predicate* and is often merely a heuristic. During the process of inference, every possible pair of nodes in the original prefix-tree acceptor is tested using the heuristic to decide whether they should be merged in the resultant acceptor.

6.4.5 Various heuristics

All heuristics developed so far for this problem have depended on matching some local properties of pairs of candidate nodes. If the heuristic does find a match, the nodes are merged. Below we sketch informally how four of these matching heuristics work.

6.4.5.1 Biermann and Feldman's k-tail heuristic

Biermann and Feldman (1972) describe a heuristic which merges states having identical 'k-tail' sets. A k-tail of a node is a string of length k or less, formed by taking a directed path from that node to an accepting state in the prefix-tree acceptor of the sample. We will refer to the states of the prefix tree acceptor in figure 6.2 by way of the unique prefix of each node. Below we denote the k-tail set of a particular node by T_{s+}^k(prefix). k is some integer value chosen by the user. Thus for the prefix tree acceptor of figure 6.2, with $k = 1$,

Language accepted, $L: (a,b)a^*(b,bb)$
Prefix tree acceptor, $PT(S^+)$:

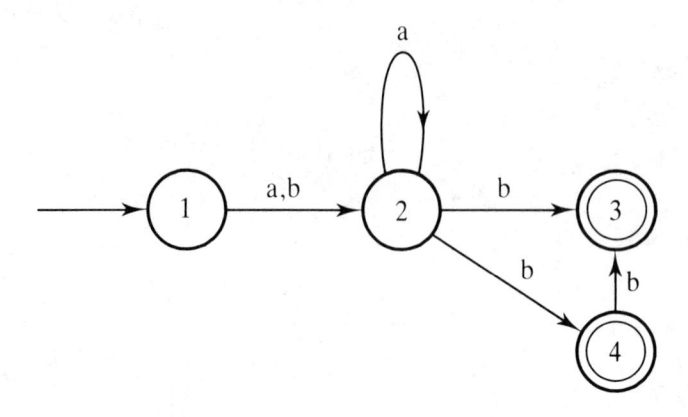

Figure 6.6 Effect of k-tail inference, $k = 2$, on prefix tree acceptor of figure 6.2

$$T^1_{S+}(\lambda) = emptyset$$
$$T^1_{S+}(a) = \{b\}$$
$$T^1_{S+}(b) = \{b\}$$
$$T^1_{S+}(\{aa\}) = \{b\}$$
$$T^1_{S+}(\{ab\}) = \{\lambda, b\}$$
$$T^1_{S+}(\{bb\}) = \{\lambda\}$$
$$T^1_{S+}(\{aab\}) = \{\lambda\}$$
$$T^1_{S+}(\{abb\}) = \{\lambda\}$$

We can now partition the original prefix set into subsets of prefixes with matching tail sets

λ,a,b,aa,ab,bb,aab,abb

The effect of having merged these nodes is shown in figure 6.6.

The reader may notice that two arcs labelled with a 'b' emanate from the state labelled '2' in this figure. This implies that a *non-deterministic* decision must be made at this point when exercising the acceptor. Such an acceptor is called a *non-deterministic acceptor* and can transformed to an equivalent *deterministic* acceptor using a procedure described by Hopcroft and Ullman (1979).

6.4.5.2 Levine's heuristic

Levine's heuristic is based on maximising and thresholding a function on each pair of states in the prefix tree acceptor (Levine, 1982). For each pair of states (u, v) in the prefix tree acceptor we compute the function

$$Stren(u,v) = \max_{i} \left[\frac{2|T^i_{S+}(u) \cap T^i_{S+}(v)|}{|T^i_{S+}(u)| + |T^i_{S+}(v)|} \right], i \geq 0$$

In order to demonstrate the algorithm, we present below the tail sets of all states in the prefix tree acceptor of figure 6.2. These tail sets are equivalent to k-tail sets with k set to infinity. In figure 6.7 we show the 2-dimensional matrix representing the computation of $Stren$ for all pairs of states.

$$\begin{aligned}
T_{S+}(\lambda) &= \{ab, bb, aab, abb\} \\
T_{S+}(a) &= \{b, ab, bb\} \\
T_{S+}(b) &= \{b\} \\
T_{S+}(\{aa\}) &= \{b\} \\
T_{S+}(\{ab\}) &= \{\lambda, b\} \\
T_{S+}(\{bb\}) &= \{\lambda\} \\
T_{S+}(\{aab\}) &= \{\lambda\} \\
T_{S+}(\{abb\}) &= \{\lambda\}
\end{aligned}$$

For purposes of thresholding, the user provides a value $Stren$ between 0 and 1. If $Stren(u, v) \geq Stren$ for any pair (u, v), this pair is merged. Thus, if we choose $Stren$ to be 2/3, we get the partition representing the universal acceptor (figure 6.5). By setting $Stren$ to 4/5, we produce the following partition

λ,a,b,aa,ab,bb,aab,abb

Figure 6.8 shows the acceptor representing this partition.

6.4.5.3 Miclet's heuristic algorithm

Miclet (1980) gives an algorithm which is general in the sense that it can be used with a variety of heuristics. However, he uses it with a heuristic which is equivalent to applying Levine's heuristic with $Stren$ always set to be the lowest non-zero value represented in the matrix. As shown above, this leads to production of the universal language with our particular example.

	λ	a	b	aa	ab	bb	aab	abb
λ	1	4/5	0	0	0	0	0	0
a	4/5	1	1	1	2/3	0	0	0
b	0	1	1	1	2/3	0	0	0
aa	0	1	1	1	2/3	0	0	0
ab	0	2/3	2/3	2/3	1	1	1	1
bb	0	0	0	0	1	1	1	1
aab	0	0	0	0	1	1	1	1
abb	0	0	0	0	1	1	1	1

Figure 6.7 Matrix of Stren for all pairs of states

Language accepted, $L: (a,b)^*b^+$
Acceptor of L:

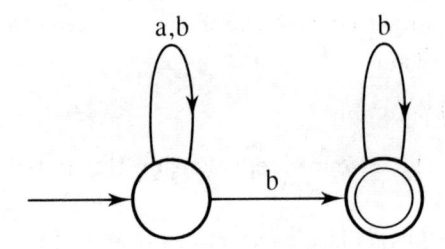

Figure 6.8 Acceptor produced from sample using Levine's algorithm, $Strn = 4/5$

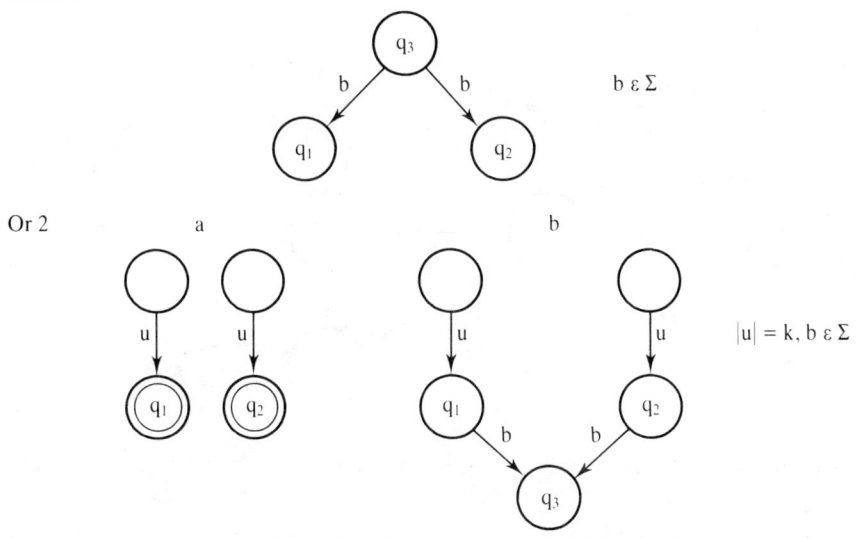

Figure 6.9 Graphical representation of conditions for merger of q_1 and q_2

6.4.5.4 Angluin's heuristic algorithm for k-reversible languages

Angluin's algorithm, like others described, uses a parameter k provided by the user (Angluin, 1982). The algorithm operates by successively merging any two states q_1 and q_2 for which one of the conditions represented in figure 6.9 holds.

In words these conditions are

1. There exist two arcs labelled with a common symbol leading out from state q_3 to q_1 and q_2.

2. Two paths labelled with a common string of length k lead to q_1 and q_2, where q_1 and q_2 are either

    (a) both accepting states, or

    (b) both have paths labelled with a common string of length 1 leading to some state q_3.

Language accepted, L: a^*b^+
Acceptor of L:

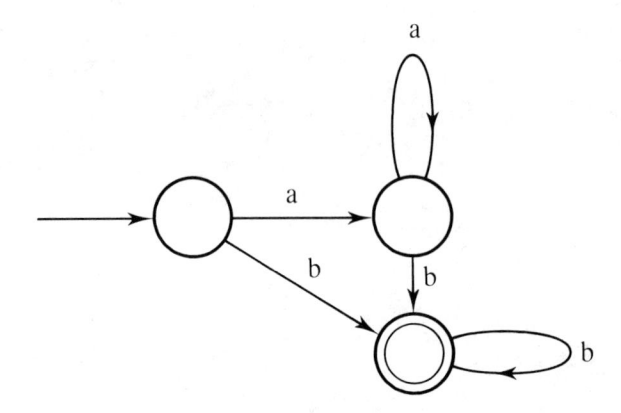

Figure 6.10 The result of applying Angluin's algorithm, $k = 1$

Figure 6.10 shows the result of applying Angluin's heuristic with $k = 1$ to the prefix tree acceptor of figure 6.2.

When minimised, this acceptor represents the language a^*b^+. Of all the results from heuristic predicates presented so far, this seems to be the most intuitively correct guess for the sample S^+. However, as Angluin's algorithm has a time complexity of $O(n^3)$ it is not practical for large samples.

6.4.6 Limitations of existing heuristics

It may be seen from inspection that a common factor of all the heuristics listed above is that $T_{S^+}(u) \cap T_{S^+}(v) \neq \emptyset$ must at least hold for $\chi(u,v)$ to be true. The following theorem shows the limitation of such a requirement.

Theorem 6.4 *For any $\chi(u,v)$ which implies $T_{S^+}(u) \cap T_{S^+}(v) = \emptyset$, the induced partition $\pi_{Pr(S^+)}$ is the trivial partition π_0 whenever $|S^+| = 1$.*

Proof. See Appendix D.

Human beings are capable of making inferential 'guesses' about regular languages from single pieces of evidence. For instance, given the string

   $aaabbb$

one might suspect L to be

a*b*

The author's k-contextual algorithm presented in section 6.6 avoids this limitation.

6.5 An efficient new algorithm

In section 6.4.5.4 we introduced Angluin's k-reversible algorithm. This algorithm has time complexity $O(n^3)$. In this section we describe a new algorithm, KR, which carries out Angluin's k-reversible induction in time $O(n^2)$. The definitions given in Appendix B are assumed as precursors to the following discussion.

6.5.1 Uniquely terminated acceptors

Let the finite state acceptor (FSA) A be described by the n-tuple $A = (Q, \Sigma, \delta, I, F)$. We say that A is a τ-terminated acceptor (TTA), (where $\tau \in \Sigma$ is a unique termination symbol) if and only if for any state $q \in Q$, $\delta(q, \tau) = q'$ implies $q' \in F$. Otherwise $\delta(q, \tau) = \emptyset$. that is we call a finite-state acceptor a TTA if it has the property that any transition arc is labelled with the termination symbol τ if and only if it leads into an acceptor state. It should be clear that any string w accepted by a TTA will have the form $w = u\tau v$ if and only if v is the empty string, λ, that is, the symbol τ can only be found as the last symbol of w.

The acceptor A is a *goal state acceptor* (GSA) if and only if it has a single accepting state, q_g, (called the *goal* state) and the set of states reached by a single transition from q_g, is empty. In other words, a GSA has a unique *goal* state which has no outgoing arcs.

We call any acceptor that is both a TTA and a GSA, *uniquely terminated*.

Theorem 6.5 *There exists a bijection h_τ such that any acceptor $A = \{Q, \Sigma, \delta, I, F\}$ in which $\tau \notin \Sigma$, $h_\tau(A)$ is a uniquely terminated acceptor that accepts the language $L(A).\{\tau\}$.*

Proof. See Appendix D.

We say that an acceptor A is ku-reversible if, and only if,

1. A is *uniquely terminated* and

2. $h_\tau^{-1}(A)$ is k-reversible (see definition of k-reversibility in section 6.4.5.4.

6.5.2 The *KR* algorithm

The following algorithm constructs a *ku*-reversible acceptor by augmenting the sample set S^+ to $S^+.\{\tau\}$ and using a process similar to that of Angluin's *ZR* algorithm. The final result is normalised to being a *k*-reversible acceptor using h_τ^{-1}.

Algorithm KR
Input: a nonempty positive sample S^+ and a parameter k.
Output: a k-reversible acceptor A.
*Initialisation
Let S_u^+ be $S^+.\{\tau\}$
Let $A_0 = (Q_0, \Sigma_0, \delta_0, I_0, F_0)$ be $PT(S_u^+)$.
Let π_0 be the trivial partition of Q_0.
For each $b \in \Sigma_0$ and $q \in Q_0$ let $s(\{q\}, b) = \delta_0(q, b)$ and $p(\{q\}, b) = \delta_0^r(q, b)$.
Choose some $q' \in F_0$.
Let LIST contain all pairs (q',q) such that $q \in F_0 - \{q'\}$.
Let $i = 0$.
* Merging
While LIST $\neq \emptyset$ do
begin
    Remove some element (q_1, q_2) from LIST.
    Let $B_1 = B(q_1, \pi_i), B_2 = B(q_2, \pi_i)$.
    If $B_1 \neq B_2$ then
     begin
      Let B_3 be B_1 and B_2 merged.
      Let π_{i+1} be π_i with B_3 replacing B_1 and B_2.
      For each $b \in \Sigma_0$, s-UPDATE(B_1,B_2,B_3,b) and
        pk-UPDATE(B_1,B_2,B_3,b,k).
      Increase i by 1.
     end
end
* Termination
Let $f = i$
Output $h_\tau^{-1}(A_0/\pi_f)$.

Although s-UPDATE remains the same as that described by Angluin (1982), we include it here for the sake of completeness.

Algorithm s-UPDATE
Input: blocks B_1, B_2 and B_3, and a symbol $b \in \Sigma_0$.

If $s(B_1,b)$ and $s(B_2,b)$ are nonempty then
begin
    Place $(s(B_1,b), s(B_2,b))$ on LIST.
end
If $s(B_1,b)$ is nonempty
    then let $s(B_3,b) = s(B_1,b)$
    else let $s(B_3,b) = s(B_2,b)$.

Angluin's *p*-UPDATE is replaced by *pk*-UPDATE which is described below.

Algorithm pk-UPDATE
Input: blocks B_1, B_2 and B_3, a symbol $b \in \Sigma_0$ and a k parameter.
For each $q_1 \in p(B_1,b)$ and $q_2 \in p(B_2,b)$
begin
    If q_1 and q_2 have a common k-leader in A_0/π_i then   (1)
    begin
        Place (q_1, q_2) on LIST.
    end
end
Let $p(B_3,b) = p(B_1,b) \cup p(B_2,b)$

Lemma 6.6 *Let S^+ be a non-empty positive sample, k a non-negative integer, and π_i the partition formed by KR on input S^+ and k after i steps. If some u_1v_1 and u_2v_2 are in the same non-goal block B of π_i (i.e. $B(u_1v_1, \pi_i) = B(u_2v_2, \pi_i)$, $v_1 \neq w_1\tau, v_2 \neq w_2\tau$), where $|v_1| = k = |v_2|$, then $v_1 = v_2$.*

Proof. See Appendix D.

The condition that q_1 and q_2 have a common k-leader in A_0/π_i from statement (1) of the algorithm *pk*-UPDATE can be computed efficiently and simply as follows. Let q_1 and q_2 correspond to $B(u_1v_1, \pi_i)$ and $B(u_2v_2, \pi_i)$, where $u_1v_1, u_2v_2 \in Pr(S^+)$. To check whether q_1 and q_2 have a common k-leader in A_0/π_i, we need merely check that $|v_1| = k = |v_2|$ and $v_1 = v_2$. It can be seen from lemma 6.6 that it does not matter which u_1v_1 and u_2v_2 are taken as representatives of the two blocks.

Lemma 6.7 *Let S^+ be a non-empty positive sample and k a non-negative integer. The output of algorithm KR on input S^+ and k is isomorphic to the prefix tree acceptor $PT(S^+)$ whenever k is greater than the length of the longest string within S^+.*

Proof. See Appendix D.

6.5.3 The correctness of KR

Angluin (1982) describes an algorithm, k-RI, for inducing k-reversible languages which repetitively merges any two blocks $B(q_1, \pi_i)$ and $B(q_2, \pi_i)$ from successive partitions π_i of the original prefix tree $PT(S^+)$ if, and only if, they violate the conditions of k-reversibility. We now define the conditions of ku-reversibility in a similar manner to those of Angluin's (see figure 6.9).

1. No two arcs labelled with a common symbol b ($b \in \Sigma_0$) leading out from any state q_3 lead to any other two states q_1 and q_2. That is, a ku-reversible acceptor is deterministic.

2. Given that there exist two paths labelled with a common string u of length k leading to two states q_1 and q_2, there must not also be two arcs labelled with a common symbol b ($b \in \Sigma_0$) leading from q_1 and q_2 to some other state q_3.

If either of these two conditions is present, then the states q_1 and q_2 mentioned should be merged. Diagrammatically we can represent the conditions as those shown in figure 6.11.

Lemma 6.8 *Let S^+ be a non-empty positive sample, k a non-negative integer, A_0 the prefix tree acceptor of S_u^+, and π_f the final partition found by KR on input S^+. Then π_f is the finest partition of the states of A_0 such that A_0/π_f is ku-reversible.*

Proof. See Appendix D.

Lemma 6.9 *Let S^+ be a non-empty positive sample, k a non-negative integer, A_0 the prefix tree acceptor of S_u^+, π_f the final partition found by KR on input S^+ and k, and $A = h_\tau^{-1}(A_0/\pi_f)$ the output automata. Then A is isomorphic to the automata $A' = PT(S^+)/\pi$, where π is the finest partition of the states of $PT(S^+)$ such that A' is k-reversible.*

Proof. See Appendix D.

We have thus shown that the KR algorithm is input/output equivalent to Angluin's algorithm (Angluin, 1982).

Theorem 6.10 *Let S^+ be a nonempty positive sample, k a natural number and let $A_u = h_\tau^{-1}(A_0/\pi_f)$ be the acceptor output by KR on input S^+ and k. Then $L(A)$ is the smallest k-reversible language containing S^+.*

Either 1

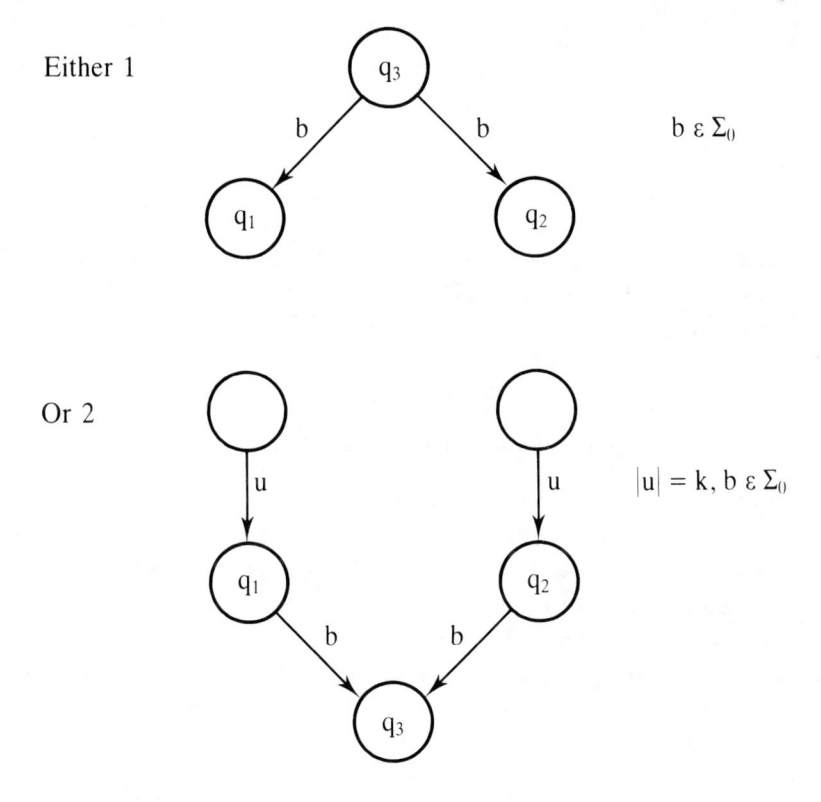

```
        q3
       /  \
      b    b            b ε Σ₀
     /      \
    q1      q2
```

Or 2

```
    ○          ○
    |u         |u        |u| = k, b ε Σ₀
    ↓          ↓
   q1         q2
     \b      b/
      ↓      ↓
        q3
```

Figure 6.11 Graphical representation of conditions for merger of q_1 and q_2

Proof. See Appendix D.

Theorem 6.11 *Let L be a nonempty k-reversible language and w_1, w_2, w_3, ... any positive presentation of L. On this input, the output A_1, A_2, A_3, ... of KR converges to $A(L)$ (that is, KR identifies L in the limit).*

Proof. See Appendix D.

6.5.4 Time complexity of KR

Theorem 6.12 *Let S^+ be a non-empty positive sample, k a non-negative integer. The algorithm KR may be implemented to run in* time $O(n^2)$ where n is

$$\left(\sum_{u \in S^+} |u|\right) + |S^+| + 1.$$

Proof. See Appendix D.

The reason that this time complexity is better than that of Angluin's algorithm is that whereas Angluin's algorithm looks at all possible mergers during each cycle, in our algorithm the search for mergers is limited by the prefix tree acceptor.

6.5.5 Updating a k-reversible guess

Angluin (1982) shows how her ZR algorithm can be modified to have good incremental behaviour. We now demonstrate how the KR algorithm described here can be modified for the same ends. Given the ku-reversible automaton $A_u = A_0/\pi_f$ computed by KR on input S^+, and given a new string w, we may easily update A_u to be the ku-reversible acceptor computed by KR on input $S^{+'} = S^+ \cup \{w\}$. The method for doing this is to start at the initial state of A_u and follow the transitions A_f makes on the input string $w\tau$. If no undefined transitions are encountered and the last state reached is the *goal* state, then A_u already accepts $w\tau$ and nothing need be done. Otherwise, add new states and transitions for each symbol of w starting with the first undefined transition (if any). Mark the last state reached by $w\tau$ as accepting, and place the pair consisting of this state and the *goal* state of A_u on LIST. Continue the merging portion of the algorithm KR until LIST is empty, and output the k-reversible acceptor $h_\tau^{-1}(A_u/\pi')$, where π' is the final partition of the states of A_u. The correctness of this procedure is verified in the same way as that of the original algorithm KR, since the order of detecting and performing required merges is immaterial.

Example 6.13 *If we run KR with a setting of $k = 0$ on the input $\{0, 00, 11, 1100\}$, we obtain A_0/π_f as shown in figure 6.12a. If we then add the string 101 to the sample and perform the updating procedure just described, we first obtain the acceptor shown in figure 6.12b. This is then 'folded up' as shown in figures 6.12c and d to obtain the final uniquely terminated acceptor. By applying h_τ^{-1} we produce the k-reversible acceptor shown in figure 6.12e which accepts strings if and only if they contain an even number of 1s.*

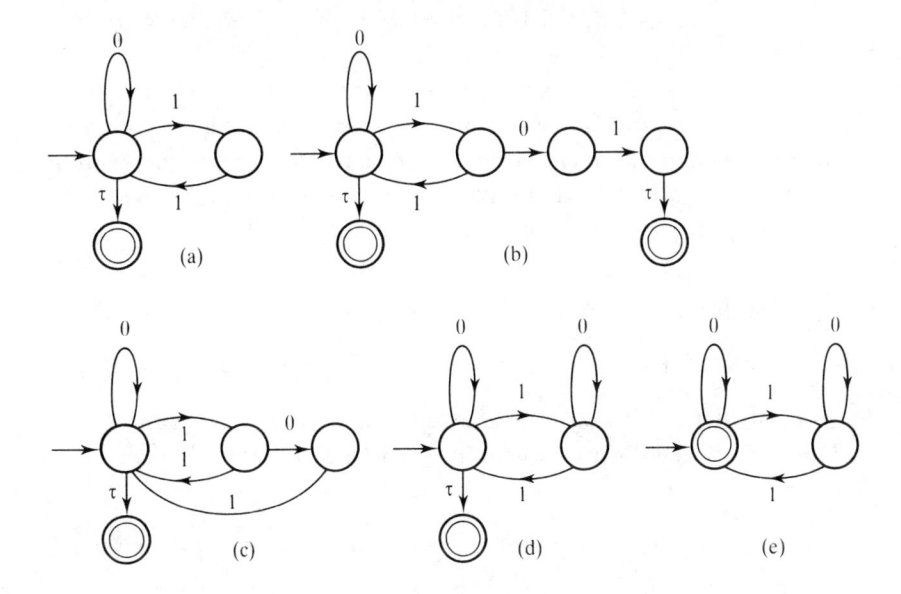

Figure 6.12 Updating a guess

6.5.6 Using negative data

negative data can be used in the same way as that described by Angluin (1982). That is, we are given a positive and negative example set (S^+, S^-), such that S^+ and S^- are disjoint finite sets of strings. We compute the k-reversible languages for $k = 0,1,2,...$ using the positive examples, S^+, until we find some k for which the inferred language does not contain any of the strings from the negative set S^-.

6.6 k-contextual languages

According to theorem 6.4, the first three algorithms reviewed in section 6.4.4 (Bierman and Feldmann, 1972; Levine, 1982; Miclet, 1980) have the common property that they require at least two examples in order to carry out any generalisation. It can also be easily shown that Angluin's k-reversible method has exactly the same limitation. However, human beings have little difficulty in hypothesising grammars from sufficiently long single strings.

The k-contextual language class described in this section has the property that the smallest k-contextual language which is consistent with a single example may contain more than one string (see example 6.21), that is algorithms which hypothesise k-contextual languages can carry out generalisation using only one example.

6.6.1 k-contextuality

First we give a language characterisation of k-contextual sets.

Definition 6.14 *Let L be a regular language. Then L is k-contextual if and only if whenever u_1vw_1 and u_2vw_2 are in L and $|v| = k$, $T_L(u_1v) = T_L(u_2v)$.*

We extend the notion of k-contextuality to cover not only languages but their corresponding acceptors.

Definition 6.15 *An acceptor A is k-contextual if and only if $L(A)$ is k-contextual.*

Remark 6.16 *If a language L is k-contextual and contains two not necessarily distinct strings u_1vw_1 and u_2vw_2, where $|v| = k$, then L also contains u_1vw_2 and u_2vw_1. This is merely an instance of definition 6.14.*

Remark 6.17 *Any 0-contextual language L containing two not necessarily distinct strings u_1w_1 and u_2w_2 also contains u_1w_2 and u_2w_1. This is a instance of remark 6.16.*

Lemma 6.18 *Any 0-contextual non-empty language L is equal to Σ^* (the universal language) where $b \in \Sigma$ if and only if there is some $ubv \in L$.*

Proof. See Appendix D.

As shown in section 6.4.4, inductive algorithms which use positive data to identify a language must avoid *over-generalisation*, that is choosing a language which is a superset of the target language. For this purpose Angluin (1982) has shown the need to define a *characteristic sample* for any class of languages. A characteristic sample of a k-contextual language L is a sample S^+ of L with the property that L is the smallest k-contextual language that contains S^+. If a characteristic sample for L is found in the sample, then proposing L is not an overgeneralisation.

Grammatical induction theory 117

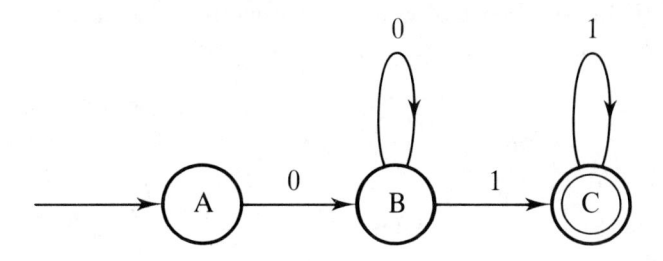

Figure 6.13 The canonical acceptor of the language 0^+1^+

Remark 6.19 $A = (Q, \Sigma, \delta, \{q_0\}, F)$ is k-contextual if and only if for all strings u_1vw_1 and u_2vw_2 accepted by A, where $|v| = k$, there is a unique state q such that $\delta(q_0, u_1v) = q = \delta(q_0, u_2v)$.

As k-contextual languages have a lot in common with k-reversible languages (it is shown later in theorem 6.24 that every k-contextual language is k-reversible), the following proof closely follows a similar proof of Angluin's.

Theorem 6.20 For any k-contextual language L there exists a characteristic sample S^+ of L.

Proof. See Appendix D.

Example 6.21 Consider the language 0^+1^+ whose canonical acceptor is shown in figure 6.13. Using the construction method of the above proof to construct a characteristic sample S^+ for this 1-contextual language, we obtain $L_A = \emptyset$, $L_B = \{0\}$, $L_C = \{1\}$ and $S^+ = \{0011\}$. Note that this is only one possible solution for S^+. Among other characteristic samples are $S^+ = \{001, 011\}$ and $S^+ = \{0000111\}$.

Clearly, a characteristic sample of a k-contextual language can consist of a single string. This is not true of any other similar language group in the literature (Angluin, 1982; Biermann and Feldmann, 1972; Levine, 1982; Miclet, 1980).

Lemma 6.22 If A is a k-contextual acceptor and A' is any subacceptor of A, then A' is a k-contextual acceptor.

Proof. See Appendix D.

6.6.2 Relationship between k-reversibility and k-contextuality

The following definition of k-reversible languages is given by Angluin (1982).

Definition 6.23 *Let L be a regular language. Then L is k-reversible if and only if whenever u_1vw and u_2vw are in L and $|v| = k, T_L(u_1v) = T_L(u_2v)$.*

Comparing this definition with that of k-contextuality (definition 6.14), gives us the following theorem.

Theorem 6.24 *Any k-contextual language L is k-reversible.*

The proof of theorem 6.24 follows trivially from the fact that the definition for k-contextuality subsumes that of k-reversibility.

6.6.3 The KC algorithm

The following algorithm constructs a k-contextual acceptor given a positive sample and a k value.

Algorithm KC
Input: a nonempty positive sample S^+ and a k parameter.
Output: a k-contextual acceptor A.
* Initialisation
Let $A_0 = (Q_0, \Sigma_0, \delta_0, I_0, F_0)$ be $PT(S^+)$.
Let π_0 be $\{\{u\} : u \in Q_0, |u| < k\}$.
Let Q_0' be $Q_0 - \bigcup \pi_0$.
Let $i = 0$.
* Merging
For each state $u_1v \in Q_0'$ where $|v| = k$ do
begin
   If there exists some block B_1 such that $B_1 = B(u_2v, \pi_i)$ then
     Let B_2 be $B_1 \cup \{u_1v\}$.
   else
     Let B_2 be $\{u_1v\}$.
   Let π_{i+1} be π_i with B_2 replacing B_1.
   Increase i by 1.
end
* Termination
Let $f = i$
Output A_0/π_f.

Note that only π_f is a complete partition of Q_0.

6.6.4 The correctness of KC

The following Lemma describes the effect of KC.

Lemma 6.25 *Let S^+ be a nonempty positive sample, k a natural number and let A_0/π_f be the acceptor output by KC on input S^+ and k. Then π_f is the finest partition of the states of A_0 such that A_0/π_f is k-contextual.*

Proof. See Appendix D.

The following theorem is analogous to a theorem proved by Angluin (1982) for her k-RI algorithm.

Theorem 6.26 *Let S^+ be a nonempty positive sample, and let A_f be the acceptor output by algorithm KC on input S^+. Then $L(A_f)$ is the smallest k-contextual language containing S^+.*

Proof. See Appendix D.

6.6.5 The running time of KC

Theorem 6.27 *The algorithm KC may be implemented to run in time $O(n)$ where n is one more than the sum of the lengths of the input strings.*

Proof. See Appendix D.

Thus the KC learning algorithm computes faster than the KR algorithm, and also uses a simpler and more natural set of constraints on acceptable solutions.

6.6.6 Identification in the limit of k-contextual languages

In this section we show that KC is able to *identify in the limit* any language L (see section 6.2). We define an operator KC_∞ which given an infinite sequence of strings $w_1, w_2, w_3, \ldots$ and a parameter k produces an infinite sequence of acceptors $A_1, A_2, A_3, \ldots$ in which

$$A_n = KC_\infty(\{w_1, w_2, \ldots, w_n\}, k) \text{ for all } n \geq 1.$$

An infinite sequence is called a *positive presentation* of a language L if and only if the range of the sequence is exactly L, that is, every element of the sequence is an element of L and vice versa. The following theorem shows that KC_∞ identifies k-contextual languages in the limit.

Theorem 6.28 *Let L be a nonempty k-contextual language for some natural number k. Let $w_1, w_2, w_3, \ldots$ be a positive presentation of L, and $A_1, A_2, A_3, \ldots$ be the output of KC_∞ on this input. Then $L(A_1)$, $L(A_2)$, $L(A_3), \ldots$ converges to L after a finite number of steps.*

Proof. See Appendix D.

6.6.7 Incremental nature of *KC*

As stated in section 1.2 expert systems are generally built in an incremental fashion. For this reason, it is desirable that any inductive tool used in the construction of expert systems produces a gradually changing output given progressive augmentation of the example set. Without this guarantee, the knowledge engineer (or expert) presenting the example material has no ability to predict the effect that any particular new example is likely to have on the system's knowledge structure. We therefore propose the following definition of incremental modification for grammatical induction algorithms.

Definition 6.29 *Let A be the acceptor output by some grammatical induction algorithm I given the positive sample S^+ and let the acceptor A' be the output of I on input $S^+ \cup \{w\}$. We say that I is* incremental *if and only A is a subacceptor of A'.*

Theorem 6.30 *Given a fixed natural number k, the algorithm KC is incremental on input k and any positive presentation of some k-contextual language L.*

Proof. See Appendix D.

6.6.8 Using negative data

Negative data can be used as follows. We are given a positive and Negative example set (S^+, S^-), such that S^+ and S^- are disjoint finite sets of strings. We compute the k-contextual languages for $k = 0, 1, 2, \ldots$ using the positive examples, S^+, until we find some k for which the inferred language does not contain any of the strings from the negative set S^-.

6.7 Use of semantic information

Gold has shown that no algorithm can identify the entire set of regular languages from positive example sentences alone (1978). Thus various approaches have been used which present a language identification algorithm with positive examples together with additional information. Generally, this additional information is sufficient to allow identification in the limit. Up until now the additional information has taken the following forms.

1. Negative examples. Angluin (1982) shows how a combination of positive and negative examples can be used to infer any finite automata in polynomial time.

2. A limit on the total number of states. Moore (1956) suggested this.

3. A value related to the compactness of the output automata. (Angluin, 1982; Biermann and Feldman, 1972; Levine, 1982) have all suggested variants on this theme.

In this section we explain a new approach to example presentation, which requires neither an *ad hoc* numerical measure, nor the need for negative data. Instead we present *semantic information* in the positive examples, by way of situation action pairs. The output of the new technique is a finite-state automaton (rather than a finite-state acceptor), which is expressed in a similar manner to Mealy machines. How variants of existing algorithms for inducing finite-state acceptors can be used in this new framework is also described.

6.7.1 Uniquely terminated Mealy machines

Let the automaton M be (Q, X, Y, δ, I, F). Q is the set of states contained in M. I is the set of initial states of M ($I \subseteq Q$). F is the set of final states of M ($F \subseteq Q$). X is the *situation* symbol set of M. Y is the *action* symbol set of M. δ is the *transition function* of M, which maps state/situation pairs of the form (q, x) to sets of action/next-state pairs of the form (y, q') where q and q' are members of Q, x is a member of the situation symbol set X, and y is a member of the action symbol set Y. We call M a *terminated* Mealy machine, in that it is similar to a form of finite state machine called a Mealy machine (see section 2.6.5). This similarity holds in all respects except that Mealy machines do not have accepting states. We call a *terminated* Mealy machine $M = (Q, X, Y, \delta, I, F)$ *deterministic* if and only if

1. I contains exactly one member, q_i and

2. $\delta(q, x) = (y, q')$ (for some $q, q' \in Q$, $x \in X$ and $y \in Y$) there exists no other $y' \in Y$, $q \in Q$ such that $\delta(q, x) = (y', q)$.

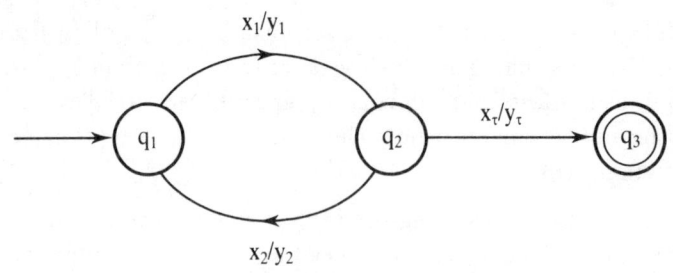

Figure 6.14 Example of a DUTMM

Let the *terminated* Mealy machine M be described by the *n-tuple* $M = (Q, X, Y, \delta, I, F)$. We extend the definition of τ-*termination* of finite state acceptors to *terminated* Mealy machines as follows. M is a τ-*terminated* Mealy machine (*TTM*) if and only if for any state $q \in Q$, $\delta(q, x_\tau) = (y_\tau, q')$ implies $q' \in F$ (where $x_\tau \in X, y_\tau \in Y$).

We also extend the definition of *goal state acceptor* to that of a *goal state* Mealy machine (GSM) as follows. The automaton M is a *GSM* if and only if it has a single accepting state q_g and the set of states reached by a single transition from q_g, $\{q : x \in X, y \in Y, F = \{q_g\}, \delta(q_g, x) = (y, q)\}$ is empty. In other words, a GSM has a unique *goal* state which has no outgoing arcs.

We call any *terminated* Mealy machine that is both a *TTM* and a *GSM*, *uniquely terminated*. In the following sections we will discuss mainly the properties of *deterministic uniquely terminated* Mealy machines (*DUTMM*). As mentioned in section 2.6.5, DUTMMs are the basis of control within modules of the Radial language (Chapter 3), and thus have special significance within this book.

Example 6.31 *Figure 6.14 is a diagrammatic representation of the DUTMM.* $M = (Q, X, Y, \delta, I, F)$ *for which* $Q = \{q_1, q_2, q_3\}$, $I = \{q_1\}$, $F = \{q_3\}$, $X = \{x_1, x_2, x_\tau\}$, $Y = \{y_1, y_2, y_\tau\}$, $\delta(q_1, x_1) = \{(y_1, q_2)\}$, $\delta(q_2, x_2) = \{(y_2, q_1)\}$, $\delta(q_2, x_\tau) = \{(y_\tau, q_3)\}$ *otherwise* $\delta(q, x) = \emptyset$ *for all other* $q \in Q$, $x \in X$, $y \in Y$.

6.7.2 Operational meaning of DUTMMs

Let $M = (Q, X, Y, \delta, \{q_i\}, \{q_g\})$ be a *DUTMM*. M can be viewed as having *semantic* properties which are similar to those of a subroutine of a programming language. M becomes *live* when called. (The term *live* is used here to indicate that M is presently executing.) M's executing state is initialised to the start state q_i. When executing some state q, M's present situation x is computed, and, using the *transition function*, the next state and next action $\delta(q, x) = (y, q')$, can be found. The next action y is executed, and on its termination, the presently executing state of M is changed to q'. If at any point M's present executing state is the goal state q_g, M returns to being *unlive*. (The term *unlive* is used to indicate that M is no longer executing.)

6.7.3 situation/action sequences

Let X be the universe of situation symbols and Y be the universe of action symbols. We call the universe of situation/action pairs $\Sigma_{sa} = (X \times Y)$. We call u a situation/action sequence if and only if $u \in \Sigma_{sa}^*$.

A *terminated* Mealy machine, $M = (Q, X, Y, \delta, I, F)$ is said to *generate* the situation/action sequence $u = (x_1, y_1)(x_2, y_2)\ldots(x_n, y_n)$ if and only if there exists a sequence of not necessarily distinct states, $q_0, q_1, q_2, \ldots q_n$ such that $(y_{i+1}, q_{i+1}) \in \delta(q_i, x_{i+1})$ for $0 \leq i \leq (n-1)$, $q_0 \in I$ and $q_n \in F$. Clearly the concept of '*generation*' of sequences by terminated Mealy machines' is analogous to that of '*acceptance* of strings by finite state acceptors'.

We call a set of situation/action sequences L_{sa} a situation/action language. The set of all situation/action sequences generated by some terminated Mealy machine M, $L_{sa}(M)$ is called the situation/action language of M. S_{sa}^+ is a positive sample of a situation/action language L_{sa} if and only if S_{sa}^+ is a subset of L_{sa}.

6.7.4 Mappings

In the following we assume the existence of the bijection h_b, in which for all elements $\langle s, a \rangle \in \Sigma_{sa}$

$$h_b(\langle s, a \rangle) = sa$$

where sa is an element of Σ. Similarly for all $sa \in \Sigma$

$$h_b^{-1}(sa) = \langle s, a \rangle$$

where $\langle s, a \rangle$ is an element of Σ_{sa}.

Lemma 6.32 *Given the bijection h_b which maps elements of Σ_{sa} to the universal alphabet Σ, there exists a bijection h_a which maps terminated Mealy machines to FSAs.*

Proof. See Appendix D.

124 Inductive Acquisition of Expert Knowledge

Lemma 6.33 *Given the bijection h_b which maps elements of Σ_{sa} to Σ, there exists a bijection h_u which maps situation/action sequences to strings.*

Proof. See Appendix D.

Lemma 6.34 *Given the bijection h_u which maps situation/action sequences to strings, there exists a bijection h_{S^+} which maps sets of situation/action sequences into sets of strings.*

Proof. The existence of this mapping and its inverse mapping, $h_{S^+}^{-1}$ can be shown trivially and is thus omitted.

6.7.5 The *SKR* algorithm

Let M be a terminated Mealy machine. We extend the usage of the term k-reversible to Mealy machines by saying that if $A = h_a(M)$ and A is k-reversible then M is also called k-reversible.

The following algorithm uses only a positive situation/action sequence sample in order to find the k-reversible Mealy machine with minimal value of k which produces the sequence.

Algorithm SKR
Input: a nonempty positive situation/action sample S_{sa}^+.
Output: the minimal-k reversible terminated Mealy machine M_f
    and k's final value f.
* Initialisation
Let $k = 0$.
Let S^+ be $h_s(S_{sa}^+)$.
While $k \leq$ (the maximum length of a sequence in S_{sa}^+) $+ 1$ do until M_k is deterministic
begin
  Let A_k be $KR(S^+, k)$.
  Let M_k be $h_a^{-1}(A_k)$.
  If M_k is not deterministic
  then increase k by 1.
end
* Termination
If M_k is not deterministic
  then
    fail.
  else

    begin
        Let $f = k$
        Output (M_f, f).
    end

Note that SKR can end in failure if the sample S_{sa}^+ inherently leads to a non-deterministic Mealy machine M_k for all settings of k.

6.7.6 Correctness of SKR

Theorem 6.35 *Let S_{sa}^+ be a positive sample of situation/action sequences. Given S_{sa}^+ as input, the algorithm SKR will output, when it can, the pair (M_f, f) where f is the smallest value of k such that M_k is both k-reversible and deterministic. Otherwise, if no such pair exists, SKR will fail.*

Proof. See Appendix D.

6.7.7 k-contextual sequence induction

The algorithm SKC which creates k-contextual Mealy machines given situation/action sequences is a trivial adaptation of SKR with a call to KC replacing that to KR. In fact, Biermann and Feldman's k-tail algorithm (Biermann and Feldmann, 1972) can be similarly adapted to work within a situation/action sequence environment with the accompanying advantage of eliminating the need for an arbitrary k parameter.

Chapter 7

Sequence Induction Applications

7.1 Introduction

In this chapter we describe six small but varied applications of the KR and SKR induction algorithms of Chapter 6.

Inductive algorithms, such as ID3 (see Appendix A and Quinlan, 1979), take sample descriptions of a static world and produce generalisations of these descriptions. For many real world problems, it is more appropriate for descriptions of activities to be given as sequences of static descriptions changing over time.

In this chapter, the application of sequence induction (see Chapter 6) in a varied set of domains is described. Our intention is to investigate the applicability of sequence induction techniques within RuleMaster. In Chapter 6 a number of algorithms for carrying out grammatical induction were described and it was shown that one of these algorithms, that of Angluin (section 6.4.5.4), gave better results than any of the others. However, it was noted that Angluin's k-reversible algorithm runs in time $O(n^3)$ and is thus not practical for large samples. Nevertheless, in section 6.5 an algorithm (KR) was given which is input/output equivalent to Angluin's k-reversible algorithm, but runs in time $O(n^2)$. In this chapter both KR (used in section 7.2) and a sequence induction version of KR called SKR (described in section 6.7.5 and used in sections 7.3–7.7) are used.

Present state	Input symbol	Next state
0	a	1
0	b	2
1	a	1
1	b	2
2	b	2
2	τ	GOAL

Figure 7.1 Induced state transition table for sentences ab, bb, aab, abb

7.2 A simple grammar

This experiment was carried out to discover if the KR algorithm could induce the grammar a^*b^*, (zero or more as followed by zero or more bs). The algorithm requires a small integer value, k, to be given to it to tell it how much generalisation is necessary. Generally, the smaller k is, the more compact its guess. In this experiment $k = 1$, since $k = 0$ leads to an over-generalisation, the automaton having only a single state.

Given the set of sentences

$S^+ = \{ab, bb, aab, abb\}$

the KR algorithm infers the automaton which is shown as a state transition table in figure 7.1.

τ is merely a termination symbol. Thus *state 2* is shown to be an acceptor state by the fact that a termination symbol can be accepted. *State 0* is the start state of the automaton. As in Radial (see Chapter 3), the unique goal state has no outgoing arcs. In descriptions of automata given in later sections of this chapter, the symbols are situation/action pairs, and, in any system producing state example information for Rulemaker, τ would be given by the user as the situation/action pair used when control is returned from the Radial module.

The automaton shown above is not the target language a^*b^* (zero or more as followed by zero or more bs). In order to get the algorithm to find a^*b^*, it is necessary to give it the strings a and λ (empty sentence) in addition to the sentences provided. Thus the sample sentences given to the algorithm would be

$S^+ = \{\lambda, a, ab, bb, aab, abb\}$

Present State	Input symbol	Next State
0	a	1
0	b	2
0	τ	GOAL
1	a	1
1	b	2
1	τ	GOAL
2	b	2
2	τ	GOAL

Figure 7.2 Induced state transition table for sentences λ, a, ab, bb, aab, abb

The resultant automaton is shown as a state transition table in figure 7.2 and as a state transition diagram in figure 7.3.

This represents the desired automaton, although it is not minimal. Minimisation of automata is a well-understood process, and a standard algorithm could be used for this purpose.

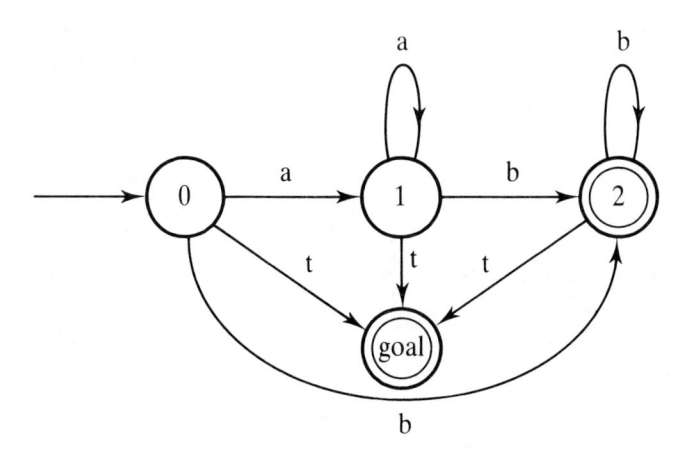

Figure 7.3 Diagrammatic representation of figure 7.2

7.3 1-bit binary adder

In the next experiment, we try to infer a 1-bit binary adder. Such a piece of circuitry can be produced automatically as a VLSI layout once the underlying finite-state machine has been designed.

Figure 7.4 shows the sequences given, together with their binary sums.

Sequences are separated in the table by double lines. Instead of the input symbols used in the previous experiment, situation/action tuples have been used. The two binary numbers to be added are given in 1-bit situation pairs, the lower order bits being presented first. The result after each input pair is given as the action.

In figure 7.5 the algorithm's solution is given as a transition table. The algorithm *SKR* (see section 6.7.5) finds that this deterministic automaton can be produced with the setting $k = 0$.

This solution is complete and correct. The two states correspond to the carry and non-carry states. Thus from seven example sums, the algorithm found a solution to an indefinite precision adder.

Situation (Input1,Input2)	Action Output	Comment
		A null sequence is legal
(0,0)	0	$0 + 0 = 0$
(0,1)	1	$0 + 1 = 1$
(1,0)	1	$1 + 0 = 1$
(1,1) (0,0)	0 1	$1 + 1 = 10$
(1,1) (1,1) (0,0)	0 1 1	$11 + 11 = 110$
(1,1) (0,1) (0,0)	0 0 1	$1 + 11 = 100$
(1,1) (1,0) (0,0)	0 0 1	$11 + 1 = 100$

Figure 7.4 Example situation/action sequences describing 1-bit binary adder

Present State	Situation (Input1,Input2)	Action Output	Next State
0	τ	NULL	GOAL
0	(0,0)	0	0
0	(0,1)	1	0
0	(1,0)	1	0
0	(1,1)	0	1
1	(0,0)	1	0
1	(0,1)	0	1
1	(1,0)	0	1
1	(1,1)	1	1

Figure 7.5 Inductively generated state transition table for a 1-bit binary adder

7.4 Traffic light controller

This example came from *Introduction to VLSI systems* by Mead and Conway. The book is a standard work of reference for VLSI technology and contains an example of a finite state circuit for controlling traffic. Here is some of the description of the problem taken directly from the book.

> The following simple example will help to illustrate the basic concepts of finite-state machines and their implementations in nMOS circuitry. A busy highway is intersected by a little-used farmroad. Detectors are installed that cause the signal C to go *high* in the presence of a car or cars on the farmroad.... . We wish to control the traffic lights at the intersection, so that in the absence of any cars waiting to cross or turn left on the highway from the farmroad, the highway lights will remain green. If any cars are detected... we wish the highway lights to cycle through caution to red and the farmroad lights then to turn green. The farmroad lights are to remain green only while the detectors signal the presence of a car or cars, but never longer than some fraction of a minute. The farmroad lights are then to cycle through caution to red and the highway lights then to turn green. The highway lights are not to be interruptible again by the farmroad traffic until some fraction of a minute has passed.

132   Inductive Acquisition of Expert Knowledge

Abbreviation	Meaning
wait	Null action
ST + HY	Start the timer and turn the highway lights yellow
ST + HR + FG	Start the timer, turn the highway lights red and turn the farmroad lights green
ST + FY	Start the timer and turn the farmroad lights yellow
ST + FR + HG	Start the timer, turn the farmroad lights red and turn the highway lights green

Figure 7.6   Meanings of action abbreviations used in figures 7.7 and 7.8

Figure 7.6 shows the meanings of actions used in figures 7.7 and 7.8. Figure 7.7 shows sequences given to the algorithm for this problem. It is assumed that the problem starts with the highway traffic lights being green.

The symbols y and n stand for *yes* and *no* respectively. The '-' symbol indicates that *any* non-clashing value of the attribute can be taken at this point.

Figure 7.8 shows the transition table of the automaton produced when SKR reaches the setting $k = 0$. Again the automaton is complete and correct according to the book. The states correspond to

1. **Highway lights are green.** Traffic is travelling along the main highway.

2. **Highway lights have changed to yellow.** The timer has been started and the automaton is waiting for the short timeout.

3. **Highway lights have turned yellow.** The farmroad lights are green. The timer has been restarted. The automaton is waiting for either the long timeout or for cars to stop flowing along the farmroad.

4. **The farmroad lights have turned yellow.** The timer has been restarted again and the automaton is waiting for the short timeout.

Sequence induction applications   133

Situation (Farmroad cars, Long time-out, Short time-out)	Action	Comment
		Null sequence acceptable
(n, -, -)	wait cars	Waiting for farmroad
(y, y, -)	ST + HY	A complete cycle of
(-, -, y)	ST + HR + FG	changing the lights
(-, -, y)	ST + FY	with no waiting
(-, -, y)	ST + FR + HG	
(y, y, -)	ST + HY	A complete cycle of
(-, -, n)	wait	changing the lights
(-, -, y)	ST + HR + FG	with one wait
(-, -, y)	ST + FY	
(-, -, y)	ST + FR + HG	
(y, y, -)	ST + HY	A complete cycle of
(-, -, n)	wait	changing the lights
(-, -, y)	ST + HR + FG	with two waits
(y, n, n)	wait	
(-, -, y)	ST + FY	
(-, -, y)	ST + FR + HG	
(y, y, -)	ST + HY	A complete cycle of
(-, -, n)	wait	changing the lights
(-, -, y)	ST + HR + FG	with three waits
(y, n, n)	wait	
(-, -, y)	ST + FY	
(-, -, n)	wait	
(-, -, y)	ST + FR + HG	

Figure 7.7 Situation/action sequences describing a traffic light controller

Present state	Situation (Farmroad cars, long time-out, stime-out)	Action	Next state
0	τ	NULL	GOAL
0	(n, -, -)	wait	0
0	(y, y, -)	ST + HY	1
1	(-, -, y)	ST + HR + FG	2
1	(-, -, n)	wait	1
2	(-, -, y)	ST + FY	3
2	(y, n, n)	wait	2
3	(-, -, y)	ST + FR + HG	0
3	(-, -, n)	wait	3

Figure 7.8 Induced state transition table for traffic light controller

It is interesting to note that the authors of the book from which this example was taken, in order to show how the automaton works, describe it in terms of example sequences of events.

7.5 Reverse motor problem

This problem is conceptually very simple. A large electric motor is controlled by three buttons. The buttons are marked 'left', 'right' and 'stop'. When the motor is not moving, pressing the left button will cause the motor to start turning to the left, the right button to the right. The only complication is that if the motor is turning in a particular direction, any attempt to force it to turn in the opposite direction will cause the motor to stop, rather than immediately changing polarity on the motor. This is necessary due to the momentum of the motor. Obviously, the stop button is used to stop the motor if it is turning in either direction. It is assumed that the motor starts not turning in either direction. Figure 7.9 shows the sequences given to the algorithm.

Figure 7.10 shows the transition table of the automaton produced when SKR reaches a setting of $k = 1$.

As with the grammar example, with a k setting of 1, the automaton, although correct, is not minimal. The reader may have noticed that state 0 and state 1 are identical and should have been merged. It is gen-

Situation Button pushed	Action	Comment
	Null sequence acceptable	
-	motor stop leaves the motor at rest	Pushing the stop button
- -	motor stop motor stop	It does not matter how many times it is pushed
left - 	motor left motor stop when it is turning left	Any button other than left stops the motor
left left -	motor left motor left motor stop	Pushing left when it is turning left keeps it turning left
- left -	motor stop motor left motor stop	Similar
right - 	motor right motor stop when it is turning right	Any button other than right stops the motor
right right -	motor right motor right motor stop	Pushing right when it is turning right keeps it turning right
- right -	motor stop motor right motor stop	Similar

Figure 7.9 Situation/action sequences describing a motor controller

136 Inductive Acquisition of Expert Knowledge

Present state	Situation Button pushed	Action	Next state
0	τ	NULL	GOAL
0	-	motor stop	1
0	left	motor left	2
0	right	motor right	3
1	τ	NULL	GOAL
1	-	motor stop	1
1	left	motor left	2
1	right	motor right	3
2	-	motor stop	1
2	left	motor left	2
3	-	motor stop	1
3	right	motor right	3

Figure 7.10 Induced state transition table for motor controller

erally true that the automata produced are only minimal if the k setting is 0. States 0 and 1 correspond to the motor being stopped, states 2 and 3 correspond to the motor turning left and right respectively.

7.6 Algebra problem

For this experiment various different solutions of simple linear equations were presented as sequences of situation/action tuples. The same problem was tackled previously by Andrew Paterson using the static induction package ACLS (see Appendix A and Paterson, 1984). The sequences are presented along with the automaton produced. Whereas Paterson used seven attributes, it was found that only four attributes were needed when using the grammatical induction algorithm. Figure 7.11 shows the meanings of situational attributes used in figures 7.13 and 7.14, the table of sequences. Figure 7.12 gives the meanings of the actions used in figures 7.13 and 7.14. Figure 7.14 shows the transition table of the automaton produced when SKR reaches a setting of $k = 1$.

Again states 0 and 1 should be the same state. States 0 and 1 deal with repetitively multiplying out the brackets. State 5 then repetitively moves all 'x' terms to the left-hand side. State 2 repetitively moves all 'constant' terms from the right-hand side of the equation to the

Attribute	Meaning
Brackets	The equation contains at least one bracketed term
X on the right	There is a term in x on the right-hand side of the equation
Const on left	There is a constant term on the left-hand side of the equation
Similar terms	Either side of the equation contains two or more constants or terms in x
Ok	There is a single term in x on the left

Figure 7.11 Meanings of situational attributes used in figures 7.13 and 7.14

left. State 4 repetitively adds up similar terms and divides both sides through by the divisor of 'x'. It should be obvious that, by dividing the task up into these smaller tasks, the user will not need to be asked as many questions when executing the automaton (given that it is being done interactively), as in each context it can be assumed that the jobs

Action	Meaning
Divide both	Divide through both sides of the equation by the coefficient of x
Add similar	Add together any similar terms (see 'Similar terms' in Figure 7.11)
Multiply brackets	Multiply out any bracketed term by its coefficient
X to left	Move a term in x from the right to the left of the equation
Const to right	Move a constant term from the left to the right of the equation

Figure 7.12 Meanings of actions used in figures 7.13 and 7.14

Situation[†]	Action	Equation
(n,n,n,n,y)	Divide both	$3x = 6$ $x = 2$
(n,n,n,y,-) (n,n,n,n,y)	Add similar Divide both	$3x + 4x = 6$ $7x = 6$ $x = 6/7$
(n,n,n,y,-) (n,n,n,y,-) (n,n,n,n,y)	Add similar Add similar Divide both	$3x + 4x + 5x = 6$ $7x + 5x = 6$ $12x = 6$ $x = 1/2$
(y,-,-,-,-) (n,n,n,n,y)	Multiply brackets Divide both	$5(3x) = 7$ $15x = 7$ $x = 7/15$
(y,-,-,-,-) (n,n,n,y,-) (n,n,n,n,y)	Multiply brackets Add similar Divide both	$5(3x + 4x) = 7$ $15x + 20x = 7$ $35x = 7$ $x = 1/5$
(y,-,-,-,-) (y,-,-,-,-) (n,n,n,y,-) (n,n,n,n,y)	Multiply brackets Multiply brackets Add similar Divide both	$5(3x) + 6(4x) = 7$ $15x + 6(4x) = 7$ $15x + 24x = 7$ $39x = 7$ $x = 7/39$
(y,-,-,-,-) (n,y,-,-,-) (n,n,n,y,-) (n,n,n,n,y)	Multiply brackets X to left Add similar Divide both	$5(3x) = 2x + 7$ $15x = 2x + 7$ $15x - 2x = 7$ $13x = 7$ $x = 7/13$

Figure 7.13 Situation/action sequences describing algebraic equation solver

[†]Brackets, X on the right, Const on left, Similar terms, Ok.

Situation[†]	Action	Equation
		$5(3x) + 7 = 2$
(y,-,-,-,-)	Multiply brackets	$15x + 7 = 2$
(n,n,y,-,-)	C to right	$15x = 2 - 7$
(n,n,n,y,-)	Add similar	$15x = -5$
(n,n,n,n,y)	Divide both	$x = -1/3$
		$5x = 7 + 2x$
(n,y,-,-,-)	X to left	$5x - 2x = 7$
(n,n,n,y,-)	Add similar	$3x = 7$
(n,n,n,n,y)	Divide both	$x = 3/7$
		$5x = 7 + 4x + 3x$
(n,y,-,-,-)	X to left	$5x - 4x = 7 + 3x$
(n,y,-,-,-)	X to left	$5x - 4x - 3x = 7$
(n,n,n,y,-)	Add similar	$x - 3x = 7$
(n,n,n,y,-)	Add similar	$-2x = 7$
(n,n,n,n,y)	Divide both	$x = -2/7$
		$5x + 7 = 3x + 5$
(n,y,-,-,-)	X to left	$5x - 3x + 7 = 5$
(n,n,y,-,-)	C to right	$5x - 3x = 5 - 7$
(n,n,n,y,-)	Add similar	$8x = 5 - 7$
(n,n,n,y,-)	Add similar	$8x = -2$
(n,n,n,n,y)	Divide both	$x = -1/4$
		$5x + 2 = 7$
(n,n,y,-,-)	C to right	$5x = 7 - 2$
(n,n,n,y,-)	Add similar	$5x = 5$
(n,n,n,n,y)	Divide both	$x = 1$
		$5x + 2 + 3 = 7$
(n,n,y,-,-)	C to right	$5x + 3 = 7 - 2$
(n,n,y,-,-)	C to right	$5x = 7 - 2 - 3$
(n,n,n,y,-)	Add similar	$5x = 5 - 3$
(n,n,n,y,-)	Add similar	$5x = 2$
(n,n,n,n,y)	Divide both	$x = 2/5$

Figure 7.13 Continued

[†]Brackets, X on the right, Const on left, Similar terms, Ok.

140 Inductive Acquisition of Expert Knowledge

Present state	Situation[†]	Action	Next state
0	(n,n,n,n,y)	Divide both	3
0	(n,n,n,y,-)	Add similar	4
0	(y,-,-,-,-)	Multiply brackets	1
0	(n,y,-,-,-)	X to left	5
0	(n,n,y,-,-)	C to right	2
1	(n,n,n,n,y)	Divide both	3
1	(n,n,n,y,-)	Add similar	4
1	(y,-,-,-,-)	Multiply brackets	1
1	(n,y,-,-,-)	X to left	5
1	(n,n,y,-,-)	C to right	2
2	(n,n,n,y,-)	Add similar	4
2	(n,n,y,-,-)	C to right	2
3	τ	NULL	GOAL
4	(n,n,n,n,y)	Divide both	3
4	(n,n,n,y,-)	Add similar	4
5	(n,n,n,y,-)	Add similar	4
5	(n,y,-,-,-)	X to left	5
5	(n,n,y,-,-)	C to right	2

Figure 7.14 Inductively generated state transition table for the equation solver

[†]Brackets, X on the right, Const on left, Similar terms, Ok.

of the preceding contexts have been carried out satisfactorily. In order for this saving to be made however, much more example information needed to be given than in Paterson's solution, which only required nine ACLS examples.

7.7 Hanging pictures in a room

This last example is more typical of the usual situation/action problems posed for robot-like worlds. The problem is as follows. A robot is in a room which contains a door and some pictures placed on the floor against the walls on which they should be hung. The robot can start off facing in any direction and must hang all the pictures on the appropriate walls. The robot is able to see objects and knows its position (either at a wall or 'other'). The robot uses the ability to see the door to make sure it has hung all the pictures before stopping. It is able to 'turn', which involves rotating in a clockwise direction until its situation vector changes in some way. It can also move forward, again until the situation vector changes. Sub-problems such as actually hanging the picture on the chosen wall could have been developed as individual, simple automata. Figure 7.15 gives the meanings of the actions used in figures 7.16 and 7.17. Figure 7.16 shows sequences given to the algorithm.

Figure 7.17 shows the transition table of the automaton produced when SKR reaches a parameter setting of $k = 0$.

The states have an interpretation as follows:

1. The robot starts in this state and must decide what line of action is appropriate.

    (a) If the robot sees the door, it will turn, and go to state 2 from which it will do a single pass around the room looking for pictures until it sees the door again.

    (b) If it sees something other than the door or a picture on the floor, it turns in order to find one of these two.

    (c) If it sees a picture on the floor it will move forward to the picture, go to state 7 and proceed by hanging the picture and returning to state 1.

2. Having entered state 2, the robot must have seen the door at least once. Thus it is only necessary to mop up all remaining pictures and keep turning until it sees the door. This will be done in either

Action	Meaning
Forward	Keep moving forward until the situational vector changes
Turn	Keep turning clockwise until the situational vector changes
Hang picture	Hang the picture which is on the floor on the wall
Lie down	Lie down on the ground

Figure 7.15 Meanings of actions used in figures 7.16 and 7.17

142 Inductive Acquisition of Expert Knowledge

Situation (See, At)	Action	Comment
(door, -)	Turn	All pictures hung,
(other, -)	Turn	start at the door
(door, -)	Lie down	
(other, -)	Turn	All pictures hung,
(door, -)	Turn	start elsewhere
(other, -)	Turn	
(door, -)	Lie down	
(door, -)	Turn	1 picture to hang
(other, -)	Turn	start at door
(picture on the floor, -)	Forward	
(picture on the floor, wall)	Hang picture	
(other, wall)	Turn	
(other, -)	Turn	
(door, -)	Lie down	
(other, -)	Turn	Start elsewhere
(picture on the floor, -)	Forward	
(picture on the floor, wall)	Hang picture	
(other, wall)	Turn	
(door, -)	Turn	
(other, -)	Turn	
(door, -)	Lie down	

Figure 7.16 Situation/action sequences describing the robot's actions

repeating the sequence state 2–state 3–state 5–state 6–state 2, or by seeing the door in state 2 and stopping.

3. This state is part of the loop described for state 2, and contains the terminating condition that the door can be seen.

4. This state merely terminates the module unconditionally.

5. This state is part of the loop starting in state 2.

Present State	Situation (See, At)	Action	Next State
1	(door, -)	Turn	2
1	(other, -)	Turn	1
1	(picture on the floor, -)	Forward	7
2	(other, -)	Turn	3
3	(door, -)	Lie down	4
3	(picture on the floor, -)	Forward	5
4	τ	NULL	GOAL
5	(picture on the floor, wall)	Hang picture	6
6	(other, wall)	Turn	2
7	(picture on the floor, wall)	Hang picture	8
8	(other, wall)	Turn	1

Figure 7.17 Inductively generated state transition table for the robot controller

6. This state is part of the loop starting in state 2.

7. This state is part of the loop starting in state 1.

8. This state is part of the loop starting in state 1.

Dufay and Latombe (1984) describe a similar method of automatically programming robots. They use an inductive algorithm which is essentially the same as that of Miclet (1980) (see section 6.3). In their system, low-level robot sequences are generated by a planner and fed into an inductive algorithm. The resultant generalised finite-state automaton is represented in a robot programming language for execution. The robot program contains not only manipulator directives but also tests to be carried out on the world state.

7.8 Conclusion

The problems described in sections 7.3–7.5 are conceptually different from those in sections 7.6–7.7. The difference lies in the fact that whereas in the first three, a particular world situation is assumed for the start state (the highway lights start off being green in the traffic light example) the latter problems make no such assumptions (the robot can start anywhere in the room, facing in any direction). Although the first examples could be developed with this 'any situation starts' approach, this does not seem typical of problems occurring in engineering as a whole. It is also interesting to note that whereas each problem is fairly difficult, it was automatically broken into a number of smaller and simpler problems.

Angluin's k-reversible algorithm (section 6.4) seems to be very powerful, and capable of dealing with building complex automata from a skimpy presentation of sample sequences. Moreover, our efficient version of this algorithm (section 6.5) runs at quite acceptable speeds, typically around 10–20 seconds for the automata presented in this chapter. As stated in section 7.7, the method of constructing robot plans from example sequences has also been investigated by Dufay and Latombe (1984). However, they used a simpler inductive algorithm, essentially the same as that described by Miclet (section 6.3). Angluin (1982) has shown Miclet's algorithm to be merely a special case of k-reversible induction. We therefore conclude that our method has a wider scope than that of Dufay and Latombe.

Chapter 8
Chess Strategies

8.1 Introduction

8.1.1 Computer chess research

In the study of expert system development, Michie (1982) has noted that use of chess expertise as a testbed domain is ideal in many respects. The domain is non-trivial though finitely bounded. It has a wealth of recorded expertise going back many centuries which has certainly not yet been fully exercised. Whereas chess specialists have developed a depth of understanding which is at least comparable with the expertise of more lucrative disciplines, expert-level chess players are generally more readily available for consultation.

Early work in programming computers to play chess was concentrated around efficiently implementing Shannon's chess playing strategy (Shannon, 1950). This employs extensive lookahead in order to compute approximations to the best next move. As this failed to produce results comparable with human expert play, recent research has focussed on more knowledge-rich approaches. Bratko and Michie (1980) described such a knowledge-based system, AL1, based partly on earlier work by Huberman (1968). AL1's *advice module* generated a list of preference ordered pieces of advice. A separate *search module* used the board-state and advice list to produce a 'forcing tree' which was applied as a strategy for play. As with all solutions in which knowledge must be hand-coded, the knowledge acquisition process becomes a developmental bottleneck.

Quinlan (1979) suggested a method of bypassing this bottleneck by using inductive inference. Quinlan's algorithm, ID3 (see Appendix A), based on Hunt's CLS algorithm (Hunt, 1966), was used to build decision trees which classified endgame positions as won, drawn or lost. A vector of attribute values is used to describe any particular position. This vector together with a class value comprises an example classification. Although the solutions were exhaustively proved correct and ran five times faster than hand-crafted algorithms, they were also completely incomprehensible to chess experts.

In order to get round this understandability barrier, Shapiro and Niblett (1982) introduced the notion of *structured induction*, in which a chess expert is required to decompose the endgame classification rules hierarchically; each sub-problem can then be solved inductively. While this approach avoids the problem of incomprehensibility, unfortunately it introduces a new bottleneck of problem structuring.

Paterson (1983) has described an attempt to automatically structure the KPK chess endgame domain from example material, using the statistical clustering algorithm CLUSTER (Michalski and Chilauski, 1983). The results however have not been very promising as the machine's suggested hierarchy does not have any significance to experts. Paterson suggested that the primary reason for failure seemed to lie in the fact that although the example set was a rich enough source of knowledge to be used for rule construction, additional information is necessary to indicate any higher-level structure. This conjecture turned out to be false, demonstrated by the successful automatic structuring of the chess ending KPa7KR (Chapter 9).

8.1.2 Sequence induction

In Chapter 6 an efficient implementation of two sequence induction techniques, k-reversible induction and k-contextual induction was described. The k-contextual algorithm used for the experiments described here requires only positive examples. The necessary constraint on solutions is that the finite state acceptor produced must be equivalent to the minimum sized k-contextual language containing the positive examples (see Chapter 6). As described in section 6.7, when dealing with sequences of ID3-like examples, we can use the semantic content provided by the situational vector as an additional constraint mechanism, thus circumventing the need to supply the algorithm with the arbitrary measure required by all similar algorithms in the literature (Angluin, 1982; Biermann and Feldman, 1972; Levine, 1982; Miclet, 1980). For this we employ the *SKC* algorithm described in section 6.7.7.

Situations in which sequence induction can be employed are many and varied (see Chapter 7). If we understand well what the properties of the algorithm being used are, we can often take advantage of various presentation and solution constraints for different scenarios. Several such properties are described and proved elsewhere in this book (see Chapter 6). For our purposes, the most important property of the k-contextual algorithm is that successive solutions are *incremental* (see section 6.6.7). Accordingly, as more examples were added, the automaton output by the algorithm developed in a controlled and predictable fashion.

Informally, 0-contextual problems are those for which a deterministic automaton can be formed using the situation attributes alone. For k-contextual problems ($k > 0$), situations in which different actions must be taken given the same attribute settings must be distinguishable on the basis of a k-length history of situation/action pairs.

8.2 The problem: KBBKN

Programming strategies for chess endgames is a notoriously difficult task. Zuidema commenting on two Algol 60 programs written for the King and Rook against King (KRK) endgame illustrates the difficulties by noting that 'A small improvement entails a great deal of expense in programming effort and program length. The new rules will have their exceptions too' (Zuidema, 1974).

In a project being carried out at the Turing Institute, the extremely complex chess endgame KBBKN is being studied with the aid of the world-class chess endgame specialist John Roycroft, and even this chess authority admits to being out of his depth. In the only definitive study of KBBKN, written in 1851, Horwitz and Kling claimed that with White-to-move (WTM), the game is drawn in all but trivial cases. For over a century this claim remained uncontested, until in 1983 Thompson revealed by exhaustive computation that almost all positions are forced wins for White, with a maximum length win of 66 moves being obtainable from 32 different positions (Roycroft, 1983; Thompson, 1986) This surprising result adds to the pressure on the international chess community to revise the 50-move rule. According to this rule, if 50 full moves are made without a capture, castling or pawn move a draw can be declared. However, clearly it may take up to 66 moves to force a win for a particular side. Thompson's computations have brought to light the existence of even longer minimax optimal paths in some other end-games.

The Turing Institute study involves two phases. In the first, Roycroft has studied the domain intensely with the aim of developing a sufficient set of primitive attributes. It is in this first phase that the

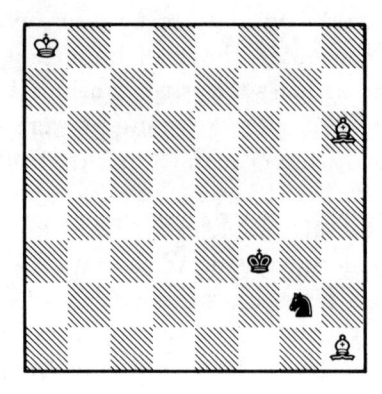

148   Inductive Acquisition of Expert Knowledge

Figure 8.1 The initial position, WTM

author has carried out the evaluation of sequence induction as a knowledge acquisition tool. In the second phase, it is intended that Roycroft's descriptions be matched against Thompson's exhaustive database for KBBKN.

Roycroft's first task was to select a sub-strategy within the KBBKN domain of an appropriate size and complexity for the application of sequence induction. The choice fell on the first section of one of the exceptional 66-move forced wins for White.

8.2.1   Initial position

Play commences from the position shown in figure 8.1.

Taking symmetry and slightly altered starting positions into account, this position is equivalent, in terms of the number of moves to a forced win, to several other similar positions. As this equivalence can be taken into account by the careful choice of terms when devising the expert system, we will ignore this extra dimension to the problem.

8.2.2   Goal position

The aim of White in this sub-strategy is to liberate the dark-squares-White-bishop (wB(dark)) from the corner in no more than 12 moves. In order to achieve this it is necessary that

(A) dark-squares-White-bishop (wB(dark)) prevents Black's king (bK) from attacking and capturing White's-bishop-on-square-h1 (wBh1). This is illustrated in figures 8.2, 8.3 and 8.4.

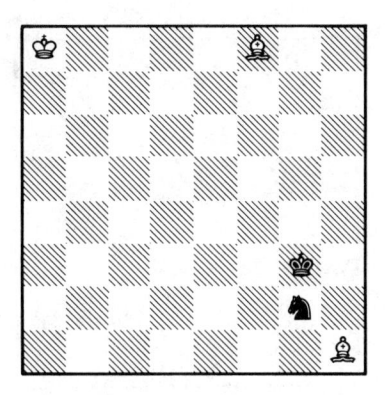

Figure 8.2 wb(dark) prepares to prevent bK from moving to h2, WTM

(B) White's king (wK) moves to support the attack of wBh1 on Black's-knight-on-square-g2 (bNg2) (see figure 8.5).

Play achieving (A) is trivially described and encoded. However, attaining (B) is complicated considerably by White's choice of delaying tactics, employed to impede wK approaching h3. It was for this second goal that we used sequence induction to capture Roycroft's description.

8.2.3 Attributes and actions

Roycroft was asked to give an exposition of play which included a set of sequences of moves together with a running commentary displaying points of interest. From this four positional attributes (based

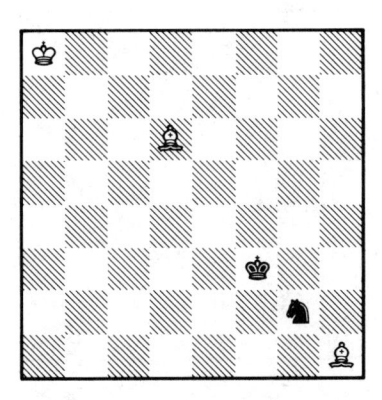

Figure 8.3 bK retreats after being checked by wB(dark), WTM

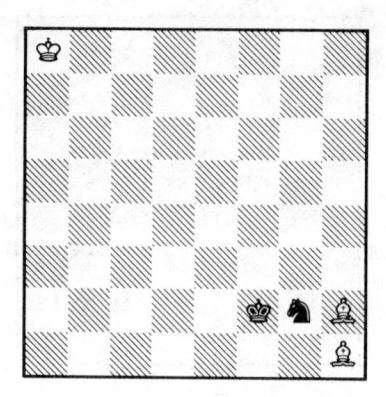

Figure 8.4 wB(dark) takes up fortified position, WTM

on Roycroft's use of adjectival phrases), four action schemas taken by White (corresponding to verb phrases) and six sequences of play were extracted. The attributes were as follows:

(B1) Is White free to take bN? y/n

(B2) Is wK on the same diagonal as the release position (h3)? y/n

(B3) Can wBh1(dark) move? y/n

(B4) Is the direct diagonal position closest to the release position covered? y/n

The actions were

(Ba) wK approaches release position (h3) by moving along rank or file.

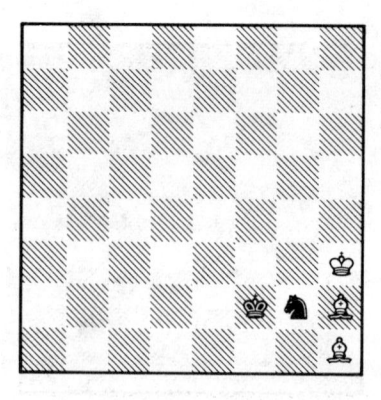

Figure 8.5 The goal of liberating wB(dark), bN forced to retreat, BTM

(**Bb**) wK moves to non-check position closest to release position on direct diagonal.

(**Bc**) wB(dark) moves out of corner along its diagonal.

(**Bd**) White takes bN.

Note that each action at this level represents a single move. However, the entire automaton to be derived represents a unit action involving several moves. Thus we might, if necessary, have a hierarchy of such actions and attributes, similar to that described by Shapiro and Niblett (shapnib) for classification (see conclusion).

8.2.4 The solution

The sequences used are given in Appendix E. These sequences were added by stepwise-refinement, the result being tested after the addition of each sequence. Very early in this process, the k-value for the solution rose from 0 to 1, where it remained during the rest of development. The number of states in the solution also grew rapidly at first to reach a steady value of 5, at which level it too stayed fixed. Altogether, this process displayed a good incremental nature.

The first six sequences represent White's response to various well-executed tactics played by Black. These were derived directly from Roycroft's description. Having by this stage generated a playing strategy that dealt adequately with more than Roycroft's described positions (the k-contextual algorithm successfully generalised solutions to a larger number of positions than those originally described) the automaton was presented and explained to Roycroft. Roycroft noted that the set of positions at which the White king can be delayed by Black was the most complex to describe. *Significantly, the state which described just these positions contained the most ID3-examples. The structure automatically imposed on the solution had a clear significance to the expert.*

As yet, with only six sequences, the solution was not able to cope with non-optimal play by Black. An additional seven sequences were added to deal with such play. The resulting k-contextual automaton is given in Appendix F in a form which can be directly translated into a Rulemaker induction file. Appendix G demonstrates the transformation carried out by ID3-like induction to produce a runnable Radial expert system. Note that all decision trees in the solution have the form of HSL decision trees (Michie, 1984). Appendix H gives the Rulemaker file corresponding to the automaton solution of Appendix F. Using this Rulemaker file, the Radial code of Appendix I was inductively generated.

8.3 Conclusion

We have demonstrated the feasibility of using sequence induction to construct expert-level chess strategies for endgame play. A great deal of further work is necessary to expand the work described here to completely cover the highly complex domain of KBBKN. However, the methodology used was found by the expert to be natural in terms of the example presentation requirements, as chess players are quite at home with describing play in terms of example move sequences. Furthermore, the bottleneck of structuring was eased, though not completely removed by the use of sequence induction. Whereas other attempts at automatic structuring have led to solutions which are not acceptable to experts, results produced by sequence induction were found to be intuitively correct by the endgame specialist John Roycroft.

In section 8.2.3 it was noted that, as the induced strategy represents a broadly defined action, it might be necessary to form a hierarchy of successively more detailed action descriptions in order to create an extensive strategy. It might be argued from this that our automatic structuring aid has gained us no ground, as it may still be necessary to do further manual structuring. We do not claim to have a complete answer to the structuring problem. However, Shapiro when constructing his structured solution of KPa7KR found that the use of more than seven examples within any particular context lead to unreadable machine induced solutions (Shapiro, 1987). We have used 13 example sequences each containing an average of four ID3-like sequences to produce a semi-structured solution in which each state's rule is derived from an average of only three examples. Thus, despite the fact that the quantity of example material used to structure this level of problem is an order of magnitude larger than that used by Shapiro, the generated solution contains a small number of easily understandable decision trees.

The k-contextual induction algorithm used has good incremental behaviour (see section 6.6.7). This algorithm has also been proved to *identify the correct solution in the limit.*

The use of two levels of induction – sequence induction and static induction – gives rise to very powerful generalisation, with solutions being output directly as runnable expert systems.

On the negative side, a form of explanation which deals satisfactorily with sequence execution has not yet been developed. It is hoped that by continued research, chess experts may be able to lead us to the most natural form of explanation required by chess players to describe sequences of play. Also, the k-contextual algorithm used for this research is written in Prolog. A more efficient implementation, with a better interface to the Radial environment is needed.

Chapter 9
Duce

9.1 Introduction

Duce[†] is a machine learning system which suggests high-level domain features (or *oracle*) to the user on the basis of a set of example object descriptions. Six transformation operators are used to compress the given examples successively by generalisation and feature construction. In this chapter, Duce is illustrated by way of its construction of a simple animal taxonomy and a hierarchical parity checker. However, Duce's main achievement has been the restructuring of a substantial expert system for deciding whether positions within the chess endgame of King-and-Pawn-on-a7 versus King-and-Rook (KPa7KR) are won-for-white or not. The new concepts suggested by Duce for the chess expert system hierarchy were found to be meaningful by the chess expert Ivan Bratko. An existing manually created KPa7KR solution, which was the basis of a recent PhD thesis is compared to the structure interactively created by Duce (Shapiro, 1987).

A second major expert system application of Duce was made within a diagnostic field of neuro-psychology. This is described in Section 9.9.

[†]This chapter describes work which was funded in part by the British Government's Alvey Logic Database Demonstrator. Research facilities were provided by the Turing Institute, Glasgow, UK. Computational facilities for the preparation of this chapter were provided by Interact R&D Corporation, Victoria, BC, Canada. A similar description appeared in the Proceedings of the International Joint Conference on Artificial Intelligence, 1987.

153

9.2 Background

It is well recognised that the acquisition of expert knowledge is the major 'bottleneck' in expert system development. However, as mentioned in Chapter 1, Michalski and Chilausky (1980) and later Quinlan (1982) have shown that this bottleneck can be considerably eased by generalising low-level data to form high-level rules. Shapiro (1982) extended this methodology to deal effectively with extensive bodies of knowledge by employing structured programming techniques. Thus the expert structures the knowledge in a top-down fashion manually, and then provides examples which can be used to inductively generate each module in the hierarchy separately. Using this technique, Shapiro and Kopec (Shapiro, 1987) created knowledge structures for correctly deciding a forced win for white in any position within the chess endgames of King-and-Pawn versus King (KPK) and King-and-Pawn-on-a7 versus King-and-Rook (KPa7KR). Both solutions were completely verified by exhaustive computation. However, using an information theoretic approach, Shapiro showed (1982) that around 80 per cent of the endgame knowledge was provided by the expert in the creation of the knowledge structure. Thus almost all the work was being done by the expert rather than by the machine. In an attempt to overcome this structuring bottleneck, Paterson (1983) tried to use the statistical clustering algorithm CLUSTER to automatically restructure the knowledge for the simpler of the two endgames, KPK. Paterson's results were not promising as the machine's suggested hierarchy did not have any significance to domain experts.

In the context of machine learning, Michalski (1986) has called the problem of originating terms *constructive induction*. CLUSTER (Michalski and Stepp, 1983), perhaps the best known constructive induction algorithm, uses a statistical clustering technique to group objects into conceptual clusters. Each object is initially described in terms of a vector of primitive attribute values. Objects are grouped using a heuristic inter-object distance metric. Rendell (1985), and Fu and Buchanan (1985) describe alternative similarity-based approaches to creating taxonomic hierarchies which work on much the same basis as CLUSTER.

9.3 Transformation-based induction

In Duce, the approach to constructive induction differs considerably from that of Michalski and Stepp (1983), Rendell (1985), and Fu and Buchanan (1985), and can be more easily compared to the deductive transformational programming techniques of Burstall and Darlington (1977). Burstall and Darlington, and later Dershowitz (1985), suggest that *deductive* program synthesis can be carried out by gradual truth-preserving transformations of a program specification. At first sight, these techniques seem not to be applicable to *inductive* inference, which, by definition, progresses by performing non-truth-preserving generalisations of the supplied training set. However, if each inductive transformation is tested against an oracle which ensures the validity of any transformation, any such inductive transformation is as legal and safe as its deductive counterparts. This use of an oracle is closely related to Sammut and Banerji's (Sammut and Banerji, 1986) method of learning concepts by asking questions. Indeed, one of the generalisation operators described in the next section is directly due to Sammut and Banerji.

Constructive induction carries out transformations which introduce new terms into the learner's vocabulary. Though such transformations can be truth-preserving, they are not what might be called semantics-preserving. Thus the primary concern in constructive induction should not be 'How can new terms be introduced into the vocabulary?' but rather 'How can meaningful new terms be introduced?' Again, by using an oracle to either name or reject machine-suggested concepts, the difficult philosophical problems involved in defining the word meaningful can be sidestepped. Given a meaningful and valid training set, every transformation of which is both meaningful and valid (by agreement of the oracle), the resultant rule set will be meaningful and valid.

9.4 Operators

Duce takes as input a set of conjunctive productions, or rules, in a form close to that of disjunctive-normal-form propositional calculus. Six operators are employed to progressively transform subsets of the rule base. These operators are described below.

1. **Inter-construction.** This transformation takes a group of rules, such as

$$X \leftarrow B \wedge C \wedge D \wedge E \quad (9.1)$$
$$Y \leftarrow A \wedge B \wedge D \wedge F \quad (9.2)$$

and replaces them with the rules

$$X \leftarrow C \wedge E \wedge Z? \qquad (9.3)$$
$$Y \leftarrow A \wedge F \wedge Z? \qquad (9.4)$$
$$Z? \leftarrow B \wedge D \qquad (9.5)$$

Here, the rule for the new concept $Z?$ (9.5) is the most specific generalisation of the rules for X (9.1) and Y (9.2).

2. **Intra-construction.** This is simply the distributive law of Boolean equations. Intra-construction takes a group of rules all having the same rule head, such as

$$X \leftarrow B \wedge C \wedge D \wedge E \qquad (9.6)$$
$$X \leftarrow A \wedge B \wedge D \wedge F \qquad (9.7)$$

and replaces them with

$$X \leftarrow B \wedge D \wedge Z? \qquad (9.8)$$
$$Z? \leftarrow C \wedge E \qquad (9.9)$$
$$Z? \leftarrow A \wedge F \qquad (9.10)$$

Note that while operator 1, inter-construction, could legitimately be applied to rules 9.6 and 9.7, the result would be less compact.

3. **Absorption.** This operator is due to Sammut and Banerji (1986), who use it to generate recursive Prolog clauses. Even though recursion is not meaningful within propositional calculus, this operator can be employed profitably in generalising rule sets. Given a set of rules, the body of one of which is completely contained within the bodies of the others, such as

$$X \leftarrow A \wedge B \wedge C \wedge D \wedge E \qquad (9.11)$$
$$Y \leftarrow A \wedge B \wedge C \qquad (9.12)$$

one can hypothesise

$$X \leftarrow Y \wedge D \wedge E \qquad (9.13)$$
$$Y \leftarrow A \wedge B \wedge C \qquad (9.14)$$

Note that the preconditions for applying this operator are stronger than those for applying inter-construction. Also, if rule 9.12 were the only rule with rule head Y, the new rule would necessarily be valid. Otherwise it is a generalisation and must be verified by the oracle. In general, asking the oracle unnecessary questions can be avoided by first attempting to answer the question deductively from the rule base.

4. **Identification.** The identification operator is again a potential generalisation, whose preconditions are stronger than those of intra-construction. A set of rules which all have the same head, the body of at least one of which contains exactly one symbol not found within the other rules, such as

$$X \leftarrow A \wedge B \wedge C \wedge D \wedge E \qquad (9.15)$$
$$X \leftarrow A \wedge B \wedge Y \qquad (9.16)$$

can be replaced by the rules

$$X \leftarrow A \wedge B \wedge Y \qquad (9.17)$$
$$Y \leftarrow C \wedge D \wedge E \qquad (9.18)$$

5. **Dichotomisation.** This operator works on sets of mixed positive and negative examples. Thus a set of rules which contains positive and negative heads, and which all have some common symbols within the bodies, such as

$$X \leftarrow A \wedge B \wedge C \wedge D \qquad (9.19)$$
$$\overline{X} \leftarrow A \wedge C \wedge J \wedge K \qquad (9.20)$$
$$\overline{X} \leftarrow A \wedge B \wedge C \wedge L \qquad (9.21)$$

are replaced with the rules

$$X \leftarrow A \wedge C \wedge Z? \qquad (9.22)$$
$$\overline{X} \leftarrow A \wedge C \wedge \overline{Z?} \qquad (9.23)$$
$$Z? \leftarrow B \wedge D \qquad (9.24)$$
$$\overline{Z?} \leftarrow J \wedge K \qquad (9.25)$$
$$\overline{Z?} \leftarrow B \wedge L \qquad (9.26)$$

where the replacement is dependent on the oracle naming $Z?$. Dichotomisation is a generalisation of the the way that ID3 (Quinlan, 1982) creates the internal nodes of decision trees.

6. **Truncation.** The truncation operator, like dichotomisation, is intended for use with rule sets containing positive and negative

examples of the same concept. However, truncation generalises by dropping conditions. A set of rules which all contain the same head, such as

$$X \leftarrow A \wedge B \wedge C \wedge D \qquad (9.27)$$
$$X \leftarrow A \wedge C \wedge J \wedge K \qquad (9.28)$$

is replaced by

$$X \leftarrow A \wedge C \qquad (9.29)$$

This operator generalises in a similar manner to that of the AQ learning algorithms (Michalski and Chilauski, 1980). Its use is restricted by the precondition that the resultant rule (9.29) must not clash (be inconsistent) with any other rule within the rule base. Of all the operators, truncation is the only one which reduces the number of rules. All other operators compact the rules by shortening the average rule length.

9.5 The search algorithm

For any state of a rule base, there are many possible operator applications. Any subset of rules within the rule base R is a candidate for the application of one of the 6 operators. Thus the search-space for the 'best' operator application is of size $2^{|R|}$, the size of the power set of R. What is meant by a 'good' operator application? Since each of the operators can reduce the number of symbols in the rule base, Duce searches for the application which produces the largest symbol reduction – Occam's razor is applied. If each rule is taken as having a symbol size equal to the number of conjunctive terms in the rule body plus one (for the rule head), for each operator there exists an equation which can be used to predict the exact symbol reduction for any operator. Let R' be a subset of the rule base R, and I' be a common subset of all the bodies of rules within R'. In the following equations, $V_{operator}$ is the symbol reduction produced when the operator is applied to R'. The total number of symbols within the rule set R' is written as $total(R')$. The symbol reduction equations are:

$$V_{Inter} = (|I'| - 1).(|R'| - 1) - 2$$
$$V_{Intra} = |I'|.(|R'| - 1) - 2$$

$$V_{Absorp} = (|I'| - 1).(|R'| - 1)$$
$$V_{Ident} = |I'|.(|R'| - 1)$$
$$V_{Dichot} = |I'|.(|R'| - 2) - 4$$
$$V_{Trunc} = total(R') - |I'| - 1$$

Note that V_{Op} can take a zero or negative value, in which case there is no symbol reduction. Searching for the best operator application is clearly intractable. Moreover, there is no guarantee that such an operator application, once found, would be acceptable to the oracle. In Duce, the next operator application is chosen using a best first search through the power set of the symbols in the rule base R. Let a subset of symbols I' be found among the bodies of the rule set R', where R' is the largest subset of R containing I'. The operator application $apply(Op, I', R')$, using operator Op, is only suggested to the oracle when some I' has been found for which V_{Op} is locally maximal. Any rejection of an operator application by the oracle leads to continued search. Transformations are carried out iteratively until no further operations can reduce the rule base size further. At termination, by the nature of the operators, almost all symbols occur within a restricted number of rules. Thus, although the termination condition requires searching the entire remaining space, the search space has shrunk to manageable proportions. Since only operations which reduce the number of symbols are applied, termination is guaranteed.

9.6 Animal taxonomy

This section illustrates the behaviour of Duce when creating a simple animal taxonomy. Figure 9.1 shows the set of example animal descriptions given to Duce. In English, the first example says

> A blackbird has a beak, is black, has two legs, a tail and wings. 'blockhead-the-blackbird' is an instance of the 'blackbird' concept.

Note the inclusion of the instance set *(blockhead-the-blackbird)* within the rule. This can be used as a powerful tool for illustrating the meaning of new rules and concepts.

Figure 9.2 shows user interaction for this example set. User input is shown in bold type. When asked to induce, Duce searches for an operation and suggests an application of the truncation operator which will

160   Inductive Acquisition of Expert Knowledge

(blackbird [beak t] ∧ [colour black] ∧ [legs 2] ∧ [tail t] ∧ [wings t])
   eg (blockhead-the-blackbird)
(chimp   [colour brown] ∧ [hairy t] ∧ [legs 2] ∧ [tail t] ∧ [wings f])
   eg (maggie-the-chimp)
(eagle   [beak t] ∧ [colour golden] ∧ [legs 2] ∧ [tail t] ∧ [wings t])
   eg (egg-the-eagle)
(elephant [colour grey] ∧ [legs 4] ∧ [size big] ∧ [tail t] ∧ [trunk t] ∧
   [wings f]) eg (adult-elephant)
(elephant [colour grey] ∧ [legs 4] ∧ [size small] ∧ [tail t] ∧ [trunk t] ∧
   [wings f]) eg (baby-elephant)
(falcon   [beak t] ∧ [colour brown] ∧ [legs 2] ∧ [size big] ∧ [tail t] ∧
   [wings t]) eg (flap-the-falcon)
(gorilla [colour black] ∧ [hairy t] ∧ [legs 2] ∧ [tail f] ∧ [wings f])
   eg (ronnie-the-gorilla)
(lemur   [colour grey] ∧ [legs 2] ∧ [tail t] ∧ [wings f])
   eg (lemur-alone)
(man   [colour brown] ∧ [hairy f] ∧ [legs 2] ∧ [size big] ∧ [tail f] ∧
   [wings f]) eg (harry-the-hamite)
(man   [colour pink] ∧ [hairy f] ∧ [legs 2] ∧ [size small] ∧ [tail f] ∧
   [wings f]) eg (clap-the-caucasian)
(sparrow [beak t] ∧ [colour brown] ∧ [legs 2] ∧ [size small] ∧ [tail t] ∧
   [wings t]) eg (sparky-the-sparrow)

Figure 9.1   Initial set of animal examples

save 12 symbols. The operation is valid if, and only if, everything having four legs is an elephant. The user can either answer affirmatively ('y'), negatively ('n') or ask for illustrative examples ('i'). If Duce is asked for illustrative examples it lists the instances adult-elephant and baby-elephant. The suggestion, although consistent with the limited universe of the examples, is too general, and is rejected. Duce continues its search and finds a slightly less advantageous truncation, which would save 11 symbols. The new suggestion, that anything with four legs and no wings is an elephant is similarly rejected. There is no particular mechanism for specialising over-generalised hypotheses. This is merely a by-product of the search mechanism. On the third attempt, Duce questions whether everything that has four legs and a trunk is an elephant. Since this is affirmed, Duce replaces all elephant rules by the new more general rule and returns to the '!-' prompt.

The second generalisation, concerning man is accepted first time around, producing a saving of 9 symbols. In the third interaction,

!- induce
   TRUNCATION – (-12)
   Is (elephant   [legs 4]) a valid rule? (y/n/i) n
   TRUNCATION – (-11)
   Is (elephant   [legs 4] ∧ [wings f]) a valid rule? (y/n/i) n
   TRUNCATION – (-11)
   Is (elephant   [legs 4] ∧ [trunk t]) a valid rule? (y/n/i) y
!- induce
   TRUNCATION – (-9)
   Is (man   [hairy f] ∧ [legs 2] ∧ [tail f] ∧ [wings f])
                  a valid rule? (y/n/i) y
!- induce
   INTER-CONSTRUCTION – (-1)
     Rule:
   (?   [legs 2] ∧ [wings f])
     What shall I call ⟨?⟩? (name/n/i)   primate
!- induce
   INTER-CONSTRUCTION – (-7)
     Rule:
   (?   [beak t] ∧ [legs 2] ∧ [tail t] ∧ [wings t])
     What shall I call ⟨?⟩? (name/n/i)   bird
!- induce
   No applicable transformation

Figure 9.2   Animal taxonomy session

Duce finds that using the interconstruction operator, one symbol can be saved by defining a new concept for all things which have two legs and no wings. The user can either reject this new concept ('n'), ask for illustrative examples ('i'), or give a name for the concept. The name 'primate' is given to the concept. Duce goes on to suggest another new concept for all things which have a beak, two legs, a tail and wings. This concept is named 'bird'. When asked to search for another operator application, Duce comes back with the message, 'No applicable transformation', meaning that none of the operators reduce the rule base. The time between each prompt in this example is in the order of one second.

Figure 9.3 shows the result of the transformations. Not only is the rule base more compact, but also the new concepts have made the rules more conceptually transparent. For example, a blackbird is simply defined as a bird which is black. Note that the illustrative examples are propagated to all new rules.

162 Inductive Acquisition of Expert Knowledge

(bird   [beak t] ∧ [legs 2] ∧ [tail t] ∧ [wings t]) eg (blockhead-the-blackbird
    egg-the-eagle flap-the-falcon sparky-the-sparrow)
(blackbird   bird ∧ [colour black]) eg (blockhead-the-blackbird)
(chimp   primate ∧ [colour brown] ∧ [hairy t] ∧ [tail t]) eg (maggie-the-chimp)
(eagle   bird ∧ [colour golden]) eg (egg-the-eagle)
(elephant   [legs 4] ∧ [trunk t]) eg (adult-elephant baby-elephant)
(falcon   bird ∧ [colour brown] ∧ [size big]) eg (flap-the-falcon)
(gorilla   primate ∧ [colour black] ∧ [hairy t] ∧ [tail f]) eg (ronnie-the-gorilla)
(lemur   primate ∧ [colour grey] ∧ [tail t]) eg (lemur-alone)
(man   primate ∧ [hairy f] ∧ [tail f]) eg (clap-the-caucasian harry-the-hamite)
(primate   [legs 2] ∧ [wings f]) eg (maggie-the-chimp clap-the-caucasian
    ronnie-the-gorilla harry-the-hamite lemur-alone)
(sparrow   bird ∧ [colour brown] ∧ [size small]) eg (sparky-the-sparrow)

Figure 9.3   Resultant animal rule base

9.7 Even-parity

In Chapter 2 we analysed the advantages of structuring the even-parity problem. According to Minsky and Papert (1969) the 'parity' function is unlearnable by single-layer perceptrons. Recent techniques using multi-layered perceptron networks (Rumelhart and McClelland, 1986) have been shown to be capable of learning parity effectively. However, in the paradigm of explicit rule formation, algorithms such as ID3 (Quinlan, 1979) and AQ11 (Michalski and Chilauski, 1980) turn out to be rather inadequate when used to learn such functions. It was shown in Chapter 2 that, whereas single-level concept representations of parity have a description complexity which is necessarily non-polynomially dependent on the number of attributes, multi-level descriptions can be built whose size is only linearly dependent on the number of primitive attributes. Efficient multi-concept solutions inevitably rely on a divide-and-conquer approach. Thus the decision of the top-level concept is based on the combination of values of lower-level predicates. Each lower-level predicate has a domain which depends on a restricted subset of the total set of problem attributes.

Figure 9.4 depicts examples of 8-variable even-parity. Note that this is an extension of the 4-variable problem depicted in figure 2.1. The variables (or primitive attributes) are numbered v1 to v8, and each is bound to a value from the set f t (rather than 0 1). In the first example, the variables have even-parity, since all eight have the value t – an

(even [v1 t] ∧ [v2 t] ∧ [v3 t] ∧ [v4 t] ∧ [v5 t] ∧ [v6 t] ∧
   [v7 t] ∧ [v8 t]) eg (tttttttt)
(even [v1 t] ∧ [v2 t] ∧ [v3 t] ∧ [v4 t] ∧ [v5 f] ∧ [v6 f] ∧
   [v7 f] ∧ [v8 f]) eg (ttttffff)
(even [v1 f] ∧ [v2 f] ∧ [v3 t] ∧ [v4 t] ∧ [v5 f] ∧ [v6 f] ∧
   [v7 f] ∧ [v8 f]) eg (ffttffff)
(even [v1 f] ∧ [v2 f] ∧ [v3 f] ∧ [v4 f] ∧ [v5 f] ∧ [v6 f] ∧
   [v7 f] ∧ [v8 f]) eg (ffffffff)
(even [v1 t] ∧ [v2 t] ∧ [v3 t] ∧ [v4 t] ∧ [v5 t] ∧ [v6 t] ∧
   [v7 t] ∧ [v8 f]) eg (tttttttf)
(even [v1 t] ∧ [v2 t] ∧ [v3 t] ∧ [v4 t] ∧ [v5 f] ∧ [v6 f] ∧
   [v7 f] ∧ [v8 t]) eg (ttttfft)
(even [v1 t] ∧ [v2 f] ∧ [v3 t] ∧ [v4 t] ∧ [v5 f] ∧ [v6 f] ∧
   [v7 f] ∧ [v8 f]) eg (tttfffff)
(even [v1 f] ∧ [v2 t] ∧ [v3 t] ∧ [v4 t] ∧ [v5 t] ∧ [v6 t] ∧
   [v7 t] ∧ [v8 t]) eg (fttttttt)

Figure 9.4 Even-parity examples

even number of variables are bound to t. The 'eg' part of the example shows a string of this form. Figure 9.5 shows the session in which Duce transforms the training set of figure 9.4 into the partial, hierarchical solution of figure 9.6. The responses are based on a standard solution in which the variables are recursively broken into two equal sized sets at each level. The total set of variables have even-parity if and only if both subsets have even-parity, or both have odd-parity. The first three concept suggestions do not follow this scheme, and are rejected. The fourth is recognised as 'the second-half of the variables have even-parity' (sev). The user then affirmatively answers questions concerning the application of the absorption operator. The next suggested concept is named ffev or 'first-half of the first-half of the variables are even'. Given the original eight examples, Duce's solution is generalised to cover 16 of the 256 possible instances. If presented initially with the complete instance set, Duce tends towards a solution consisting of an 8-level deep hierarchy in which levels are used to count the number of variables set to t.

!- induce
   DICHOTOMISATION − (-6)
   (even   [v3 t] ∧ [v4 t] ∧ ?)
   (even [v3 t] ∧ [v4 t] ∧ ?)
   What shall I call ⟨?⟩? (name/n/i) n
   DICHOTOMISATION − (-5)
   (even   [v1 t] ∧ [v3 t] ∧ [v4 t] ∧ ?)
   (even [v1 t] ∧ [v3 t] ∧ [v4 t] ∧ ?)
   What shall I call ⟨?⟩? (name/n/i) n
   DICHOTOMISATION − (-5)
   (even   [v2 t] ∧ [v3 t] ∧ [v4 t] ∧ ?)
   (even [v2 t] ∧ [v3 t] ∧ [v4 t] ∧ ?)
   What shall I call ⟨?⟩? (name/n/i) n
   DICHOTOMISATION − (-4)
   (even   [v1 t] ∧ [v2 t] ∧ [v3 t] ∧ [v4 t] ∧ ?)
   (even [v1 t] ∧ [v2 t] ∧ [v3 t] ∧ [v4 t] ∧ ?)
   What shall I call ⟨?⟩? (name/n/i) sev
!- induce
   ABSORPTION − (-3)
   Is (even   sev ∧ [v1 f] ∧ [v2 t] ∧ [v3 t] ∧ [v4 t])
               a valid rule? (y/n/i) y
!- induce
   ABSORPTION − (-9)
   Is (even   sev ∧ [v1 f] ∧ [v2 f] ∧ [v3 t] ∧ [v4 t])
               a valid rule? (y/n/i) y
   Is (even   sev ∧ [v1 f] ∧ [v2 f] ∧ [v3 f] ∧ [v4 f])
               a valid rule? (y/n/i) y
   Is (even   sev ∧ [v1 t] ∧ [v2 f] ∧ [v3 t] ∧ [v4 t])
               a valid rule? (y/n/i) y
!- induce
   DICHOTOMISATION − (-2)
   (even   sev ∧ [v3 t] ∧ [v4 t] ∧ ?)
   (even sev ∧ [v3 t] ∧ [v4 t] ∧ ?)
   What shall I call ⟨?⟩? (name/n/i) ffev
!- induce
   ABSORPTION − (-1)
   Is (even   ffev ∧ [v3 t] ∧ [v4 t] ∧ v) a valid rule? (y/n/i) y
!- induce
   ABSORPTION − (-1)
   Is (even   ffev ∧ sev ∧ [v3 f] ∧ [v4 f]) a valid rule? (y/n/i) y
!- induce
   TRUNCATION − (-7)
   Is (even   ffev ∧ sev) a valid rule? (y/n/i) n
No applicable transformation

Figure 9.5 Parity session

(even   ffev ∧ sev ∧ [v3 t] ∧ [v4 t]) eg (ffttffff ttttffff tttttttt)
(even   ffev ∧ sev ∧ [v3 f] ∧ [v4 f]) eg (ffffffff)
(ffev   [v1 t] ∧ [v2 t]) eg (ttttffff tttttttt)
(ffev   [v1 f] ∧ [v2 f]) eg (ffttffff)
(sev   [v5 t] ∧ [v6 t] ∧ [v7 t] ∧ [v8 t]) eg (ttttttttt)
(sev   [v5 f] ∧ [v6 f] ∧ [v7 f] ∧ [v8 f]) eg (ttttffff)
(even sev ∧ [v3 t] ∧ [v4 t] ∧ effev) eg (ffttttttt tttffff)
(even ffev ∧ [v3 t] ∧ [v4 t] ∧ esev) eg (ttttffft tttttttf)
(ffev [v1 t] ∧ [v2 f]) eg (tttffff)
(ffev [v1 f] ∧ [v2 t]) eg (fttttttt)
(sev   [v5 t] ∧ [v6 t] ∧ [v7 t] ∧ [v8 f]) eg (tttttttf)
(sev   [v5 f] ∧ [v6 f] ∧ [v7 f] ∧ [v8 t]) eg (ttttffft)

Figure 9.6   Resultant parity rule base

9.8   Recreation of the KPa7KR structure

Both the animal taxonomy and parity problems have highly restricted domains. The real test of Duce's capabilities has been the attempt to restructure Shapiro and Kopec's expert system (Shapiro, 1987) for deciding whether positions within the chess endgame of King-and-Pawn-on-a7 versus King-and-Rook (KPa7KR) are won-for-white or not. The domain contains around 200,000 positions. Shapiro generated a database of all positions, labelling each with its minimax backup value of forced win-for-white or not. A set of 36 primitive board features were calculated for each position. Since many positions had the same feature vector and won-for-white value, the number of distinct examples was reduced to 3196. With this number of examples, Duce's search-space for applying the first operation is 2^{3196} (see Section 9.5), or approximately 10^{1000}. Nilsson (1980) states that the complete game tree for chess has approximately 10^{120} nodes; even that well-known hard problem has a considerably smaller search space than that attempted here.

For the purposes of the experiment, Shapiro provided a randomly chosen board position for each example. Thus the initial rule base given to Duce consisted of examples of the form

(won-for-white   feature1 ∧ feature2 ∧ .. feature36) eg (position)

Two chess experts, Ivan Bratko and Tim Niblett, helped in giving oracle answers to questions asked by Duce. The rule base started with 118,252 symbols. The first suggestion reduced 21,606 of these, a reduction

Pa7
  bxqsq
  rimmx
  stlmt
  Delayed-queening
    hdchk
    Mate-threat
      bkxbq
      bkxwp
      qxmsq
      rxmsq
      r2ar8
    WK-on-a8
      blxwp
      r2ar8
      simpl
      wkna8
    WK-in-check
      bkxcr
      mulch
      rimmx
      rkxwp
      thrsk
      wknck
    Black-attacks-queening-square-soon
        bknwy
        bkona
        bkon8
        skrxp
        wkovl
    Double-attack-threat
      bkblk
      bkxbq
      cntxt
      katri
      wkpos
      Black-advantage-from-potential-skewer
        bkspr
        reskd
        reskr
        r2ar8
        skach
        wkcti
  Delayed-skewer
    bkxbq
    dsopp
    dwipd
    skewr
    spcop
    wtoeg

Figure 9.7 Human expert's KPa7KR problem decomposition

Pa7
    bxqsq hdchk
    rimmx spcop
    stlmt
    Delayed-queening-1
        bknwy bkon8
        dsopp mulch
        rxmsq skach
        skrxp wkna8
        Delayed-queening-2
            bkblk
            White-king-in-check-delay
                bkxcr bkxwp
                cntxt simpl
                skewr wknck
                wtoeg
            Skewer-threat
                bkspr rkxwp
                r2ar8 rkxwp
                wkcti wkovl
                wkpos
            Double-attack-threat-2
                bkona bkxwp
                bkxbq blxwp
                dwipd katri
                reskr
    Mate-threat-1
        cntxt wkna8
        Mate-and-double-attack
            bkblk bkxbq
            bkxcr katri
            thrsk
            Mate-and-double-attack-safe-from-promoted-queen
                dsopp qxmsq
                r2ar8 rkxwp
                wkcti wknck
        Mate-threat-2
            bkon8 bkspr
            bkxcr r2ar8
            skrxp thrsk
            wknck wkovl
            Mate-threat-safe-from-promoted-q
                bkxbq blxwp
                dsopp dwipd
                rkxwp rxmsq
                simpl skewr
                wtoeg
    Double-attack-1
        bkblk bkona
        bkspr bkxcr
        bkxwp blxwp
        dwipd skrxp
        Potential-double-attack-useful-to-black
            bknwy bkxbq
            cntxt katri
            r2ar8 wkcti
            wknck wkovl
            wkpos

Figure 9.8 KPa7KR knowledge structure generated by Duce

of around 20%. After three questions, around 60% of the rule base had been reduced. After 41 transformations, the rule base had been reduced to 553 rules, and contained a total of 9050 symbols. At this point there were still applicable operations, but symbol reductions had been reduced to the low hundreds.

In questions 3 and 5, in which new concepts were introduced, the size of the common set of symbols, Int, was too large for a comprehensible rule description. It is here that the illustrative board positions were indispensible. For this experiment, a domain-dependent graphics front-end was built into Duce which gave the user the ability to peruse a large number of board positions representing the concept and counterconcept. Without this graphical device, new concepts could not have been recognised and named. As it was, concepts were named with confidence within the presentation of 20–40 board positions. It was rarely necessary to reject new concepts and generalisations suggested by Duce in the KPa7KR experiment.

Figure 9.7 shows the structure created manually by Shapiro and Kopec, which took an estimated six man months of effort. Figure 9.8 shows Duce's solution. Duce carried out the 41 oracle agreed transformations during a single working day. The computation time between each question was in the order of a minute. It should be noted that where Shapiro and Kopec have used nine hierarchically arranged concepts, Duce has used thirteen. Duce's solution also contains 553 rules and 9050 symbols where Shapiro and Kopec's manually created solution contains the equivalent of around 225 productions and around 1000 symbols. Although Duce's solution could have been made more compact by applying more transformations or by generating decision trees for each concept using ID3, it seems unlikely that this would have resulted in a solution which was as compact as that of Shapiro and Kopec.

By virtue of the operators used by Duce, the KPa7KR solution is guaranteed correct by construction.

9.9 Neuropsychology application

A second structuring experiment was carried out using Duce at Interact Corporation, Canada. In this, Duce was used to construct a problem decomposition for deciding on dysfunction of the left parietal brain area of children with learning disabilities. The input to the algorithm consisted of 227 diagnosed cases. Each case contained the results of a battery of approximately 100 binary-valued clinical tests. Each case was marked with a diagnosis of normal/abnormal left parietal lobe by the resident clinical neuropsychologist, Dr Russell. Using these cases, Duce carried out an interactive session in which Russell was asked to answer a total of 53 questions. During and subsequent to the construction of the rulebase, a set of 48 independent cases were used to test the performance of the new rule-set. Since the cases and generated rules were inherently noisy, a majority-vote mechanism was used for rule evaluation. After all 53 questions had been answered, 43 of the 48 test cases agreed with Russell's diagnosis – 90% agreement. In contrast, an existing expert system developed by Russell had only a 63% agreement rate with Russell's diagnoses over the same test data. While Duce's structured rulebase took 2–3 man-days to build and verify, the equivalent part of the hand-built expert system is conservatively estimated to have taken 2–3 man-months to generate, improve and verify.

In parallel with the supervised construction of the Duce rulebase, Duce was run on the same cases in unsupervised mode. In this mode, all generalisation questions were answered affirmatively and all new concepts were arbitrarily named. Performance with unsupervised learning stabilised after 27 questions to a level of 25% agreement with Russell's diagnoses of the same test cases.

Unlike the endgame experiment in which an exhaustive example set was used, the neuropsychological example set was relatively sparse. As a consequence, whereas no rejections were necessary in the case of the chess experiment, an average of ten rejections were required per acceptance with the neuropsychological data. This seems to indicate the need for expert supervision of Duce where sparse data is involved, and explains the dramatic difference in verification results between the supervised and unsupervised data.

The structure of the rulebase created by Russell working with Duce is shown in Figure 9.9. This hierarchical structure contains groups of rules associated with each node of the network. The sub-types implied by this hierarchy were, according to Russell, 'clinically significant', and relate directly to neuropsychological sub-types based on Wide-range-achievement-test (WRAT) results in arithmetic, reading and spelling.

9.10 Conclusion

Duce is a program which, with the aid of a human oracle, discovers useful new concepts. AM (Lenat, 1981), an early concept discovery

```
LPAb    LPAb_GoodV
        LPAb_PoorA1
          LPAb_PoorA
        LPAb_BadA1
          LPAb_BadA1_RS_AST
        LPAb_BadA
          LPAb_BadA_PoorS
            LPAb_BdA_PrS_BadAST_GdSSPT
          LPAb_BadA_BadAST
            LPAb_BadA_AST_S1
              LPAb_BadA_AST_S
              LPAb_BadA_AST_S1_V
```

Figure 9.9 Structure of neuropsychological expert system constructed by Duce

program, was criticised by Ritchie and Hanna (1984) for the obscurity of the techniques involved. Unlike AM, Duce uses a simple and explicit set of six operators to create and refine concepts. In addition, the meaning-giving agent, implicitly present within any machine learning system, is explicitly represented as the oracle within Duce.

Extensive search is used to decrease the number of questions asked by Duce of the oracle. However, in what circumstances is the use of an oracle either justified or feasible? In this respect it is worth noting that, on the basis of a meagre number of empirical studies, the ratio of oracle rejections to acceptances seems to be inversely related to the percentage of examples provided from the domain. In the parity problem, where Duce was supplied with a sparse set of examples, a large number of rejections were necessary (figure 9.5). In the more complex KPa7KR chess domain, Duce was given an exhaustive set of examples, and required almost no rejections from the oracle. Thus it might be expected that in domains in which a moderate amount of example material is available the oracle would need to reject a moderate number of proposals. Further research is necessary to show the truth of this hypothesis.

Duce works with statements in propositional logic. One way of extending this would be to attempt using similar techniques within other representations. Both Banerji (1987) and Muggleton and Buntine (1988) have looked at the problem of constructive induction within first-order calculus. This seems one of the most exciting directions for the future development of Machine Learning techniques.

Appendix A
ACLS, ID3 and CLS

The induction algorithm used within Rulemaker is called ACLS (Analog Concept Learning System (Paterson and Niblett, 1982)). This algorithm is an extended version of Quinlan's ID3 algorithm (Quinlan, 1979). In turn ID3 was developed from Hunt's CLS (1966). The same algorithm is used within other commercially available expert system products such as Extran (A-Razzak *et al*, 1984).

Inducing a decision tree can be thought of as generating a tree, each node of which has a number of examples associated with it. The algorithm for inducing a rule is as follows.

1. Create root node of tree and associate with entire example set. Present-node = root-node

2. If all examples at present-node have the same class then stop

3. Choose best attribute to split examples at current node. This is done using the information theoretic measure described below. The attribute chosen may be either logical or an integer. If it is logical the tree is split with one branch for each value of the attribute. If it is an integer, a binary split is performed by partitioning the examples on either side of a threshold value. The threshold is chosen to split the examples optimally.

4. The examples at the current node are associated with the new branch nodes according to the value of the split attributes.

5. The process is repeated for each branch recursively from step 2.

A.1 The entropy function

The following account is excerpted from the *ACLS User Manual* (Paterson and Niblett, 1982).

The choice of an attribute on which to split at any node is performed using an information theoretic measure, described below. The attribute which has the 'best' value according to this measure is used.

The algorithm used in Rulemaker works rather differently for integer-valued attributes than for logical attributes. We will consider the logical attributes first.

As explained above, at any node we have a set of N attribute vectors. Let us consider a simple example of what can happen. Assume there are two class-values, C_1 and C_2 and assume that the attribute under consideration takes two values V_1 and V_2. If we split our N attribute vectors using the assumed attribute we would get the following 2×2 table.

	C_1	C_2
V_1	p_{11}	p_{12}
V_2	p_{21}	p_{22}

In this case p_{ij} is the probability of one of the attribute vectors having value V_i for the attribute and class-value C_j. We can now define the *entropy* of the initial state before splitting on the attribute. This is:

$$-((p_{11} + p_{21})\ln(p_{11} + p_{21}) + (p_{12} + p_{22})\ln(p_{12} + p_{22}))$$

By splitting on the attribute, it is easy to see that we have decreased the entropy, which is now:

$$-(p_{11}\ln(p_{11}) + p_{12}\ln(p_{12}) + p_{21}\ln(p_{21}) + p_{22}\ln(p_{22}))$$

The difference (initial entropy − final entropy) is a measure of the usefulness of the attribute. The attribute with the highest value of this difference is the one on which we split. In the case above, this difference is:

$$p_{11}\ln(p_{11}/(p_{11} + p_{21})) + p_{12}\ln(p_{12}/(p_{12} + p_{22}))$$
$$+ p_{21}\ln(p_{21}/(p_{11} + p_{21})) + p_{22}\ln(p_{22}/(p_{12} + p_{22}))$$

This example is easily generalised. If we have M class values and N possible values for a particular attribute, the measure to be maximised is:

$$\sum_{i=1}^{N}\sum_{j=1}^{M} p_{ij} \ln \frac{p_{ij}}{\sum_{k=1}^{M} p_{ik}}$$

Again p_{ij} represents the probability of the ith value of the attribute occurring with the jth class value.

Now let us consider what happens with an integer-valued attribute. In this case, not only do we need to calculate the value of the measure but we also have to compute the value on which to split the attribute.

Let us assume that we have N attribute vectors $V_1, \ldots, V_N$ and that we are concerned with attribute A. We can further assume that the attribute vectors are ordered in increasing value of A.

For each i ($1 < i < N$) we can split the vectors into two subsets, $\{V_1, \ldots, V_i\}$ and $\{V_{i+1}, \ldots, V_N\}$. These subsets define a value of the evaluation function defined above. We choose the minimum value as the value of the evaluation function for A. If this value occurs for subsets $\{V_1, \ldots, V_j\}$ and $\{V_{j+1}, \ldots, V_N\}$, we split the attribute at an A value midway between the values at V_j and V_{j+1}.

Appendix B
Definitions

Below we present some basic definitions from set theory and formal language theory which are used in Chapter 6 and Appendix C. The notation used roughly follows that of Angluin (1982).

$|S|$ the *cardinality* of the set S.

2^S the *power set* of S, $2^S = \{S' : S' \subseteq S\}$. $|2^S| = 2^{|S|}$.

Σ a finite alphabet with cardinality $|\Sigma| \geq 2$.

Σ^* the infinite set of strings made up of zero or more letters from Σ.

λ the empty string.

uv the concatenation of the strings u and v.

$|u|$ the length of string u.

w^r the reverse of the string w.

L a *language* L is any subset of Σ^*.

L^r the reverse of L, $L^r = \{w^r : w \in L\}$.

$Pr(L)$ the prefixes of elements of L, $Pr(L) = \{u : \text{for some } v, uv \in L\}$.

$T_L(u)$ the left-quotient of u in L, $T_L(u) = \{v : uv \in L\}$.

$T_L^k(u)$ the k-tails of u in L, $T_L^k(u) = \{v : v \in T_L(u), |v| \leq k\}$.

178 Inductive Acquisition of Expert Knowledge

S^+ a *positive sample* S^+ of L is any finite subset of L.

π_S a *partition* of some set S, π_S, is a set of pairwise disjoint non empty subsets of S such that the union of all sets in π_S is equal to S.

$B(s, \pi_S)$ the unique *block* (element) of π_S containing s, where $s \in S$.

refines given two partitions, π and π', π *refines* π' if and only if every block of π' is a union of blocks of π.

$\chi_{\pi_S}(u, v)$ the characteristic predicate of a partition over S is defined as

$$\chi_{\pi_S}(s, s') = \begin{cases} true & \text{if } s, s' \in S,\ B(s, \pi_S) = B(s', \pi_S) \\ false & otherwise \end{cases}$$

χ_{π_S} can easily be shown to be an *equivalence relation*. A relation R is an equivalence relation if and only if it has the properties of being *reflexive* (for all $s \in S^+$, $\chi_{\pi_S}(s, s)$ is true), *transitive* ($\chi_{\pi_S}(s, s')$ and $\chi_{\pi_S}(s', s'')$ implies $\chi_{\pi_S}(s, s'')$) and *symmetric* ($\chi_{\pi_S}(s, s')$ implies $\chi_{\pi_S}(s', s)$).

A an acceptor is a tuple $A = (Q, \Sigma, \delta, I, F)$, where Q is the non-empty finite *state set*, Σ is the input alphabet, $\delta : 2^Q \times \Sigma \to 2^Q$, is the *transition function*. The transition function for strings $\delta^*: 2^Q \times \Sigma^* \to 2^Q$, is defined using the recursive definition
$\delta^*(Q', \lambda) = Q'$
$\delta^*(Q', bu) = \delta^*(\delta(Q', b), u)$

where $q \in Q$, $b \in \Sigma$ and $u \in \Sigma^*$, $I \subseteq Q$ is the set of *initial states*, and $F \subseteq Q$ is the set of *final states*. A *deterministic acceptor* is defined similarly, the difference being that I, δ and δ^* represent single element sets. When dealing with deterministic acceptors, we will write q_0 for the initial state set $I = \{q_0\}$, $\delta(q, b) = q'$ for $\delta(\{q\}, b) = \{q'\}$ and $\delta^*(q, u) = q'$ for $\delta^*(\{q\}, u) = \{q'\}$.

$L(A)$ the regular language $L(A)$ recognised by A consists of strings u which are accepted by A, that is $\delta^*(I, u) \in F$.

δ^r the reverse transition function δ^r is defined as
$$\delta^r(Q', a) = \{q' : q \in \delta(q', a)\} \text{ for all } a \in \Sigma, q \in Q$$

A^r the reverse of the acceptor A is $A^r = (Q, \Sigma, \delta^r, I, F)$. Diagrammatically, A^r is A with the initial and final states swapped and all transition arcs reversed in direction. It can easily be shown that $L(A^r) = (L(A))^r$.

In the following, let $A = (Q, \Sigma, \delta, I, F)$ and $A' = (Q', \Sigma', \delta', I', F')$ be two acceptors.

a-successor for some $q, q' \in Q, a \in \Sigma$, q is an a-successor of q' if and only if $q \in \delta(q', a)$.

k-follower a string u is said to be a k-follower of a state $q \in Q$ if and only if $|u| = k$ and $\delta(q, u) \neq \emptyset$. Every state has exactly one 0-follower, namely λ.

k-leader a string u is a k-leader of a state $q \in Q$ if and only if $\delta^r(q, u^r) \neq \emptyset$. Every state also has exactly one 0-leader, λ.

isomorphic we say that A is *isomorphic* to A' if and only if there exists a bijective mapping $h : Q \to Q'$ such that $h(I) = I'$, $h(F) = F'$, and for every $q \in Q$ and $b \in \Sigma$, $h(\delta(q, b)) = \delta'(h(q), b)$. In other words, two acceptors are isomorphic if a renaming of their states makes them identical.

subacceptor A' is a *subacceptor* of A if and only if $Q' \subseteq Q$, $I' \subseteq I$, $F' \subseteq F$ and for every $q' \in Q'$ and $b \in \Sigma$, $\delta'(q', b) \subseteq \delta(q', b)$. Alternatively, A' is a subacceptor of A if and only if $L(A') \subseteq L(A)$. Diagrammatically a subacceptor is formed from an acceptor by removing some nodes and arcs from the transition diagram of the original acceptor.

A/π_Q let π_Q be some partition of Q, the state set of A. $A' = A/\pi_Q$, the *quotient* of A and π_Q is defined as follows. Q' is the set of blocks of π_Q. I' is the set of blocks of π_Q that contain at least one element of I. Similarly, F' is the set of blocks of π_Q that contain at least one element of F. Block B_2 is a member of $\delta'(B_1, a)$ if and only if there exists $q_1 \in B_1$ and $q_2 \in B_2$ such that $q_2 \in \delta(q_1, a)$.

$A(L)$ the *canonical* or *minimal acceptor* for a language L, $A(L) = (Q, \Sigma, \delta, I, F)$ is defined as follows

$$
\begin{aligned}
Q &= \{T_L(u) : u \in Pr(L)\}, \\
I &= \{T_L(\lambda)\} && \text{if } L \neq \emptyset, \text{otherwise } I = \emptyset, \\
F &= \{T_L(u) : u \in L\}, \\
\delta(T_L(u), a) &= T_L(ua) && \text{if } u, ua \in Pr(L).
\end{aligned}
$$

Note that the canonical acceptor $A(L)$ has the minimum number of states possible for an acceptor of L. Any acceptor A' which is *isomorphic* to $A(L)$ is called canonical.

$PT(S^+)$ if S^+ is a positive sample of L, we define the *prefix tree acceptor* of S^+, $PT(S^+) = (Q, \Sigma, \delta, I, F)$, as

$$
\begin{aligned}
Q &= Pr(S^+), \\
I &= \{\lambda\} && \text{if } S^+ \neq \emptyset, \text{otherwise } I = \emptyset, \\
F &= S^+, \\
\delta(u, a) &= ua && \text{whenever } u, ua \in Pr(S^+).
\end{aligned}
$$

Appendix C
Heuristics Used in the Literature

Although the heuristics described in Biermann and Feldmann (1972), Levine (1982), Miclet (1980) were not originally described in terms of the function χ of IM1, predicates giving equivalent results can easily be described and compared in this manner. Unfortunately, Angluin's k-reversible algorithm (Angluin, 1982) cannot be described in terms of IM1. However, the use of IM1 (section 6.4.2) considerably eases the coding and testing of the other three algorithms.

C.1 Biermann and Feldman's k-tail predicate

Biermann and Feldman's heuristic is functionally equivalent to the predicate

$$\chi(u,v) = \begin{cases} true & \text{if } T_{S+}^k(u) = T_{S+}^k(v) \\ false & \text{otherwise} \end{cases}$$

where k is some positive integer supplied by the user (Biermann and Feldman, 1972). The resultant acceptor A is more compact the smaller k is. Biermann and Feldman proved that given the correct value of k for the target language, their algorithm will identify in the limit an acceptor A which when minimised is *isomorphic* to $A(L)$. However, the correct value of k cannot be determined without first knowing what $A(L)$ is. Biermann and Feldman show that, by using a hashing function to merge states, it is possible to carry out induction using this predicate in $O(n)$ time.

C.2 Levine's heuristic

Although Levine (1982) applied his heuristic algorithm primarily to inference of tree systems, he shows that it is also possible to use it for inference of finite acceptors. Levine defines a strength function which measures the maximum overlap between pairs of tail sets.

$$Stren(u,v) = \max_i \left[\frac{2|T^i_{S+}(u) \cap T^i_{S+}(v)|}{|T^i_{S+}(u)| + |T^i_{S+}(v)|} \right], i \geq 0$$

The heuristic predicate he uses is

$$\chi(u,v) = \begin{cases} true & \text{if } Stren(u,v) \geq Strn \\ false & \text{otherwise} \end{cases}$$

where $Strn$ is a user defined parameter in the range 0 to 1. As with Biermann and Feldman's k parameter, the acceptor has a compactness which is roughly proportional to the value of $Strn$. The calculation of $Stren$ itself has an upper bound time complexity of $O(n)$, thus giving the complete algorithm a time complexity of $O(n^3)$ when using IM1.

C.3 Miclet's algorithm

Miclet (1980) designed a heuristic algorithm based on statistical clustering techniques. The algorithm uses a distance function to do successive clustering and merging of states. Although this is a fairly general methodology, in his examples he uses a heuristic which approximates in its results to one described fully by Angluin (1982). The heuristic identifies in the limit the maximally sized *zero-reversible* language containing the input sample. The heuristic is the simplest of all those presented here. The zero-reversible heuristic described by Angluin is equivalent to

$$\chi(u,v) = \begin{cases} true & \text{if } T_{S+}(u) \cap T_{S+}(v) \neq \emptyset \\ false & \text{otherwise} \end{cases}$$

Angluin in (1982) presents a method of computing A using this heuristic in approximately $O(n)$ time.

C.4 Angluin's algorithm

Angluin (1982) has shown that there are a class of languages, that she calls *k-reversible*, which can be identified in the limit. The acceptor

A is defined to be 'deterministic with lookahead k' if and only if for any pair of distinct states q_1 and q_2, if $q_1, q_2 \in I$ or $q_1, q_2 \in \delta(q_3, a)$ for some $q_3 \in Q$ and $a \in \Sigma$, then there is no string that is a k-follower of both q_1 and q_2. This guarantees that any nondeterministic choice in the operation of A can be resolved by looking ahead k symbols past the current one.

An acceptor A is defined to be *k-reversible* if and only if A is deterministic and A^r is deterministic with lookahead k. A language L is defined to be *k-reversible* if and only if there exists a *k-reversible* acceptor A such that $L = L(A)$.

Angluin presents an algorithm which, starting with the prefix tree acceptor, successively refines acceptors by merging any two states q_1 and q_2 which violate the condition of k-reversibility. The algorithm continues this process until no such pair of states q_1 and q_2 exist. As no more than n mergers can be made (the prefix tree acceptor contains only n nodes), and $O(n^2)$ comparisons must be made for each merger, the time complexity of the algorithm is $O(n^3)$. Angluin shows that her heuristic will identify in the limit any particular language in any of the classes of k-reversible languages. However, she also shows that not all regular languages are members of a k-reversible language class.

Appendix D
Proofs

In this appendix we provide proofs for lemmas and theorems from Chapter 6.

Theorem 6.5 *There exists a bijection h_τ such that any acceptor $A = \{Q, \Sigma, \delta, I, F\}$ in which $\tau \notin \Sigma$, $h_\tau(A)$ is a uniquely terminated acceptor that accepts the language $L(A).\{\tau\}$.*

Proof. The mapping function h_τ is as follows. Let $A = (Q, \Sigma, \delta, I, F)$. Now we construct the uniquely terminated acceptor $A_u = h_\tau(A) = (Q_u, \Sigma_u, \delta_u, I_u, F_u)$ with $Q_u = Q \cup \{q_g\}$ (where q_g is the *goal* state), $\Sigma_u = \Sigma \cup \tau$, $\delta_u(q_f, \tau) = \{q_g\}$ for all $q_f \in F$, $\delta_u(q, b) = \delta(q, b)$ for all $q \in Q$, $b \in \Sigma$ and $\delta_u(q_g, b') = \emptyset$, $b' \in \Sigma_u$, $I_u = I$, $F = \{q_g\}$. Clearly A_u is a *TTA* since all arcs leading to q_g are labelled with τ. It is also a *GSA* since q_g is unique and $\delta_u(q_g, b') = \emptyset$, $b' \in \Sigma_u$.

In order to show that h_τ is a bijection, we need to prove the existence of the inverse function h_τ^{-1}. Let A_u be a uniquely terminated acceptor $A_u = (Q_u, \Sigma_u, \delta_u, I_u, F_u)$ where $F_u = \{q_g\}$. Now we construct the finite state acceptor $A = h_\tau^{-1}(A_u) = (Q, \Sigma, \delta, I, F)$ with $Q = Q_u - \{q_g\}$, $\Sigma = \Sigma_u - \tau$, $\delta(q, \tau) = \emptyset$ for all $q \in Q$, $\delta(q, b) = \delta_u(q, b)$ for all $q \in Q - F$, $\delta(q_f, b) = \delta_u(q_f, b)$ for all $q_f \in F$ where $b \in \Sigma$. $I = I_u$, $F = \{q : q \in Q_u, \delta_u(q, \tau) = \{q_g\}\}$. Given that A_u is uniquely terminated, clearly A is by definition a finite-state acceptor since it is fully specified and does not accept any symbols other than those of Σ. □

Lemma 6.6 *Let S^+ be a non-empty positive sample, k a non-negative integer, and π_i the partition formed by KR on input S^+ and k after i steps. If some $u_1 v_1$ and $u_2 v_2$ are in the same non-goal block B of π_i (i.e. $B(u_1 v_1, \pi_i) = B(u_2 v_2, \pi_i)$, $v_1 \neq w_1 \tau, v_2 \neq w_2 \tau$, where $|v_1| = k = |v_2|$, then $v_1 = v_2$.*

Proof. From inspection of KR, two strings $u_1 v_1$ and $u_2 v_2$ are in the same block B of π_i only if at some step j, previous to i, $B(u_1 v_1, \pi_j)$

was merged with $B(u_2v_2, \pi_j)$. Let the pair (q_1, q_2) be the pair of states representing $B(u_1v_1, \pi_{j'})$ and $B(u_2v_2, \pi_{j'})$, placed on LIST during some step j', previous to j. (q_1, q_2) can have been placed on LIST only either

1. during initialisation, in which case v_1 and v_2 are terminated by a τ symbol (i.e. $v_1 = w_1\tau, v_2 = w_2\tau$ and are within a goal block B_g of π_i). However, Lemma 6.6 only applies to non-goal blocks *or*

2. by *pk*-UPDATE. *pk*-UPDATE would only merge q_1 and q_2 if they had a common k-leader in A_0, i.e. $v = v_1 = v_2$ and $|v| = k$ *or*

3. by *s*-UPDATE. As A_0 is $PT(S_u^+)$, which is by definition deterministic, *s*-UPDATE would only merge q_1 and q_2 if they were both b-successors ($b \in \Sigma_0 - \{\tau\}$) of some state q_3. Also, as A_0 is deterministic, q_3 must have been formed by a similar chain of 0 or more merges by *s*-UPDATE preceded by a *pk*-UPDATE. Thus all strings leading into q_1 and q_2 must have a common tail of at least length k. □

Lemma 6.7 *Let S^+ be a non-empty positive sample and k a non-negative integer. The output of algorithm KR on input S^+ and k is isomorphic to the prefix tree acceptor $PT(S^+)$ whenever k is greater than the length of the longest string within S^+.*

Proof. Let π_f be the partition formed by KR on input S^+ and k, and let $u_1v_1w_1$ and $u_2v_2w_2$ be two members of S^+. During initialisation, A_0 is set to be $PT(S_u^+)$ where S_u^+ is $S^+.\{\tau\}$. By Lemma 6.6 u_1v and u_2v are only within the same non-goal block B of π_f when $|v_1| = k = |v_2|$ and $v_1 = v_2$. However, since k is greater than the longest string within S^+, there can exist no such substrings v_1 and v_2 of length k. Thus no non-goal state of A_0 will be merged. However, all and only goal states are placed on LIST during initialisation, thus all such goal states are merged into a single goal state. Therefore the output of KR, $h_\tau^{-1}(A_0/\pi_f)$ must be isomorphic to $PT(S^+)$ by the definition of h_u^{-1} (proof of Theorem 6.5). □

Lemma 6.8 *Let S^+ be a non-empty positive sample, k a non-negative integer, A_0 the prefix tree acceptor of S_u^+, and π_f the final partition found by KR on input S^+. Then π_f is the finest partition of the states of A_0 such that A_0/π_f is ku-reversible.*

Proof. If the pair (q_1, q_2) is ever placed on LIST, then q_1 and q_2 must be in the same block of the final partition, that is, $B(q_1, \pi_f) = B(q_2, \pi_f)$. Thus in order to prove that KR always produces a ku-reversible acceptor, it suffices to show that two states q_1 and q_2 are always placed on

LIST if and only if they violate the conditions of *ku*-reversibility. From inspection of KR, it can be seen that (q_1,q_2) can have been placed on LIST only either

1. during initialisation.

    (a) This corresponds to all those occurrences of condition (2) (figure 6.11) in which $b = \tau$.

    (b) Owing to the initialisation of LIST all occurrences of condition (2) (figure 6.11) in which $b = \tau$ will be found and merged.

2. by *pk*-UPDATE.

    (a) This corresponds to all those occurrences of condition (2) (figure 6.11) in which $b \neq \tau$.

    (b) As A_0 has the graphical form of a tree (each state has a maximum of one arc leading into it), and condition (2) depicts a graph containing a state (q_3) with two arcs leading into it, q_3 must have been formed as the product of a merger. Following this merger, q_1 and q_2 would have been placed on LIST. Thus such conditions will always be found.

3. by *s*-UPDATE.

    (a) This corresponds to all those occurrences of condition (1) (figure 6.11).

    (b) Since A_0 is deterministic, the state q_3 depicted in condition (1) of figure 6.11 must have been formed as the product of a merger. Following this merger, q_1 and q_2 would have been placed on LIST by *s*-UPDATE. Again, such conditions will always be found.

We have shown that the states (q_1,q_2) will be merged in cases 1–3 *only if* the conditions of *ku*-reversibility are violated. Also we have shown in all cases 1–3 that (q_1,q_2) are always placed on LIST *if* the conditions of *ku*-reversibility are violated. Thus $A_u = A_0/\pi_f$ is *ku*-reversible.

It remains to show that if π is any partition of Q_0 such that A_0/π is *ku*-reversible then π_f refines π. We prove by induction that π_i refines π for $i = 0, 1, \ldots f$. Clearly, π_0 refines π. Suppose $\pi_0, \pi_1, \ldots \pi_i$ all refine π and π_{i+1} is obtained from π_i in the course of processing (q_1, q_2) for LIST. Since π_i refines π, $B(q_1, \pi_i)$ is a subset of $B(q_1, \pi)$ and $B(q_2, \pi_i)$ is a subset of $B(q_2, \pi)$, so to show that π_{i+1} refines π, it suffices to show that $B(q_1, \pi) = B(q_2, \pi)$.

Either (q_1, q_2) was first placed on LIST during the initialisation stage or not. If so, then q_1 and q_2 are both accepting states, and since A_0/π is ku-reversible and thus by definition is a GSA, it has only one accepting state, so $B(q_1, \pi) = B(q_2, \pi)$. Otherwise, (q_1, q_2) was first placed on LIST in consequence of some previous merge, let us say the merge to produce π_j from π_{j-1}, where $0 < j \leq i$. Then $(q_1, q_2) = (s(B_1, b), s(B_2, b))$ (resp. $(p(B_1, b), p(B_2, b))$) where B_1 and B_2 are the blocks of π_{j-1} merged in forming π_j and b is some symbol. Then q_1 and q_2 are b-successors (resp. b-predecessors) of two states in some block B of π_j. Since π_j refines π by the induction hypothesis, q_1 and q_2 are b-successors (resp. b-successors) of some block B' in π, and since A_0/π is ku-reversible, $B(q_1, \pi) = B(q_2, \pi)$. Thus in either case π_{i+1} refines π, and by induction we conclude that π_f refines π. □

Lemma 6.9 *Let S^+ be a non-empty positive sample, k a non-negative integer, A_0 the prefix tree acceptor of S_u^+, π_f the final partition found by KR on input S^+ and k, and $A = h_\tau^{-1}(A_0/\pi_f)$ the output automata. Then A is isomorphic to the automata $A' = PT(S^+)/\pi$, where π is the finest partition of the states of $PT(S^+)$ such that A' is k-reversible.*

Proof. From the definitions of k-reversibility and the mapping h_τ^{-1}, since A_0/π_f is ku-reversibility, it follows that $h_\tau^{-1}(A_0/\pi_f)$ is k-reversible.

It is necessary to show that if $B(w_1, \pi_f) = B(w_2, \pi_f)$ then $B(w_1, \pi) = B(w_2, \pi)$, $w \neq u\tau v$. Mergers made under condition (figure 6.11)

1. are the same

2. $b \in \Sigma_0 - \{\tau\}$ merges are for k-reversible reasons. $b = \tau$, q_1 and q_2 would be accepting states.

Thus merges are made in the same way as those for conditions of Angluin's k-reversibility for all states other than goal states. All and only necessary states are merged (proof of 6.8). Thus A is isomorphic to the automata $A' = PT(S^+)/\pi$, where π is the finest partition of the states of $PT(S^+)$ such that A' is k-reversible. □

Theorem 6.10 *Let S^+ be a nonempty positive sample, k a natural number and let $A_u = h_\tau^{-1}(A_0/\pi_f)$ be the acceptor output by KR on input S^+ and k. Then $L(A)$ is the smallest k-reversible language containing S^+.*

Proof. As KR is input/output equivalent to Angluin's algorithm, k-RI, and Angluin proves this to be true for k-RI, it clearly holds for KR (Angluin, 1982). □

Theorem 6.11 *Let L be a nonempty k-reversible language and $w_1, w_2, w_3, \ldots$ any positive presentation of L. On this input, the output $A_1, A_2, A_3, \ldots$ of KR converges to $A(L)$ (i.e. KR identifies L in the limit).*

Proof. As KR is input/output equivalent to Angluin's algorithm, k-RI, and Angluin also proves this to be true for k-RI, it clearly holds for KR (Angluin, 1982). □

Theorem 6.12 *Let S^+ be a non-empty positive sample, k a non-negative integer. The algorithm KR may be implemented to run in time $O(n^2)$ where n is*

$$\left(\sum\nolimits^{u \in S^+} |u|\right) + |S^+| + 1.$$

Proof. During initialisation, S_u^+ is composed as $S^+ . \{\tau\}$. Let $n = \left(\sum\nolimits^{u\tau \in S_u^+} |u\tau|\right) + 1 = \left(\sum\nolimits^{u \in S^+} |u|\right) + |S^+| + 1.$

The prefix tree acceptor $A_0 = PT(S_u^+)$, which can have no more than n states can be constructed in time $O(n)$. Similarly, the time taken to output the final acceptor $h_\tau^{-1}(A_0/\pi_f)$ is $O(n)$. As A_0 is a tree, it contains $n - 1$ transition arcs and thus there are exactly $n - 1$ s and p relations. Thus s-UPDATE and pk-UPDATE can effectively merge a total maximum of $n - 2$ pairs of s and p relations respectively. Since s-UPDATE takes constant time, the sum of times for all calls of s-UPDATE is $O(n)$. For any triple B_1, B_2 and b passed to pk-UPDATE, pk-UPDATE will compare all pairs $q_1 \in p(B_1, b)$ and $q_2 \in p(B_2, b)$ for merger of q_1 and q_2. This pair of predecessor arcs will never be used for comparison again since B_1 and B_2 are merged into a single block B_3. As there are $n - 1$ p relations in the prefix tree, this leads to a maximum of $\frac{(n-1)(n-2)}{2}$ comparisons, that is $O(n^2)$. Each comparison can be computed in a constant time proportional to k using Lemma 6.6. Block mergers can be carried out in time $O(n)$ using set union. Since block merger can happen at most $n - 1$ times, the total time for mergers is $O(n^2)$ Thus since no component of the algorithm takes more than time $O(n^2)$, the entire algorithm will run in time $O(n^2)$. □

Theorem 6.4 *For any $\chi(u, v)$ which implies $T_{S^+}(u) \cap T_{S^+}(v) = \emptyset$, the induced partition $\pi_{Pr(S^+)}$ is the trivial partition π_0 whenever $|S^+| = 1$.*

Proof. Let $S^+ = \{w\}$. Let two distinct prefixes of w be u_1 and u_2. Let $T_{S^+}(u_1) = \{v_1\}$ and $T_{S^+}(u_2) = \{v_2\}$. As u_1 and u_2 are distinct prefixes of w, $|u_1| \neq |u_2|$ and $|w| = |u_1| + |v_1| = |u_2| + |v_2|$. Thus $v_1 \neq v_2$, $T_{S^+}(u_1) \neq T_{S^+}(u_2)$ and $\chi(u_1, u_2)$ will always be false. As no mergers would ever be made, $\pi_{Pr(S^+)} = \pi_0$. □

Lemma 6.18 *Any 0-contextual non-empty language L is equal to Σ^* the universal language where $b \in \Sigma$ if and only if there is some $ubv \in L$.*

Proof. Let L be a nonempty 0-contextual language. We prove by induction that $L = \Sigma^*$ where $b \in \Sigma$ if and only if there is some $ubv \in L$. Let w be an element of L. Since $w = \lambda.w = w.\lambda$, it follows from Remark 6.17 that λ is an element of L. By the inductive hypothesis we suppose that L contains all members of Σ^* of length less than or equal to n. Now suppose that $|ubv| = n+1$. The strings u, v and b are all members of L since they are all of length less then n. Since $u.\lambda, \lambda.b \in L$, by Remark 6.17 $ub \in L$. Similarly, since $ub, \lambda.v \in L$, by Remark 6.17 $ubv \in L$, which completes the inductive step and the proof. □

Theorem 6.20 *For any k-contextual language L there exists a characteristic sample S^+ of L.*

Proof. If $L = \emptyset$ then $S^+ = \emptyset$ is a characteristic sample of L so suppose $L \neq \emptyset$. Let $A = (Q, \Sigma, \delta, \{q_0\}, F)$ be the canonical acceptor of L. For each $q \in Q$ let L_q denote the set of k-leaders of q in A. For each pair $q \in Q$ and $x \in L_q$ let $u(q,x)$ be some string u such that $\delta(q_0, ux) = q$. The sample S^+ is defined as containing all strings u of length less than k which are in L, some string $u(q,x)xbv \in L$ for each $q \in Q$, $x \in L_q$, $b \in \Sigma$, and some string $u(q_f, x)x \in L$ for each $q_f \in F$, $x \in L_{q_f}$. No other strings are in S^+. Lemma 6.18 establishes that in the case $k = 0$, $L = \Sigma^*$ where $b \in \Sigma$ if and only if there is some $ubv \in L$. Thus S^+ is a characteristic sample of L for $k = 0$ if for every $b \in \Sigma$ there is some string of the form $ubv \in S^+$, which is so by the definition of S^+. Suppose $k \geq 1$.

Let L' be any k-contextual language containing S^+. We must show that L is contained in L'. Clearly, any element of L of length less than k is in S^+ and therefore in L'. We show by induction that for every $w \in Pr(L)$ of length at least k, $T'_L(w) = T'_L(u(q,x),x)$, where x is the suffix of w of length k and $q = \delta(q_0, w)$. If w has length exactly k, then $w = x$ and $u(q,x) = \lambda$, so this condition is satisfied. Using the inductive hypothesis we suppose that for every $n \geq k$ this condition is satisfied for all strings $w \in Pr(L)$ of length at most n. Suppose w is any element of $Pr(L)$ of length $n+1$. Let $w = w'axb$, where $|x| = k-1$ and $a, b \in \Sigma$. By the inductive hypothesis $T'_L(w'ax) = T'_L(u(q,ax)ax)$, where $q = \delta(q_0, w'ax)$. Thus $T'_L(w) = T'_L(u(q,ax)axb)$. Let $q' = \delta(q,b) = \delta(q_0, w)$. Then S^+ contains the strings $u(q,ax)axbv_1$ and $u(q', xb)xbv_2$, so L contains these strings. By Remark 6.19, this implies that $T'_L(u(q,ax)axb) = T'_L(u(q', xb)xb)$, so $T'_L(w) = T'_L(u(q', xb)xb)$, completing the induction step.

Now let w be any element of L of length at least k, and let x be the suffix of w of length k. Then $T'_L(w) = T'_L(u(q_f, x)x)$, where $q_f \in F$. The string $u(q_f, x)x$ is contained in S^+ by construction and therefore is in L'. Hence w is in L', which completes the proof that L is contained in L'. Thus L is the smallest k-contextual language containing S^+, and S^+ is a characteristic sample of L. □

Lemma 6.22 *If A is a k-contextual acceptor and A' is any subacceptor of A, then A' is a k-contextual acceptor.*

Proof. Let k be a natural number, $A = (Q, \Sigma, \delta, I, F)$ be some k-contextual acceptor, and $A' = (Q', \Sigma', \delta', I', F')$ be a subacceptor of A. A' is a subacceptor of A only if $\delta'(q', b) \subseteq \delta(q', b)$ for all $q' \in Q'$ and $b \in \Sigma$. Let us assume that A' is not k-contextual. Thus by Remark 6.19 $\delta'(q_0, u_1 v) \neq \delta'(q_0, u_2 v)$ for some $u_1 v w_1, u_1 v w_1 \in L(A')$, $|v| = k$. We can show trivially by mathematical induction that since by the definition of subacceptors (see Appendix B) $\delta'(q', b) \subseteq \delta(q', b)$ for all $q' \in Q', b \in \Sigma'$, it follows that $\delta'(q', w) \subseteq \delta(q', w)$ for all $w \in \Sigma'^*$. Remark 6.19 shows that $\delta(q_0, u_1 v) = \delta(q_0, u_2 v) = \{q\}$. Thus since $\delta'(q', w) \subseteq \delta(q', w)$ for all $w \in \Sigma'^*$, it follows that both $\delta'(q_0, u_1 v) \subseteq \{q\}$ and $\delta'(q_0, u_2 v) \subseteq \{q\}$. However $\delta'(q_0, u_1 v) \neq \emptyset$ and $\delta'(q_0, u_2 v) \neq \emptyset$ since $u_1 v w_1, u_2 v w_2 \in L(A')$. Thus $\delta'(q_0, u_1 v) = \delta'(q_0, u_2 v) = \{q\}$. This contradicts our assumption that A' is not k-contextual. Therefore A' is k-contextual. □

Lemma 6.25 *Let S^+ be a nonempty positive sample, k a natural number and let A_0/π_f be the acceptor output by KC on input S^+ and k. Then π_f is the finest partition of the states of A_0 such that A_0/π_f is k-contextual.*

Proof. Let $A_0 = (Q_0, \Sigma_0, \delta_0, I_0, F_0)$. By inspection, we note that the initialisation and merging sections of KC guarantee that every state of Q_0 will be placed into exactly one block of π_f. Thus π_f is a partition of Q_0, and A_0/π_f is a legal acceptor. Furthermore a trivial inductive argument can be employed to show that every block B of π_f contains either a single state $u \in Q_0$ for which $|u| < k$, or all states $uv \in Q_0$ for which uv has a particular suffix v of length k.

Let $u_1 v w_1$ and $u_2 v w_2$ be two strings in a language L, where $|v| = k$. By Definition 6.14, L is k-contextual if and only if $T_L(u_1 v) = T_L(u_2 v)$, i.e. $u_1 v$ and $u_2 v$ lead to the same state in $A(L)$. Since all states $uv \in Q_0$ for which uv has a particular suffix v of length k are contained within the same block of π_f it follows that $u_1 v$ and $u_2 v$ lead to the same state in A_0/π_f for any $u_1 v w_1, u_2 v w_2 \in S^+$. Thus A_0/π_f is k-contextual.

It remains to show that if π is any partition of Q_0 such that A_0/π is k-contextual, then π_f refines π. Let us assume the opposite, i.e. there exists some π which refines π_f where π is not equal to π_f and $L = L(A_0/\pi)$ is k-contextual. Thus at least one block of π_f is the union of more than one block of π. But as all blocks of π_f contain either singletons or contain all states $uv \in Q_0$ for which uv has a particular suffix v of length k there must exist at least two blocks of π containing states with the same k-leader. Let these two blocks B_1 and B_2 contain u_1v and u_2v respectively, where v is the common k-leader. This implies that $T_L(u_1v) \neq T_L(u_2v)$ and therefore L is not k-contextual; which contradicts the original assumption and shows that π_f refines all partitions π for which A_0/π is k-contextual. This completes the proof. □

Theorem 6.26 *Let S^+ be a nonempty positive sample, and let A_f be the acceptor output by algorithm KC on input S^+. Then $L(A_f)$ is the smallest k-contextual language containing S^+.*

Proof. Lemma 6.25 shows that $L(A_f)$ is a k-contextual language containing S^+. Let L be any k-contextual language containing S^+, and let π be the restriction of the partition π_L to the elements of $Pr(S^+)$. If A_0 denotes the prefix tree acceptor for S^+, then Lemma 6.1 shows that A_0/π is isomorphic to a subacceptor of $A(L)$, and Corollary 6.2 shows that $L(A_0/\pi)$ is contained in L. From Lemma 6.22, $L(A_0/\pi)$ is k-contextual. Thus by Lemma 6.25 π_f refines π, so $L(A_0/\pi_f)$ is contained in $L(A_0/\pi)$. Consequently, $L(A_f)$ is contained in L, and $L(A_f)$ is the smallest k-contextual language containing S^+. □

Theorem 6.27 *The algorithm KC may be implemented to run in time $O(n)$ where n is one more than the sum of the lengths of the input strings.*

Proof. Let S^+ be the set of input strings and n be one more than the sum of the lengths of strings in S^+. The prefix tree acceptor $PT(S^+)$ can be constructed in time $O(n)$ and contains no more than n states. Both π_0 and Q_0' can be created in a single pass over all strings in S^+, and thus also take time $O(n)$. Since Q_0' contains at most n strings and each pass through the iteration can be completed in constant time given a hashing mechanism for finding the appropriate block B_1, merging also takes $O(n)$ time. The output automaton A_0/π_f can also be created in time $O(n)$. Since no operation takes more than time $O(n)$ it follows that the algorithm KC completes within time $O(n)$. □

Theorem 6.28 *Let L be a nonempty k-contextual language for some* natural number k. Let $w_1, w_2, w_3, \ldots$ be a positive presentation of L, and $A_1, A_2, A_3, \ldots$ be the output of KC_∞ on this input. Then $L(A_1)$, $L(A_2)$, $L(A_3)$, $\ldots$ converges to L after a finite number of steps.

Proof. By Theorem 6.20, L contains a characteristic sample. Let N be sufficiently large that $w_1, w_2, \ldots, w_N$ contains a characteristic sample for L. For $n \geq N$, $L(A_n)$ is the smallest k-contextual language containing $w_1, w_2, \ldots, w_N$, by definition of KC_∞ and Theorem 6.26. Thus $L(A_n) = L$, by the definition of a characteristic sample (Definition 6.14). □

Theorem 6.30 *Given a fixed natural number k, the algorithm KC is incremental on input k and any positive presentation of some k-contextual language L.*

Proof. Let k be a natural number, S^+ be a positive sample, w be some string, $A = PT(S^+)/\pi = (Q, \Sigma, \delta, I, F)$ be the output of KC on input k and S^+, and $A' = PT(S^+ \cup w)/\pi' = (Q', \Sigma', \delta', I', F')$ be the output of KC on input k and $S^+ \cup \{w\}$. We need to show that A is a subacceptor of A'.

By definition A is a subacceptor of A' if and only if $Q \subseteq Q', I \subseteq I', F \subseteq F'$ and $\delta(q, b) \subseteq \delta'(q, b)$ for all $q \in Q$ and $b \in \Sigma$. Following a similar argument to that of Lemma 6.25, we get that $\pi = \{\{u\} : uv \in S^+, |u| < k\} \cup \{B_v : xvz \in S^+, |v| = k, uv \in B_v\}$ and $\pi' = \{\{u\} : uv \in S^+ \cup \{w\}, |u| < k\} \cup \{B_v : xvz \in S^+ \cup \{w\}, |v| = k, uv \in B_v\}$. Thus for every block $B = \{u\}$ in π for which $uv \in S^+, |u| < k$ there exists one and only one corresponding block $B' = \{u\}$ in π'. Similarly, for every block B_v in π there is a corresponding block B_v' in π'. It follows from the definition of quotient that $Q \subseteq Q', I \subseteq I', F \subseteq F'$ and $\delta(q, b) \subseteq \delta'(q, b)$ for all $q \in Q$ and $b \in \Sigma$. Thus A is a subacceptor of A'. □

Lemma 6.32 *Given the bijection h_b which maps elements of Σ_{sa} to the universal alphabet Σ, there exists a bijection h_a which maps terminated Mealy machines to FSAs.*

Proof. First we prove the existence of h_a by construction. Let $M = (Q_m, X, Y, \delta_m, I_m, F_m)$ be a terminated Mealy machine. h_a constructs an FSA $A_a = (Q_a, \Sigma, \delta_a, I_a, F_a)$. For every state $q \in Q_m$ there is exactly one state $q' \in Q_a$. For every initial state $q_i \in I_m$ there is exactly one state $q_i' \in I_a$. For every final state $q_f \in F_m$ there is exactly one state $q_f' \in F_a$. $\delta_a(q_a, b) = q_a'$ if and only if $\delta_m(q_m, x) = (y, q_m')$, the pairs of states (q_m, q_a) and (q_m', q_a') correspond in M and A_a, and $h_b((x, y)) = b$.

In order to show that h_a is a bijection, we need to prove the existence of the inverse mapping h_a^{-1}. This is also done by construction. Let $A_a = (Q_a, \Sigma, \delta_a, I_a, F_a)$ be a FSA. h_a^{-1} constructs a terminated Mealy machine $M = (Q_m, X, Y, \delta_m, I_m, F_m)$. For every state $q \in Q_a$ there is exactly one state $q' \in Q_m$. For every initial state $q_i \in I_a$ there is exactly one state $q_i' \in I_m$. For every final state $q_f \in F_a$ there is exactly one state $q_f' \in F_m$. $\delta_m(q_m, x) = (y, q_m')$ if and only if $\delta_a(q_a, \dot{u}) = q_a'$, the pairs of states (q_m, q_a) and (q_m', q_a') correspond in M and A_a, and $h_b^{-1}(b) = (x, y)$. $\square$

Lemma 6.33 *Given the bijection h_b which maps elements of Σ_{sa} to Σ, there exists a bijection h_u which maps situation/action sequences to strings.*

Proof. h_u is very simply proved by construction. Let the situation action sequence u_{sa} be $(x_1, y_1)(x_2, y_2)\ldots(x_n, y_n)$. h_u constructs the string $u = b_1 b_2 \ldots b_n$ such that $h_b((x_i, y_i)) = u_i$, $1 \leq i \leq n$.

The existence of the inverse mapping, h_u^{-1} can be shown trivially and is thus omitted. $\square$

Theorem 6.35 *Let S_{sa}^+ be a positive sample of situation/action sequences. Given S_{sa}^+ as input, the algorithm SKR will output, when it can, the pair (M_f, f) where f is the smallest value of k such that M_k is both k-reversible and deterministic. Otherwise, if no such pair exists, SKR will fail.*

Proof. By inspection SKR will output the required pair (M_k, k) for the lowest value of k between 0 and the maximum length of sequence within $S_s a^+$, given that M_k is k-reversible and deterministic. According to Lemma 6.7, output of algorithm KR on any input S^+ and k is isomorphic to the prefix tree acceptor $PT(S^+)$ whenever k is greater than the length of the longest string within S^+. Thus if M_k is not deterministic when k is one greater than the maximum length of any string within S^+, M_i is non-deterministic for all i greater than k, since all such M_i are isomorphic to the prefix tree acceptor of S^+. $\square$

Appendix E
Example Move Sequences

The following is a description of the example sequences used in Chapter 8.

E.1 Actions

(Ba) wK approaches release position (such as h3) by moving along rank or file

(Bb) wK moves to non-check position on direct diagonal which is closest to release position

(Bc) wB(light) moves out of corner along its diagonal

(Bd) white takes bN

E.2 Attributes

(B1) white free to take bN

(B2) wK on the same diagonal as release position

(B3) wBh1 can move

(B4) (wK on direct diagonal) and (direct diagonal position closest to release position is covered)

196 Inductive Acquisition of Expert Knowledge

E.3 Black plays optimally

E.3.1 Sequence 1

Starts from wKa8 and bN does delaying check

B1	B2	B3	B4	Action	Position	Move
n	n	n	n	Ba	wKa8 wBh1 wBh2 bKf3 bNg2	wKb8
n	n	n	n	Ba	wKb8 wBh1 wBh2 bKf2 bNg2	wKc8
n	y	n	n	Bb	wKc8 wBh1 wBh2 bKf3 bNg2	wKd7
n	y	n	n	Bb	wKd7 wBh1 wBh2 bKf2 bNg2	wKe6
n	y	n	n	Bb	wKe6 wBh1 wBh2 bKf1 bNg2	wKf5
n	y	n	n	Ba	wKf5 wBh1 wBh2 bKf1 bNe3	wKg5
n	n	n	n	Bb	wKg5 wBh1 wBh2 bKf1 bNg2	wKg4
n	y	n	n	Bb	wKg4 wBh1 wBh2 bKf2 bNg2	wKh3
n	-	y	n	Bc	wKh3 wBh1 wBh2 bKf1 bNf3	wBa8

The '-' in the last line allows the algorithm to generalise to the case in which bN releases wB(light).

E.3.2 Sequence 2

Starts from wKb7 and bN does delaying check

B1	B2	B3	B4	Action	Position	Move
n	n	n	n	Ba	wKb7 wBh1 wBh2 bKf2 bNg2	wKc7
n	n	n	n	Ba	wKc7 wBh1 wBh2 bKf3 bNg2	wKd7
n	y	n	n	Bb	wKd7 wBh1 wBh2 bKf2 bNg2	wKe6
n	y	n	n	Bb	wKe6 wBh1 wBh2 bKf1 bNg2	wKf5
n	y	n	n	Ba	wKf5 wBh1 wBh2 bKf1 bNe3	wKg5
n	n	n	n	Bb	wKg5 wBh1 wBh2 bKf1 bNg2	wKg4
n	y	n	n	Bb	wKg4 wBh1 wBh2 bKf2 bNg2	wKh3
n	-	y	n	Bc	wKh3 wBh1 wBh2 bKf1 bNf3	wBa8

E.3.3 Sequence 3

Starts from wKb8 and bN does delaying check

B1	B2	B3	B4	Action	Position	Move
n	n	n	n	Ba	wKb8 wBh1 wBh2 bKf2 bNg2	wKc8
n	y	n	n	Bb	wKc8 wBh1 wBh2 bKf3 bNg2	wKd7
n	y	n	n	Bb	wKd7 wBh1 wBh2 bKf2 bNg2	wKe6
n	y	n	n	Bb	wKe6 wBh1 wBh2 bKf1 bNg2	wKf5
n	y	n	n	Ba	wKf5 wBh1 wBh2 bKf1 bNe3	wKg5
n	n	n	n	Bb	wKg5 wBh1 wBh2 bKf1 bNg2	wKg4
n	y	n	n	Bb	wKg4 wBh1 wBh2 bKf2 bNg2	wKh3
n	-	y	n	Bc	wKh3 wBh1 wBh2 bKf1 bNf3	wBa8

E.3.4 Sequence 4

Starts with wKa8 and bN does not do delaying check

B1	B2	B3	B4	Action	Position	Move
n	n	n	n	Ba	wKa8 wBh1 wBh2 bKf3 bNg2	wKb8
n	n	n	n	Ba	wKb8 wBh1 wBh2 bKf2 bNg2	wKc8
n	y	n	n	Bb	wKc8 wBh1 wBh2 bKf3 bNg2	wKd7
n	y	n	n	Bb	wKd7 wBh1 wBh2 bKf2 bNg2	wKe6
n	y	n	n	Bb	wKe6 wBh1 wBh2 bKf1 bNg2	wKf5
n	y	n	n	Bb	wKf5 wBh1 wBh2 bKf2 bNg2	wKg4
n	y	n	n	Bb	wKg4 wBh1 wBh2 bKf1 bNg2	wKh3
n	-	y	n	Bc	wKh3 wBh1 wBh2 bKf2 bNf3	wBa8

E.3.5 Sequence 5

Starts with wKg4

B1	B2	B3	B4	Action	Position	Move
n	y	n	n	Bb	wKg4 wBh1 wBh2 bKf1 bNg2	wKh3
n	-	y	n	Bc	wKh3 wBh1 wBh2 bKf2 bNf3	wBa8

E.3.6 Sequence 6

Starts with wKh3

B1	B2	B3	B4	Action	Position	Move
n	-	y	n	Bc	wKh3 wBh1 wBh2 bKf2 bNf3	wBa8

E.4 Black plays badly

E.4.1 Sequence 7

Starts with wKa8 after bK has left bN undefended (en prise)

B1	B2	B3	B4	Action	Position	Move
y	-	n	n	Bd	wKa8 wBh1 wBh2 bKe2 bNg2	wB x N!

E.4.2 Sequence 8

Starts with wKa8 and bK leaves bN as first move

B1	B2	B3	B4	Action	Position	Move
n	n	n	n	Ba	wKa8 wBh1 wBh2 bKf3 bNg2	wKb8
y	-	n	n	Bd	wKb8 wBh1 wBh2 bKe3 bNg2	wB x N!

E.4.3 Sequence 9

Starts with wKg4 and bK leaves bN as first move

B1	B2	B3	B4	Action	Position	Move
n	y	n	n	Bb	wKg4 wBh1 wBh2 bKf1 bNg2	wKh3
y	-	n	n	Bd	wKh3 wBh1 wBh2 bKe1 bNg2	wB x N!

E.4.4 Sequence 10

Starts with wKb8, bN does not do delaying check but allows the release of wB

B1	B2	B3	B4	Action	Position	Move
n	n	n	n	Ba	wKb8 wBh1 wBh2 bKf2 bNg2	wKc8
n	-	y	n	Bc	wKc8 wBh1 wBh2 bKf2 bNd1	wBc6

E.4.5 Sequence 11

Starts with wKe6, bN does delaying check and then allows the release of wB

B1	B2	B3	B4	Action	Position	Move
n	y	n	n	Bb	wKe6 wBh1 wBh2 bKf1 bNg2	wKf5
n	y	n	n	Ba	wKf5 wBh1 wBh2 bKf1 bNe3	wKg5
n	-	y	n	Bc	wKg5 wBh1 wBh2 bKf1 bNd1	wBc6

E.4.6 Sequence 12

Starts with wKe6, bN does delaying check and then allows itself to be taken (by moving to g4).

B1	B2	B3	B4	Action	Position	Move
n	y	n	n	Bb	wKe6 wBh1 wBh2 bKf1 bNg2	wKf5
n	y	n	n	Ba	wKf5 wBh1 wBh2 bKf1 bNe3	wKg5
y	-	n	n	Bd	wKg5 wBh1 wBh2 bKf1 bNg4	wKg4!

E.4.7 Sequence 13

Starts with wKd7, bN checks allowing itself to be taken by wB(dark)

B1	B2	B3	B4	Action	Position	Move
n	y	n	n	Bb	wKd7 wBh1 wBh2 bKf2 bNg2	wKe6
y	y	y	n	Bd	wKe6 wBh1 wBh2 bKf2 bNf4	B x N

Appendix F
Results of Sequence Induction

The following is the result of the sequence induction on the sequences of Appendix E.

F.1 Actions

(Ba) wK approaches release position (such as h3) by moving along rank or file

(Bb) wK moves to non-check position on direct diagonal which is closest to release position

(Bc) wB(light) moves out of corner along its diagonal

(Bd) white takes bN

F.2 Attributes

(B1) white free to take bN

(B2) wK on the same diagonal as release position

(B3) wBh1 can move

(B4) (wK on direct diagonal) and (direct diagonal position closest to release position is covered)

F.3   State machine

	B1	B2	B3	B4		(Action,NextState)
STATE 0						
	n	-	y	n	⇒	(Bc,GOAL)
	n	n	n	n	⇒	(Ba,1)
	n	y	n	n	⇒	(Bb,2)
	y	-	n	n	⇒	(Bd,GOAL)
STATE 1						
	n	-	y	n	⇒	(Bc,GOAL)
	n	n	n	n	⇒	(Ba,1)
	n	y	n	n	⇒	(Bb,2)
	y	-	n	n	⇒	(Bd,GOAL)
STATE 2						
	n	-	y	n	⇒	(Bc,GOAL)
	n	y	n	n	⇒	(Bb,2)
	n	y	n	y	⇒	(Ba,3)
	y	-	n	n	⇒	(Bd,GOAL)
	y	y	y	n	⇒	(Bd,GOAL)
STATE 3						
	n	-	y	n	⇒	(Bc,GOAL)
	n	n	n	n	⇒	(Bb,4)
	y	-	n	n	⇒	(Bd,GOAL)
STATE 4						
	n	y	n	n	⇒	(Bb,2)

Appendix G
Automata after ACLS Induction

The following is the result of applying ACLS induction to the state machine of Appendix F.

G.1 Actions

(Ba) wK approaches release position (such as h3) by moving along rank or file

(Bb) wK moves to non-check position on direct diagonal which is closest to release position

(Bc) wB(light) moves out of corner along its diagonal

(Bd) white takes bN

G.2 Attributes

(B1) white free to take bN

(B2) wK on the same diagonal as release position

(B3) wBh1 can move

(B4) (wK on direct diagonal) and (direct diagonal position closest to release position is covered)

G.3 State description

STATE 0
[B1]
    y : ⇒ (Bd, GOAL)
    n : [B3]
        y : ⇒ (Bc, GOAL)
        n : [B2]
            y : ⇒ (Bb, 2)
            n : ⇒ (Ba, 1)

STATE 1
[B1]
    y : ⇒ (Bd, GOAL)
    n : [B3]
        y : ⇒ (Bc, GOAL)
        n : [B2]
            y : ⇒ (Bb, 2)
            n : ⇒ (Ba, 1)

STATE 2
[B1]
    y : ⇒ (Bd, GOAL)
    n : [B3]
        y : ⇒ (Bc, GOAL)
        n : [B4]
            y : ⇒ (Ba, 3)
            n : ⇒ (Bb, 2)

STATE 3
[B1]
    y : ⇒ (Bd, GOAL)
    n : [B4]
        y : ⇒ (Bc, GOAL)
        n : ⇒ (Bb, 4)

STATE 4
(Bb, 2)
GOAL

Appendix H
KBBKN Rulemaker Induction File

The following is the file corresponding to the state machine of Appendix F.

MODULE: wKsupp
  DECLARATIONS:
[INTENT: "move wK to support the attack of wBh1 on bNg2"]
  ACTIONS:
    wKapp [prints "wK approaches release position (eg. h3)" ;
      advise " by moving along rank or file"]
    wKnonc [prints "wK moves to non-check position on direct"
      prints " diagonal which is closest to"
      advise " the release position (eg. h3)"]
    wBout [print "wB(light) moves out of corner along its"
      advise " diagonal"]
    wtakes [advise "white takes bN"]
  CONDITIONS:
    wcantake [ask "Is white free to take bN? " "y,n"]
        y n
    wKinck   [ask "Is the wK in check? " "y,n"]
        y n
    wKond [ask "Is wK on same diagonal as release position? "
      "y,n"] y n
    wBcanmv [ask "Can the cornered wB now move? " "y,n"]
        y n
    diagcvr [prints "Is the wK on the direct diagonal and
      prints " the direct diagonal position closest
      ask " to the release position is covered" "y,n"]
        y n

STATE: zero
 EXAMPLES:
 n n - y n ⇒ (wBout,GOAL)
 n n n n n ⇒ (wKapp,1)
 n n y n n ⇒ (wKnonc,2)
 y n - n n ⇒ (wtakes,GOAL)
STATE: one
 EXAMPLES:
 n n n n n ⇒ (wKapp,1)
 n n y n n ⇒ (wKnonc,2)
 y n - n n ⇒ (wtakes,GOAL)
STATE: two
 EXAMPLES:
 n - y n y ⇒ (wKapp,3)
 n n - y n ⇒ (wBout,GOAL)
 n n y n n ⇒ (wKnonc,2)
 y n - n n ⇒ (wtakes,GOAL)
STATE: three
 EXAMPLES:
 n n - y n ⇒ (wBout,GOAL)
 n n n n n ⇒ (wKnonc,4)
 y n - n n ⇒ (wtakes,GOAL)
STATE: four
 EXAMPLES:
 n n y n n ⇒ (wKnonc,2)

Appendix I
KBBKN Radial Code

The following Radial module was generated from the Rulemaker file given in Appendix H. The module was partially verified against the KBBKN data-base (see section 8.2) using a sample set of sequences. However, the test sequences used were not exhaustive.

MODULE wKsupp IS
  INTENT: "move wK to support the attack of wBh1 on bNg2"
  STATE: zero
  IF (ask "Is white free to take bN? " "y,n") IS
    "y" : (advise "White takes bN", GOAL)
    ELSE IF (ask "Can the cornered wB now move? " "y,n") IS
      "y" : (advise "wB(light) moves out of corner along its diagonal",
        GOAL)
      ELSE IF (ask "Is wK on same diagonal as release position? "
        "y,n") IS
        "y" : (advise "wK moves to non-check position on direct
          diagonal which is closest to the release position
          (eg. h3)", two)
        ELSE (advise "wK approaches release position (eg. h3)
          by moving along rank or file", one)
  STATE: one
  IF (ask "Is white free to take bN? " "y,n") IS
    "y" : (advise "White takes bN", GOAL)
    ELSE IF (ask "Can the cornered wB now move? " "y,n") IS
      "y" : (advise "wB(light) moves out of corner along its diagonal",
        GOAL)
      ELSE IF (ask "Is wK on same diagonal as release position? "
        "y,n") IS
        "y" : (advise "wK moves to non-check position on direct
          diagonal which is closest to the release position

                        (eg. h3)", two)
            ELSE (advise "wK approaches release position (eg. h3)
                by moving along rank or file", one)
STATE: two
   IF (ask "Is white free to take bN? " "y,n") IS
      "y" : (advise "White takes bN", GOAL)
      ELSE IF (ask "Can the cornered wB now move? " "y,n") IS
         "y" : (advise "wB(light) moves out of corner along
                  its diagonal", GOAL)
         ELSE IF (ask "Is the wK on the direct diagonal and the
                     direct diagonal position closest to the release
                     position is covered? " "y,n") IS
            "y" : (advise "wK approaches release position (eg. h3)
                    by moving along rank or file", three)
            ELSE (advise "wK moves to non-check position on
                   direct diagonal which is closest to the release
                   position (eg. h3)", two)
STATE: three
   IF (ask "Is white free to take bN? " "y,n") IS
      "y" : (advise "White takes bN", GOAL)
      ELSE IF (ask "Is the wK on the direct diagonal and the
                  direct diagonal position closest to the release position
                  is covered? " "y,n") IS
         "y" : (advise "wB(light) moves out of corner along its
                 diagonal", GOAL)
         ELSE (advise "wK moves to non-check position on
                direct diagonal which is closest to the release position
                (eg. h3)", four)
STATE: four
   (advise "wK moves to non-check position on direct diagonal
   which is closest to the release position (eg. h3)", two)
GOAL OF wKsupp

Bibliography

D. Angluin (1982) Inference of reversible languages. *JACM*, 29:741–765.

D. Angluin (1982) A note on the number of queries needed to identify regular languages. *Information and Control*, 51(1):76–87.

D. Angluin (1978) On the complexity of minimum inference of regular sets. *Information and Control*, 39:337–350.

D. Angluin and C.H. Smith (1983) A survey of inductive inference: theory and methods. *Computing Surveys*, 15(3):237–269.

M. A-Razzak, T. Hassan, and R. Pettipher (1984) Extran-7: a Fortran-based software package for building expert systems. In M.A. Bramer, editor, *Research and Development in Expert Systems*, pages 23–30, Cambridge University Press, Cambridge.

B. Arbab and D. Michie (1985) Generating rules from examples. In *IJCAI-85*, pages 631–633, Kaufmann, Los Altos, CA.

R.B. Banerji (1987) Learning in the limit in a growing language. In *IJCAI-87*, pages 280–282, Kaufmann, Los Angeles, CA.

A.W. Biermann and J.A. Feldman (1972) On the synthesis of finite-state machines from samples of their behaviour. *IEEE Transactions on Computers*, C(21):592–597.

D.G. Bobrow and M. Stefik (1983) *The LOOPS manual*. Xerox, Palo Alto, CA.

I. Bratko (1983) *Generating human-understandable decision rules*. Working paper, E. Kardelj University Ljubljana, Ljubljana, Yugoslavia.

I. Bratko and D. Michie (1980) A representation of pattern-knowledge in chess endgames. In M. Clarke, editor, *Advances in Computer Chess*, pages 31–56, Edinburgh University Press, Edinburgh.

R.M. Burstall and J. Darlington (1977) A transformation system for developing recursive programs. *Journal of the Association for Computing Machinery*, 24:44–67, 1977.

R. Dechter and D. Michie (1984) *Induction of plans.* TIRM 84-006, The Turing Institute, Glasgow.

N. Dershowitz (1985) Synthesis by completion. In *IJCAI-85*, pages 208–214, Kaufmann, Los Altos, CA.

R.O. Duda, J. Gashnig, and P.E. Hart (1979) Model design in the prospector consultant program for mineral exploration. In D. Michie, editor, *Expert Systems in the Microelectronic Age*, pages 153–167, Edinburgh University Press, Edinburgh.

B. Dufay and J.C. Latombe (1984) An approach to automatic robot programming based on inductive learning. *International Journal of Robotics Research*, 3(4):3–20.

L. Fagan, J. Kunz, E. Feigenbaum, and J. Osborne (1979) Representation of dynamic clinical knowledge measurement interpretation in the intensive care unit. In *IJCAI-79*, pages 260–262, Kaufmann, Los Altos, CA.

E.A. Feigenbaum (1979) Themes and case studies of knowledge engineering. In D. Michie, editor, *Expert Systems in the Microelectronic Age*, pages 3–25, Edinburgh University Press, Edinburgh.

E.A. Feigenbaum and P. McCorduck (1984) *The Fifth Generation: artificial intelligence and Japan's computer challenge to the world.* Joseph, London.

K.S. Fu and T.L. Booth (1975) Grammatical inference: introduction and survey. *IEEE Transactions on Systems, Man, Cybernetics*, 5:95–111,409–423.

L.M. Fu and B.G. Buchanan (1985) Learning intermediate concepts in constructing a hierarchical knowledge base. In *IJCAI-85*, pages 659–666, Kaufmann, Los Altos, CA.

E.M. Gold (1978) Complexity of automaton identification from given data. *Information and Control*, 37:302–320.

E.M. Gold (1967) Language identification in the limit. *Information and Control*, 10:447–474.

D. Haussler (1988) Quantifying inductive bias: AI learning algorithms and Valiant's learning framework. *Artificial intelligence*, 36:177 – 221.

J.E. Hopcroft and J.D. Ullman (1979) *Introduction to Automata and Formal Languages*. Addison-Wesley, Reading, MA.

Horwitz and Kling (1851) *Chess Studies*. Skeet, London.

B.J. Huberman (1968) *A program to play chess end-games*. CS 106, Computer Science Department, Stanford.

E.B. Hunt, J. Marin, and P.T. Stone (1966) *Experiments in Induction*. Academic Press, New York.

Intellicorp (1984) *The Knowledge Engineering Environment*. Intellicorp, Menlo Park, CA.

D.B. Lenat (1981) On automated scientific theory formation: A case study using the AM program. In J.E. Hayes and D. Michie, editors, *Machine Intelligence 9*, Horwood, New York.

B. Levine (1982) The use of tree derivatives and a sample support parameter for inferring tree systems. *IEEE Transactions on Pattern Analysis and Machine Intelligence*, 4:25–34.

R. McLaren (1984) *Expert Ease User Manual*. ITL-KnowledgeLink, Glasgow.

W.J. Van Melle (1980) *System Aids in Constructing Programs*. PhD thesis, University of Michigan.

R.S. Michalski (1983) A theory and methodology of inductive learning. In R. Michalski, J. Carbonnel, and T. Mitchell, editors, *Machine Learning: An Artificial Intelligence Approach*, pages 83–134, Tioga, Palo Alto, CA.

R.S. Michalski (1986) Understanding the nature of learning: issues and research directions. In R. Michalski, J. Carbonnel, and T. Mitchell, editors, *Machine Learning: An Artificial Intelligence Approach*, pages 3–25, Kaufmann, Los Altos, CA.

R.S Michalski and R.L. Chilausky (1980) Learning by being told and learning from examples: an experimental comparison of the two methods of knowledge acquisition in the context of developing an expert system for soybean disease diagnosis. *International Journal of Policy Analysis and Information Systems*, 4(2):125–161.

R.S. Michalski and R. Stepp (1983) Learning from observation: conceptual clustering. In R. Michalski, J. Carbonnel, and T. Mitchell, editors, *Machine Learning: An Artificial Intelligence Approach*, pages 331–364, Tioga, Palo Alto, CA.

D. Michie (1982) Computer chess and the humanisation of technology. *Nature*, 299:391–394.

D. Michie (1985) Expert systems and robotics. In D. Nof, editor, *Handbook of Industrial Robotics*, pages 419–436, Wiley, New York.

D. Michie (1982) Measuring the knowledge content of expert programs. *The Bulletin of the Institute of Mathematics and its Application*, 18:216–220, November 1982.

D. Michie (1984) Quality control of induced rule-based programs. In *The Fifth Generation*, GS Institute, London.

D. Michie (1986) The superarticulacy phenomenon in the context of software manufacture. *Proceedings of the Royal Society of London*, A 405:185–212, 1986.

D. Michie, S. Muggleton, C. Riese, and S. Zubrick (1984) RuleMaster: a second-generation knowledge-engineering facility. In *Proceedings of the First Conference on Artificial Intelligence Applications*, pages 591–597, IEEE Computer Soc..

L. Miclet (1980) Regular inference with a tail clustering method. *IEEE Transactions on Systems, Man, Cybernetics*, 10:737–743, 1980.

M. Minsky (1975) A framework for representing knowledge. In P. Winston, editor, *The Psychology of Computer Vision*, pages 211–277, Mcgraw-Hill, New York.

M. Minsky and S. Papert (1969) *Perceptrons*. MIT Press, MA.

E.F. Moore (1956) Gedanken-experiments on sequential machines. In C.E. Shannon and J. McCarthy, editors, *Automata Studies*, pages 129–153, Princeton University Press, Princeton, NJ.

J. Moses (1975) *A MACSYMA primer*. Technical Report Mathlab Memo No. 2, Computer Science Laboratory, MIT.

I. Mozetic, I. Bratko, and N. Lavrac (1984) *The derivation of medical knowledge from a qualitative model of the heart*. Technical Report, Josef Stefan Institute, Ljubljana, Yugoslavia.

S.H. Muggleton (1987) Duce, an oracle based approach to constructive induction. In *IJCAI-87*, pages 287–292, Kaufmann.

S.H. Muggleton (1988) A strategy for constructing new predicates in first order logic. In *Proceedings of the Third European Working Session on Learning*, pages 123–130, Pitman.

S.H. Muggleton and W. Buntine (1988) Machine invention of first-order predicates by inverting resolution. In *Machine Learning 5*, pages 339–352, Kaufmann.

T. Niblett (1985) YAPES: Yet Another Prolog Expert System. *CC-AI: the journal for integrated study of artificial intelligence, cognitive science and applied epistemology*, 2(2):3–30.

N.J. Nilsson (1980) *Principles of Artificial Intelligence*. Tioga, Palo Alto, CA.

NTIS (1969) *Use of the Skew T, Log P Diagram in Analysis and Forecasting. Air Weather Service Manual AWSM*. Technical Report NTIS AD695603, National Technical Information Service, Springfield, VA.

T.W. Pao and J.W. Carr III (1978) A solution of the syntactical induction-inference problem for regular languages. *Computer Languages*, 3:53–64.

A. Paterson (1983) *An attempt to use CLUSTER to synthesise humanly intelligible subproblems for the KPK chess endgame*. Technical Report UIUCDCS-R-83-1156, Univ. Illinois, Urbana, IL.

A. Paterson (1984) *Computer Induction in a Tutorial Context*. University of Edinburgh, (M.Phil. Thesis), Edinburgh.

A. Paterson and T. Niblett (1982) *ACLS User Manual*. ITL-KnowledgeLink, Glasgow.

K. Popper (1972) *Conjectures and Refutations: The Growth of Scientific Knowledge*. Routledge and Kegan Paul, London.

J.R. Quinlan (1979) Discovering rules from large collections of examples: a case study. In D. Michie, editor, *Expert Systems in the Micro-electronic Age*, pages 168–201, Edinburgh University Press, Edinburgh.

J.R. Quinlan (1982) Semi-autonomous acquisition of pattern-based knowledge. In D. Michie, editor, *Introductory readings in expert systems*, pages 192–207, Gordon and Breach, New York.

L. Rendell (1985) Substantial constructive induction using layered information compression: tractable feature formation in search. In *IJCAI-85*, pages 650–658, Kaufmann.

C. Riese (1984) *Transformer fault detection and diagnosis using Rule-Master by Radian*. Technical report, Radian Corporation, Austin, Texas.

G.D. Ritchie and F.K. Hanna (1984) AM: a case study in AI methodology. *Artificial Intelligence*, 23(3):249–268.

J. Roycroft (1983) A prophesy fulfilled. *EG magazine*, November 1983.

D.E. Rumelhart and J.L. McClelland (1986) Learning internal representations by error propogation. In *Explorations in the Micro-Structure of Cognition Vol. 1 : Foundations*, pages 318–362, MIT Press, Cambridge, MA.

C. Sammut and R.B Banerji (1986) Learning concepts by asking questions. In R. Michalski, J. Carbonnel, and T. Mitchell, editors, *Machine Learning: An Artificial Intelligence Approach. Vol. 2*, pages 167–192, Kaufmann, Los Altos, CA.

C.E. Shannon (1950) Programming a computer for playing chess. *Phil. Mag.*, 41:256–275.

A. Shapiro and T. Niblett (1982) Automatic induction of classification rules for a chess endgame. In M.R.B. Clarke, editor, *Advances in Computer Chess*, pages 73–91, Pergammon, Oxford.

A.D. Shapiro (1987) *Structured Induction in Expert Systems*. Addison-Wesley, Wokingham.

A.D. Shapiro and D. Michie (1986) A self-commenting facility for inductively synthesised endgame expertise. In D.F. Beal, editor, *Advances in Computer Chess*, pages 147–165, Pergammon, Oxford.

E.Y. Shapiro (1983) *Algorithmic program debugging*. MIT Press.

E.H. Shortliffe and B. Buchanan (1975) A model of inexact reasoning in medicine. *Mathematical Biosciences*, 23:351–379.

K. Thompson (1986) Private letter to J. Roycroft. *EG magazine*, January.

S. Zubrick (1988) Validation of a weather forecasting expert system. In J.E. Hayes, D. Michie, and J. Richard, editors, *Machine Intelligence 11*, pages 391–422, Oxford University Press, Oxford.

S. Zubrick (1984) *Willard: a severe thunderstorm forecasting system using RuleMaster by Radian*. Technical report, Radian Corporation, Austin, Texas.

C. Zuidema (1974) Chess, How to program the exceptions? *Afdeling informatica*, IW21/74.

Index

a-successor, 179
Absorption, 156
abstract data types, 48
accept, 96
ACLS, 19, 54, 136, 173, 203
action, 54, 63, 150
ACTIONS, 54
adder, 40
advice module, 145
algebra, 136
algorithmic programming, 41
alphabet, 177
Alvey, 153
AM, 170
Angluin, 7, 98, 99, 107, 112, 127
animal taxonomy, 153, 159
animals, 36
applications, 8, 38, 83, 86, 90, 127, 168, 201
Arbab, 5
ARCH, 66
arch, 63
artificial respiration, 57
ask, 47
attribute, 15, 150
auto-pilot, 84
automatic programming, 4
automatic structuring, 6

Banerji, 155
Biermann, 7, 103, 181
bijection, 185
binary, 39
binary adder, 130
blocks, 63, 178

Booth, 99
bottleneck, 146, 154
Bratko, 5, 145, 153, 165
Buchanan, 154
Buntine, 170
Burke, 83
Burstall, 155

C, 35, 39, 57
canonical, 98
canonical acceptor, 101, 180
cardinality, 177
Carr, 98
carry, 40, 130
causal model, 38
characteristic predicate, 103, 178
characteristic sample, 117, 193
chess, 2, 9, 10, 15, 145, 165
chess endgame, 145, 153
Chilausky, 154
CHILD, 66
choking, 57
CIGOL, 170
class, 20
class-value, 174
classification, 2, 38
clear, 68
clinically significant, 169
CLUSTER, 6, 146, 154
commercial packages, 4
commercial product, 35
compaction, 168
complexity, 22
comprehensibility, 5, 31
computable funtions, 17

215

concatenation, 177
CONDITIONS, 54
constructive induction, 154, 155
context, 41
control, 3, 6, 8
coordinate, 49
correctness, 112, 119, 125
coverage, 89

daily routine, 40
Darlington, 155
data type, 50
database, 148
debug, 3
Dechter, 63
decision tree, 5, 14, 20, 36, 43, 145, 173
DECLARATIONS, 54
declarative, 38
deduction, 13
deductivist, 4
definitions, 177
delaying check, 196
Dershowitz, 155
design, 39
deterministic acceptor, 178
deterministic with lookahead k, 183
Dichotomisation, 157
domain, 2
dont care, 56
Duce, 6, 8, 10, 15, 153
Duce operators, 155
Duce questions, 160
Dufay, 142
DUTMM, 28, 39, 122

EARL, 9, 51, 83, 90
effectiveness, 16
empty string, 177
EMYCIN, 38, 41
entails, 14

entropy, 174
equivalence relation, 178
even-parity, 20
EXAMPLES, 56
examples, 3, 14, 15, 19, 37, 97
Expert Ease, 68
expert systems, 1, 2, 4, 14, 34, 83, 86, 90
explanation, 1, 3, 8, 33, 35, 47, 51, 152
external information, 60
Extran, 173

feature construction, 153
Feigenbaum, 33
Feldman, 7, 103, 181
final state, 178
finite automata, 7, 9, 19, 24–31, 39, 40, 96, 99, 100, 104, 112, 121, 128, 129, 147
finite state acceptor, 96, 178
finite-state acceptor, 25
finite-state machine, 95
first-order logic, 38
forcing tree, 145
formal language theory, 95
formalism, 5, 14
FORTRAN, 47
frames, 38
Fu, 99, 154

game-playing, 14
GENARCH, 71
generalisation, 4, 13, 37, 85
generalise, 157
GENERIC, 48
GOAL, 46
goal, 63
goal state, 39
goal state acceptor, 109
Gold, 97
Golds theorem, 98

goto, 30, 41
grammar, 14, 128
grammatical induction, 7, 95, 128
graphics, 168
guesses, 14

hanging pictures problem, 138
Hartford Steam Boiler Company, 9, 90
Haussler, 17
Heimlich, 57
heuristics, 96, 100, 103, 181
hierarchy, 34, 57, 64, 65, 154
Horn clauses, 38
Horwitz, 147
Huberman, 145
human subset language, 5
Hunt, 145, 173

ID3, 19, 20, 35, 127, 145, 173
Identification, 157
identification in the limit, 17, 97, 98, 113, 119, 121, 189
illustrative examples, 168
IM1, 99, 181
IN, 47
incremental learning, 114, 120, 147, 193
induction, 3, 4, 8, 13, 15, 18, 36
inductivist, 4
inference networks, 38
infix, 50
input, 39
instantiated modules, 48
insurance, 91
integer-valued attributes, 174
INTENT, 47, 51
Inter-construction, 155
Interact, 153, 168
internal state, 39
international chess community, 147

Intra-construction, 156
irrelevance, 36
isomorphic, 179, 180

k-contextual, 97, 115, 190
k-follower, 179
k-leader, 179
k-reversible, 97, 107, 127, 182
k-tail, 103, 177
KBBKN, 147, 195
KC algorithm, 118
Kling, 147
knowledge, 2
knowledge engineers, 3, 30
Kopec, 154, 168
KPa7KR, 146, 154, 165
KPK, 154
KR algorithm, 110, 127, 186
KRK, 147
ku-reversible, 109

language, 177
Latombe, 142
learnability, 97
learning disabilities, 168
left parietal brain area, 168
left-quotient, 177
Levine, 105, 182
linear equations, 136
LISP, 60
logic, 4, 13
logic programming, 33, 38
logical-valued attributes, 174
lookahead, 145

machine learning, 1, 4, 10, 153
MACSYMA, 1
majority-vote, 169
mapping, 123
Marvin, 156
mathematical induction, 18
matrix, 105
Mealy machine, 26, 96

Mealy machines, 121
meaning, 155
medical expert systems, 14
merging, 101
meteorology, 36, 86
Michalski, 154
Michie, 2, 5, 10, 51, 63, 145
Miclet, 105, 142, 182
minimax, 147
minimisation, 129
Minsky, 162
model, 14
module, 38, 44, 45
module types, 45
Moore machine, 26
MYCIN, 2, 34, 52

NASA, 83
National Weather Service, 8, 86
negative examples, 98, 115, 120
negative examples, 16, 157
neural networks, 162
neuro-psychology, 10, 168
next state function, 39
Niblett, 8, 20, 35, 146, 165
Nilsson, 165
non-deterministic acceptor, 104, 125
non-optimal play, 151
noughts and crosses, 46
NP-hard, 98
NSSFC, 86

object-oriented model, 38
Occams razor, 158
oil, 91
operator, 153
operator properties, 50
oracle, 16, 98, 153, 155, 168
ordering, 15
ordering explanation, 53
OUT, 46

output, 39
over-generalisation, 103, 116, 128

Pao, 98
Papert, 162
parity, 25, 97, 162
parity (structured), 21
parity (unstructured), 20
partial certainty, 33
partition, 178
Paterson, 136, 146, 154
perceptons, 162
planning, 63, 138
polynomial time, 95
Popper, 14, 17
positive examples, 16, 98
positive presentation, 119
positive sample, 178
power set, 177
precedence, 51, 66
predicate calculus, 13
prediction, 89
prefix, 103, 177
prefix tree acceptor, 99, 180
PRIMITIVE, 47
primitive, 71
primitive attributes, 162
print, 49
prints, 57
probability, 174
production rules, 37
program synthesis, 155
Prolog, 34, 50, 152, 156
proofs, 185
propositional logic, 14, 38
provable, 14

query, 98
questions, 155
Quinlan, 19, 145, 154, 173
quotient, 179

Radial, 9, 19, 28–30, 34, 35, 38–51, 53, 57, 59, 60, 63, 96, 128, 151, 207
Radial program structure, 42
Radial syntax, 41
Radian, 8, 83
read, 49
reads, 57
reasoning, 3
recursion, 30, 68
refines, 178
reflexive, 178
regular expression, 96
regular languages, 95, 183
release position, 150, 201
Rendell, 154
reverse motor problem, 134
Riese, 9, 83, 90
robot, 71, 138
Roycroft, 147
rule, 19
rule language, 8
Rulemaker, 34, 38, 53, 65, 84, 128, 151, 173, 205, 207
Rulemaker syntax, 54
RuleMaster, 1, 8, 10, 18, 33–36, 38, 39, 52, 53, 57, 60, 63, 64, 68, 71, 73, 74, 83, 85, 91, 93, 95, 127
rules, 14, 37
Russell, 169

Sammut, 155
scheduling, 39
screening, 92
sequence induction, 125
search, 158
SELS, 91
semantic information, 120
semantics-preserving, 155
sequence induction, 6, 9, 18, 24, 127, 146, 201

sequences, 6, 151, 195
Shannon, 145
Shapiro, 6, 8, 15, 20, 35, 51, 146, 154, 165, 168
Shepherd, 71
SHUTTLE, 83
SILENT, 47, 51
single example, 7
situation-action sequences, 123
situation, 15, 63
SKC algorithm, 146
SKR algorithm, 124, 127, 136
space-shuttle, 83
splitting, 174
start state, 39
STATE, 54
state transition diagram, 40
state transition table, 40, 128
static descriptions, 5
static induction, 6, 18
statistics, 89
Stepp, 155
stepwise-refinement, 151
STORAGE, 49
structured induction, 5, 146
subacceptor, 179
support facilities, 35
symbol reduction, 158
symbol reduction equations, 158
symmetric, 178
symmetry, 148
syntax, 13

tail set, 105
taxonomy, 154
termination symbol, 128
TEST, 54, 57
test, 54
testing, 8
text, 16, 98
theory, 95
Thompson, 147

thunderstorms, 86
time, 127
time complexity, 7, 100, 113, 119, 182
TITAN, 83
tower, 78
trace information, 95
traffic light controller, 131
transformer, 90
transitive, 178
troubleshooting, 83
Truncation, 157
truth-preserving, 155
turbo engineer, 48
Turing Institute, 147

umbrella, 43, 54
uniquely terminated, 109, 185
universal acceptor, 103
universal language, 98
Universal Turing machine, 29
UNIX, 35, 48, 60
unsupervised learning, 169
USNWS, 89

validation, 16, 51, 89, 90, 92, 169
value-returning, 46
variables, 30
verification, 89, 169, 207
visibility, 42
VLSI, 130, 131
VM, 3, 34
vocabulary, 155

well-formed-formula, 13
WILLARD, 8, 36, 52, 83, 86
world, 14
world-model, 73
worst-case, 20
WRAT, 169

zero-reversible, 182

Zubrick, 8, 83, 86
Zuidema, 147